THE OTHER MISSISSIPPI

A STATE IN CONFLICT WITH ITSELF

David G. Sansing

The Nautilus Publishing Company

OXFORD, MISSISSIPPI

© copyright 2018, David G. Sansing

THE NAUTILUS PUBLISHING COMPANY
426 South Lamar Blvd., Suite 16
Oxford, Mississippi 38655
Tel: 662-513-0159
www.nautiluspublishing.com

First Edition

Photo credits: p. 4 courtesy of Square Books; p. 6 © Houston Cofield; p. 10 © Martin Dain; p. 17 © University Communications; p. 42 courtesy of The Nautilus Publishing Company; p. 63 (top) courtesy of Lisa Howorth, (bottom) photo by Tim Ivy; p. 78 © University Communications; p. 147 map researched and drawn by Deborah Freeland; p. 158 © University Communications; p. 197 courtesy of UM Athletics; p. 206 courtesy of *Harvard* magazine; p. 213 courtesy of UM Athletics; p. 218 © University Communications; p. 224 © University Communications; p. 252, 276 photos by Getty Images; p. 282 © University Communications; p. 298 courtesy of *The Oxford Eagle*; p. 312 courtesy of Deborah Freeland; p. 311 © TimeWarner.

Library of Congress Cataloging-in-Publication Data has been applied for.
ISBN: 978-1-936-946-39-6

Printed in Canada

10 9 8 7 6 5 4 3 2 1

To
Elizabeth, David, Cindy, Beth, John, Jeannie, Perry
Cherish, Mary Love, Kimberly, Max, Michael, and Lizzie

CONTENTS

CONTENTS

INTRODUCTION

In the early 1980s I presented a lecture, titled "The Other Mississippi," at the Oxford-Lafayette County Historical Society. Richard Howorth, the distinguished owner of Square Books and a major figure in the intellectual history of Mississippi, especially of Oxford and Lafayette County, was at that meeting, and he suggested that I write a book about The Other Mississippi. Well, almost forty years later, here it is. Things take time in Mississippi.

The first use of the term "The Other Mississippi" that I have found was the title of an article in the March 1963 issue of the *New South*, a journal published by the Southern Regional Council in Atlanta. Written in the aftermath of the Meredith Crisis at Ole Miss, that article includes commentaries by Duncan Gray, Jr., Karl Wiesenburg, a group of 28 young Methodist ministers, and others who endorsed the Civil Rights Movement. The editor declared that these and Other Mississippians like them would "help redeem the state." I have found no other use of the term prior to my lecture at the Oxford-Lafayette County Historical Society. The only other published reference I have found to the term was a book by Bob Carney titled *The Other Mississippi: Especially the 1920s and 1930s*, which he published in 1994 and is a somewhat laudatory account of Mississippi during those years. In 1974, Carl N. Degler published a fascinating history of *The Other South*.

Although I was born in Mississippi, I have lived most of my life in The Other Mississippi. One of my earliest memories, and my first awareness of

The Other Mississippi, occurred when I was about five or six years old. In my hometown of Greenville, the Queen City of the Delta, which historian James Cobb calls "The Most Southern Place on Earth," I had a little friend who lived just down the street. We were playmates, but one day I missed him. I looked for him, but he didn't come out to play for several days. Then he came back, and I asked him where he had been. He told me that he had been over in the hills to visit some of his kinfolks.

The hills? What are hills, I asked him. The little world I lived in, on Theobald Street and on South Hinds Street, was flat, and I mean flat. I did not know about hills. I do not recall any of the words he used to describe that strange terrain, but I remember how excited I was to hear about the hills and about how much I wanted to see those things called hills.

Many years later, when I was giving one of my first lectures on Mississippi history at Ole Miss, I discussed the various soil regions in Mississippi. As I lectured on the differences between the Delta and the North Central Hills, I remembered my childhood friend telling me about the hills.

Another childhood experience that I remember so well were the times that an elderly lady in my neighborhood would gather some of the children in her yard, which was down the street from a Chinese grocery store, and give us cookies and lemonade. In that Delta neighborhood there were black and brown and white and yellow children. As we were enjoying her cookies and swinging in her large swing, she would talk to us about being friends and loving each other, although we looked different, and the color of our skin was different. She would often read to us her favorite Bible verse, "A soft answer turneth away wrath, but grievous words stir up anger." Her simple acts of kindness erased whatever prejudice there may have existed in my heart and soul.

Another enduring early encounter I had with The Other Mississippi occurred when I was in junior high school. I was working at a supermarket called the A&P Store. I swept floors, restocked the shelves, sacked groceries, and carried them out to the cars for the ladies. The men, of course, carried out their own. Among the ten or twelve workers at the store was a young black guy who was about my age. His name was Sonny. I don't remember his last name, if I ever even knew it. Of course, we went to different schools, but we were buddies; I liked him, and he liked me.

One year, as Christmas approached, the store manager told all of us to come back to the stockroom after the store closed. He said he was going to give us a Christmas party and wanted us to draw names so we could exchange gifts at the party. When we all got to the stockroom, he gave us a piece of paper, told us to write our name on it, and drop it in the basket, and then we would draw a name. As he was explaining all of this, I noticed that Sonny was not there. I did not understand why he was not there. I told the manager that Sonny was not there and asked him if he wanted me to go get him.

I remember that he was not ugly or angry with me, but after a moment of verbal infelicity, he just told me that Sonny would not be at the party. All of the other workers at the meeting seemed to understand that, but I didn't. Why would we work together but not let him come to our Christmas party? I didn't say anything else. I don't remember if I went to the party or not. But I will never ever forget the manager's attempt to explain to me why Sonny would not be at the Christmas party.

To this day I remember the look on his face, though I cannot adequately describe it. The simple question of a kid in junior high school had forced this grown white man to try to articulate, I am sure for the first time in his life, a racial philosophy based on the theory of white supremacy that would allow Sonny to work with us every day, do the same things we did, but would not allow him to come to our Christmas party. It was intricacies such as these that Walker Percy has called "the terrible complexities of race."

Many years later I saw a documentary on William Faulkner. In one powerful scene there was a white boy and a black boy playing around and wrestling with each other, having a good time. After a few minutes of playing with the black kid, the white boy got up and began walking slowly away; he didn't even say bye, as the narrator read from Faulkner's *Go Down Moses*:

Then one day the old curse of his fathers, the old haughty ancestral pride [that] stemmed not from courage and honor but from wrong and

World-renowned Square Books

4 | David Sansing

shame, descended to him [and] he entered his heritage. He ate its bitter fruit.

When I saw that documentary, I remembered Sonny, and I wondered where he was. And I understood why the store manager had so much trouble trying to explain my Southern "heritage" to me.

In addition to the enduring influence of my Southern heritage, my family heritage also influenced me in ways that I cannot fully understand or explain. I had four brothers and four sisters, another sister had died when I was very young. Among the nine of us, growing up in the Delta, I was in the middle, and I was the dumbest of them all. Although my father had only a fourth-grade education, he was one of the smartest people I have ever known. With my parents there were eleven people who lived every day in our small house. I remember my mother would heat bricks in the fireplace, wrap them in cloth and put them at the foot of our bed to keep us warm on cold, wintry nights. I also remember bathing in a washtub on the back porch or in the back yard, and drawing water from the pump in the back yard. With eleven people living in a house, pandemonium might well have been the norm, but it wasn't. Kindness, goodness, and sweetness governed our household. I also remember, vividly, like it was yesterday, as a little boy, my father gathering us all in the living room with the kerosene lights out. I could not understand why we were sitting there in the dark. And then he reached up, pulled a string, and there was light. I will never, ever forget that moment. Remembering that experience many years later, when I was teaching American history, I had a special fondness for President Franklin D. Roosevelt and the New Deal Congress, and the TVA. Several years later, in someone else's house, I was allowed to watch a small screen in a large console with live, moving pictures. The people in that small picture were blurry, and we were told that they were in New York City, and we were seeing them on something called television. I was absolutely flabbergasted. But the old gentleman sitting next to me looked at me and mumbled, "That damn thing'll never sell." I have often wondered what he would think of cell phones and the internet. To a large extent, I am who I am because I grew up in The Other Mississippi, in Greenville.

Square Books founder Richard Howorth

Over the last forty years most young Mississippians have learned about their Mississippi heritage from three college professors who grew up in that wonderful place called Greenville, and who published high school textbooks on Mississippi history. When we were growing up, Greenville was an oasis in a state that was often troubled by racial violence. Charles Sallis, Class of 1952, the long-time, distinguished professor of history at Millsaps College, published, with James Loewen, *Mississippi, Conflict and Change* in 1974. The publication of that prize-winning textbook was a pivotal moment in the teaching of Mississippi's heritage. University of Southern Mississippi history professor Ray Skates, Class of 1952, and I, Class of 1951, also published Mississippi history textbooks. Mississippi State University history Professor John K. Bettersworth also published a popular Mississippi history textbook. My text book, *A Place Called Mississippi*, is currently used in Mississippi's public and private schools.

During my high school days, Greenville High was like a first-rate prep school with one of the finest high school faculties in the Deep South, and the dynamics of its classrooms are among my fondest memories. My eighth-grade history teacher, Miss Cuthbert, changed my life in ways that I can't explain and don't even now fully understand. My ninth-grade science teacher was Mr. Herbert, and I will never forget him. A diminutive Cora Erwin commanded her classroom with all the authority of a ship captain. The Shell sisters — we called them "Little Miss Shell" and "Big Miss Shell" — were extraordinary, as were Miss Keady, Miss McBrayer, Mr. Acree and Mr. Lukenbach, Mrs. Ward, Counselor H. L. Berryhill, and Coach Warren Averitte. All of them had an enduring impact on my life.

These high school teachers are on the Honor Roll of my memory, but I must add one more to that list. President Julius J. Hayden, who gave me my first teaching job at Perkinston Junior College in 1960, also had an enduring and immeasurable influence on my life. President Hayden lived in and welcomed me into The Other Mississippi. The ten years that I spent at Perkinston Junior College were among the best and happiest days of my life.

My high school history teacher, Mrs. Nell Thomas, was perhaps the single most important influence in my academic career. From her I learned the beauty of words and the power and force of language. I also learned about the joys of teaching. Mrs. Thomas formally introduced me to The Other Mississippi. Throughout my half century of teaching, my loftiest ambition has been to have a student feel toward me as I do toward Mrs. Thomas.

One of the most transformative early encounters I had with The Other Mississippi occurred in 1963, when Rubel Phillips, a former Democrat, a circuit court clerk of Alcorn County, and a public service commissioner, switched parties and ran for governor as a Republican. Phillips was demeaned and shamed by the press and politicians as a modern-day scalawag. This puzzled me. It was common knowledge in Mississippi that scalawags were the dregs of Southern society, men without honor or dignity who teamed up with carpetbaggers and former slaves to exploit the devastation of the Civil War for their own personal and political gain. Rubel Phillips did not in any way fit that description.

I was teaching at Perkinston Junior College in 1963, was just beginning to work on a Ph.D. in history at the University of Southern Mississippi, and was trying to decide what I would write my dissertation on. Rubel Phillips was a popular and highly regarded politician, so I began to wonder if the traditional definition of scalawags was historically accurate. I discussed this with Dr. John Gonzales, my major professor, and after some initial research, he agreed to allow me to write my dissertation on the Mississippi scalawags. Early in my research I discovered that many scalawags were numbered among Mississippi's wealthiest planters and largest slave owners, like James L. Alcorn, for whom Alcorn University was named, and Robert W. Flournoy, who owned more than a hundred slaves but after the war edited a newspaper titled Equal Rights, which championed political and social equality among the races. Alcorn and Flournoy were social and political architects who were committed to building The Other Mississippi.

In 1970, the year after I received my Ph.D. from the University of Southern Mississippi, I was appointed assistant professor of history at Ole Miss. During most of my years at Ole Miss, I was honored to occupy Professor James Silver's former office in Bondurant Hall. When I brought my family to Oxford, I felt that I had come home and that I was where I was supposed to be.

Most of these essays, articles, and speeches are edited and updated versions of those I presented at various times during my nearly fifty-year academic career, and I found it impractical to include all the different times and places I presented or published them. Because they were presented at different times and places, there is some repetition in various articles. The article on the State Ole-Miss rivalry is a revised and updated article that I prepared for an attorney who represented the NCAA in a lawsuit involving Ole Miss and Mississippi State and is used with his permission.

I especially want to thank Neil White, creative director and publisher of Nautilus Publishing Company in Oxford, for his continual support in so many ways and in particular for his publishing this book. I also want to thank Carroll Chiles Moore, associate publisher, and Sinclair Rishel, associate editor, of Nautilus for their support and diligence in preparing this manuscript for publication. Finally, I want to thank Karen Bryant for her excellent proofreading of this book.

James Silver

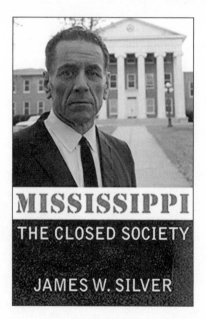

The Closed Society

I

THE OTHER MISSISSIPPI

In his speech accepting the Nobel Prize in 1950 William Faulkner said that he wrote about the human heart in conflict with itself. Most of Faulkner's greatest novels and short stories are set in his "postage stamp of native soil" in Mississippi, which like the human heart is often in conflict with itself.

When people ask me for a good history of Mississippi, I suggest they read Faulkner's *Absalom, Absalom!* and that they read it two or three times. I think it is the best history of Mississippi, and the Old South, ever written. I also suggest that they read it in one or two sittings, certainly no more than three. Faulkner's dense and towering prose should not be read in spurts.

People outside of Mississippi often ask, as Shreve McCannon asked Quentin Compson in *Absalom, Absalom!*, "What's it like there? What do they do there? Why do they live there?" Shreve was from Canada, and Quentin, Shreve's Harvard roommate, was a native Mississippian. At first Quentin told Shreve that he would have to be born there to understand Mississippi. But then he tried to explain to Shreve what it was like to live in Mississippi and to be a Mississippian. In that effort Quentin told Shreve the story of Thomas Sutpen, one of Faulkner's most enduring characters and the central figure in *Absalom, Absalom!*.

In a 1993 real-life encounter reminiscent of the fictional conversation between Shreve McCannon and Quentin Compson, Bern Keating, the renowned photographer and writer from Greenville, was picking at an avocado burger on a California patio in San Francisco when the host's daughter introduced herself and asked:

"Where are you coming from... geographically, that is?"

"Mississippi," Keating replied.

"But you seem like a nice intelligent man," she protested. "Who can you relate to in that intellectual desert? ... I mean, do you ever rap with anybody but Neanderthalers out there?"

After Keating told her that he had recently talked with Karl Malden, Ira Wallach, Carroll Baker, Robert Penn Warren, and James Jones, among others, when they visited Pulitzer Prize-winning editor Hodding Carter of the Greenville *Delta Democrat Times*, she said,

> *Oh, wow.... That crowd probably is brighter even than this California bunch, I guess.*

An image of Mississippi has been superimposed upon the American psyche, and that perception has been writ large upon the mindscape of America, from the Hallowed Halls of Harvard, across the fruited plains, beyond the purple mountains' majesty, all the way to the Golden Gate itself.

In the aftermath of World War II, a Harvard professor wrote in his classic study of Southern politics that "Northerners, provincials that they are, regard the South as one large Mississippi. Southerners, with their eye for distinction, place Mississippi in a class by itself [and] fall back on the soul-satisfying exclamation, 'Thank God for Mississippi!'" The learned professor's personal opinion was that Mississippi accentuated "the darker political strains that run throughout the South."

It is no wonder that as America entered the Civil Rights Movement in the 1960s a popular Mississippi bumper sticker read: "Mississippi: The Most Misunderstood State."

Although it has been a Closed Society for much of its history, Mississippi has also been one of the most closely monitored societies in the western world. If Mississippi sneezes, the national media gives it a glance, and if it sneezes twice, all of Europe looks, and parts of Asia. They may not cover it or report it, but they will hear it and will make a note of it.

A careful reading, however, reveals that most of those press accounts are sometimes uneven and often intemperate. In the case of television, even a quick scan reveals a picture that is just not quite in focus. But it is the nature of television to distort reality.

Mississippi, as they say in that business, is good press and has been for a long time. It may be that there is just no other place in America quite like Mississippi. People like to write about us and read about us, and Northerners in particular like to talk to us and listen to us talk. Most Mississippians are amused by the attention we get when we visit other parts of the country.

People seem somehow intrigued to find a real live Mississippian outside its natural habitat.

They may even be a little (secretly) envious. For example, Willie Morris, one of our most beloved expatriates and author of *North Toward Home*, was scored by a New York friend for wanting to change (improve?) Mississippi. His friend declared:

> *Can you imagine, there he is with... the most fertile ground in America for a writer to write about. ... Why, if I was a writer I'd use all the influence I had with the politicians and get them to put up big green signs at every point of entry into Mississippi, all along the borders, saying: POSTED. NO TRESPASSING.*

While most Mississippians might object to one or more of those "uncompliments," we take a measure of delight at being in the limelight, without bothering about, or being bothered by, the shadows such illumination may cast. We have this thing about being a Mississippian. Those of you who are not Mississippians cannot understand this. Those of you who are understand what I mean when I say to be a Mississippian is an existential predicament.

Mississippi's national image, and the perception that many Americans have of us, is not altogether inaccurate. But it is incomplete. It is a truthful image, but it is only half of the truth, and we all know that a half-truth can be as bad or worse than no truth at all. I think Mississippi has always been, and still is, misunderstood because for every trait or characteristic that is typical of Mississippi there is a corresponding opposite trait that is equally typical.

We are known for the scent of magnolias and the smell of burning crosses. Our hospitality is legendary, but so too is our hostility to outsiders.

Mississippi is a sad and lonely place; the blues were born here. But we are also exuberant and excitable, and we gave the world rock and roll.

Mississippi has the highest rate of illiteracy in the country, but we have more Pulitzer Prize winners per acre than any other state in America.

That corresponding opposite is what I call The Other Mississippi.

Unfortunately, we know a lot more about Mississippi than we do about The Other Mississippi. We know a lot about the cultured Nabobs who lived up on the high bluffs at Natchez, but we don't know much about, as Professor John Guice calls them, the Nobodies who lived at Natchez Under-the-Hill. Because of Professor William Scarborough's book, *Masters of the Big House* (2003), we know a lot about the wealthy planters who lived in the Great Mansions, but we know much less about the slaves who lived in the shacks, or the poor whites who lived in the Piney Woods, or the middle-class whites who lived in the towns and villages.

We know a lot about those gallant gentlemen whose exaggerated sense of honor prompted countless duels and other violent confrontations. But we don't know much about the daughters of Peggy Dow, like Phoebe Calvit, an "enterprising and independent widow" who, according to historian Robert V. Haynes, "was inclined toward litigation." We don't know much about Sallie Reneau, the eighteen-year-old school teacher who persuaded the legislature to establish a woman's college in 1856 so "the indigent and the opulent" women of Mississippi could acquire "the imperishable riches of a well cultivated mind." We know even less about the countless other women who labored to maintain their self worth in that gentlemen's world.

We know all about the valiant grey-clad heroes who rushed off to war in 1861. But we don't know much about The Other Mississippians, black and white, who donned the Union blue, or the chief justice of the Mississippi Supreme Court who opposed secession and was arrested during the Civil War for flying an American flag in his front yard.

David Sansing

Poverty and prejudice and illiteracy have kept Mississippi back, and backwards, but The Other Mississippians have battled poverty and prejudice throughout our history. And for every Mississippi politician who has shamed its name, there have been others to make it proud.

In 1884 most Southerners opposed the Blair Bill that provided federal aid to public schools because it was "a form of charity" and an insult to "Southern honor." But Senator LQC Lamar made an impassioned speech in support of the bill because it was "a decided step toward the solution of the race problem," which he said was a "problem of illiteracy." Although Lamar had drafted Mississippi's Ordinance of Secession, he was a statesman of The Other Mississippi, and he delivered the eulogy of Senator Charles Sumner in 1874 that some historians cite as the "burial of the bloody shirt" and the beginning of the reunion of the North and the South.

James K. Vardaman was self-educated; he had no college degrees; he read law in his cousin's law office in Winona, and was a racial demagogue. John Sharp Williams studied in two European universities, received a law degree from the University of Virginia, and was a racial moderate. In the 1907 senatorial election, out of 118,344 votes cast, John Sharp Williams defeated James K. Vardaman by a margin of 648 votes.

In the next senatorial election in 1911 Vardaman was elected to the U.S. Senate, and in 1917 Senator Vardaman was one of only six senators who voted against America's declaration of war against Germany and later opposed America's entry into the League of Nations. But Senator John Sharp Williams was a floor leader for that legislation and received President Woodrow Wilson's personal and public commendation.

Everyone knows about Senator Theodore G. Bilbo, and few would be surprised to learn that *Life* magazine in 1939 rated him one of the worst and least competent members of the United States Senate. But many would be surprised to learn that *Life* rated Senator Pat Harrison, Mississippi's Other Senator, as one of the Senate's most respected and most competent members.

Mississippi's segregated churches received a great deal of negative press during the Civil Rights Movement. But the 1962 manifesto, *Born of Con-*

viction, supporting civil rights and signed by twenty-eight mostly young Methodist ministers, was not well-noted nor long remembered.

The image of Governor Ross Barnett standing in the doorway in defiance of the Supreme Court's order to admit James Meredith to Ole Miss in 1962 is still vivid in America's memory. But few remember that his successor, Governor Paul B. Johnson, Jr., in his inaugural address counseled Mississippians to accept the civil rights of African Americans and admonished them:

> *Hate, or prejudice or ignorance will not lead Mississippi while I sit in the governor's chair... if I must fight, it will not be a rear-guard defense of yesterday... it will be an all-out assault of our share of tomorrow.*

Hardly anyone remembers, if they ever even knew, that two "good ole boys" from The Other Mississippi, Willie Morris and Turner Catledge, edited *Harper's* magazine and *The New York Times* in the 1960s. When he was writer-in-residence at Ole Miss in the 1980s, Willie loved to tell his Oxford friends that he and Turner Catledge would talk at cocktail parties on the roof of some high-rise overlooking that Great Metropolis and decide what America would read in the days and weeks to come. Both of these "good ole boys" have left us their memoirs. Catledge in *My Life and The Times* (1971), and Morris in *New York Days* (1993).

Many may remember the anxiety and the fear of disorder that preceded the massive public school integration in Mississippi in the spring of 1970. Public school teachers, the foot soldiers in the army of The Other Mississippi, made that transition successful. But few are aware that black football players like Walter Payton helped make that transition safe and acceptable.

A year after Mississippi's public schools were integrated, Bill Waller, a transformational figure in the history of The Other Mississippi, was elected governor, and for the first time since Reconstruction, blacks were appointed to state boards and agencies and to positions in state law enforcement. And too few remember that Governor Waller declared October 20, 1973, "Walter Payton Day" throughout the state of Mississippi.

William Winter

In 1980 William Winter, another hero in the army of The Other Mississippi, was elected governor and inaugurated a period of racial reconciliation that has culminated in the election of more blacks to public office in The Other Mississippi than in any other state in the nation.

Through the years many pundits have dismissed Mississippi as a "cultural wasteland," but during its darkest days, the arts and letters flourished in The Other Mississippi.

It may not be too much to say that The Other Mississippi taught the world to sing.

The blues were born here, and we gave the world B.B. King.

Rock and roll was also born here, and Elvis changed the way the world sings.

Country music, the most popular musical style in America, was elevated to an art form by Jimmie Rodgers of Meridian, who was the first inductee into the Country Music Hall of Fame.

Leontyne Price, one of The Other Mississippi's gifts to grand opera, received a forty-two-minute standing ovation after her 1961 New York Metropolitan Opera debut. Fewer still know that the first African American diva was Elizabeth Taylor Greenfield, the Black Swan. Born in Natchez, the Black Swan performed for Queen Victoria in Buckingham Palace on May 10, 1854.

The Other Mississippi's literary tradition is a marvel in the world of letters and includes William Faulkner, Eudora Welty, Richard Wright, and Tennessee Williams. Those literary giants did not stifle the creative spirit in Mississippi but inspired wave after wave of other great writers including Margaret Walker Alexander, Shelby Foote, Willie Morris, Richard Ford, Beth Henley, Mildred D. Taylor, Clifton Taulbert, Barry Hannah, Jesmyn Ward, Greg Iles, Kathryn Stockett, John Grisham, and Natasha Trethewey.

Mississippi's radical editors and racist newspapers are known and well-remembered, while those other voices "crying in the wilderness" are not, but they were there. Voices like Hazel Brannon Smith, a Pulitzer Prize winner; and Ira Harkey, a Pulitzer Prize winner; Hodding Carter, a Pulitzer Prize winner; and the *Clarion Ledger*, a Pulitzer Prize winner that was edited by Charles Overby.

It is said that history does not repeat itself. Mark Twain said history may not repeat itself but it does rhyme. I believe that history happened to Mississippi, not once but twice, during the cataclysm we call the Civil War, and during the social revolution we call the Civil Rights Movement.

Most Mississippi politicians in the 1950s, like their forbears in the 1850s, appealed to the fears and frustrations so deeply imbedded in all of us. In the 1850s, and in the 1950s, Mississippi's leaders were measured not by competence, but by eloquence, not by theories of government, but by theories of race and history.

To some, history is not what was, but what might have been, or what they wish had been. History may be made by the sword, but it is written by the pen, and no one should doubt which is the mightier.

In 1875, the year the Democratic Party regained control of state government after Reconstruction, a Mississippi poetess addressed the state convention of the Democratic Press Association and implored them:

> *To you we look in this trying hour*
> *To you, who wield the Press' power*
> *The pen must win what the sword has lost*
> *For our beautiful, beautiful South.*

Her pleading, "The pen must win what the sword has lost," was heeded not only by pundits and preachers and professors and politicians, it was validated by Mississippi's official historian. In 1898 Dunbar Rowland, the founding director of the Mississippi Department of Archives and History, and a prolific historian, offered this version of our past:

> *Twenty-three years have passed into history since Adelbert Ames,*
> *the last of the "Carpet Baggers," was driven from his high position as*
> *governor of Mississippi by... an outraged and indignant people. ... The*
> *state was turned over as so much prey to the hungriest and cruelest flock*
> *of human vultures that ever cursed mankind. The blighting curse of*

negro rule was patiently borne by the people of Mississippi until 1875...
until every white man in the state took a solemn oath before high heav-
en that he would free himself and his posterity from such a disgrace, or
die in the attempt.

Now read the 1900 official, or "snow white version," of Mississippi's history that Dunbar Rowland would proclaim and preserve in Mississippi's archival records:

> *From 1817 to 1861 Mississippi... was a land of brave men, fair*
> *women and eloquent statesmen. ... Nothing in nature is more beautiful*
> *than the cotton fields of the state during the picking season. ... As the*
> *work proceeds the peculiar melody... bursts forth, and there is actual*
> *joy in the sound. Men and women who sing while they toil are happy.*
> *The black toilers were happy in their work. ... The Southern slave was*
> *joyous and mirth-loving.*
>   *The Mississippi planter was magnificent and great in everything.*
> *... He was the ablest expounder of a constitutional democracy, and yet*
> *he belonged to an aristocracy the most exclusive that America has ever*
> *seen. ... It is impossible to picture in words the wife mother of a Missis-*
> *sippi plantation home... the grandest, noblest and best type of woman*
> *that ever brought joy and happiness to the world.*
>   *Descended from a long line of distinguished ancestry, she was tru-*
> *ly noble, pure and beautiful. ... Of all the characters of history... the*
> *Southern woman should be enshrined in fame's proudest niche. ... The*
> *grand and noble men and women of the "Old South" are rapidly pass-*
> *ing away. Their memories, deeds, and virtues must be preserved by*
> *their sons and daughters. They must be preserved on the living pages of*
> *history... in story, poetry, song, in sculptured marble... so that they will*
> *endure forever and forever.*

Dunbar Rowland was the official custodian of Mississippi history, and he reiterated the antebellum creed that slavery was a positive good, the ordained condition of the African race, and that white men were noble and born to rule.

In the years following Reconstruction, sharecropping replaced slavery, tenant farming became a new form of bondage, blacks were disfranchised, and fidelity to the "Cult of the Lost Cause" became the creed by which white Mississippians were measured.

"It's all now you see," Faulkner said, "the past is never dead; it's not even past."

When the white power structure regained complete control of public affairs in the 1890s, they began what Professor Neil McMillan has called a Dark Journey, and Mississippi became a closed society.

From 1892, when former Governor Robert Lowry and William McCardle published *A History of Mississippi For Use in Schools*, until 1963, when Ole Miss history professor James W. Silver published *Mississippi, The Closed Society*, Dunbar Rowland's version of Mississippi history was the prevailing official view of Mississippi's past, especially in public schools.

Professor Silver's controversial study prompted a reexamination of Mississippi history among both academics and laymen that culminated in the 1973 publication of *A History of Mississippi*, a two-volume study edited by Richard Aubrey McLemore, and the 1974 publication of *Mississippi, Conflict and Change*, a high school textbook written by James W. Loewen and Charles Sallis.

Dr. McLemore, a former professor of history and president of the University of Southern Mississippi, was appointed Director of the Mississippi Department of Archives and History in 1969. The two volume history he edited was written by recognized scholars and was a dramatic departure from Dunbar Rowland's "official" version of Mississippi's troubled history.

But nothing is easy in Mississippi.

When Loewen and Sallis published their 1974 textbook, which challenged the legitimacy of the white power structure and celebrated the role blacks and poor whites had played in Mississippi history, the state textbook agency did not approve *Conflict and Change* for adoption. That rejecti prompted a federal lawsuit by Loewen and Sallis. In 1980 a federal court ruled that the Mississippi adoption agency did not have legal reasons to reject the textbook, and at the next adoption cycle *Mississippi, Conflict and Change* was approved and adopted by schools across the state.

The controversy over the textbook agency's refusal to approve the Loewen and Sallis book elevated the issue of public school textbooks to a high-level discussion. That controversy led to the publication of several new Mississippi history books that were similar in scope and perspective to *Mississippi, Conflict and Change* and introduced high school students to The Other Mississippi.

To recognize The Other Mississippi is not to excuse the bigots. And a million acts of kindness can never make up for the murders of innocent black people. Nor does it exempt Mississippi from the scorn that such despicable acts, which were sanctioned by the closed society and condoned by the power structure, have rightfully called down upon it.

To recognize The Other Mississippi is to declare that in Mississippi's darkest hours all were not racists; all were not bigots, all did not condone injustice. It is to recognize that some whites and many blacks stood up and called out against injustice and prejudice. And many of them, like Medgar Evers and Vernon Dahmer, and Clyde Kennard and Fannie Lou Hamer, gave their last full measure to the cause of justice and freedom and human dignity.

To recognize The Other Mississippi is preface to the claim that The Other Mississippians are taking their state back from the racists and the reactionaries and all those who think Mississippi's finest hour has passed.

Some will dispute this, but Mississippi is not like it used to be. It is different; it is better than it was, and it is no longer a closed society. In the end, Mississippians almost always do what is right. We may falter; we may debate and deliberate much too long before we act, but we almost always do the right thing.

There is still prejudice and ignorance and poverty in Mississippi, and there are still acts of injustice and even violence. But those despicable acts are no longer sanctioned by the state, and racial discrimination is no longer an official state policy. There was a time in Mississippi when racial discrimination was a matter of public policy in the same way that the speed limit was a public policy. But that is no longer true. There are no laws on our books that differentiate and discriminate on the basis of race; our constitution has been purged, and Mississippi's Supreme Court is at last a tribunal in the truest sense of that word.

To say all of this is not to say that The Other Mississippi has won and that the battle is over. The struggle against injustice and ignorance and poverty may never be over. So, the true goal then, may not be to win the battle, but to never quit the struggle.

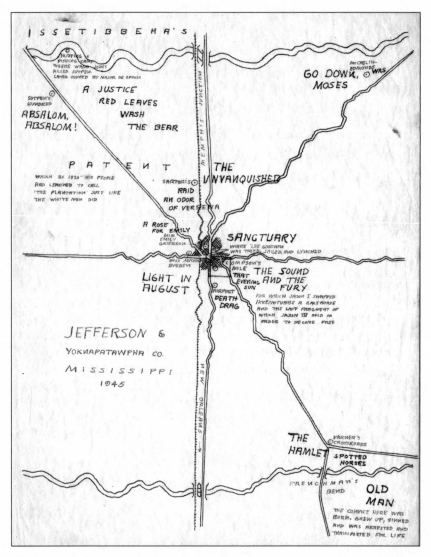

Faulkner's County

2

History of Northern Mississippi

Faulkner and Yoknapatawpha
Conference, 1974
Opening Lecture

Any standard historical atlas of the United States will indicate to the most casual observer that there is a political and geographic subdivision designated Mississippi. There are fifty such subdivisions, and collectively they constitute the United States. However, Mississippi is not just a state of the Union, it is a state of mind; it is more than a constituency, it is a condition. To most Mississippians there is a difference between the Mississippi penciled in on a map and that Mississippi charted by a magic marker. In the next forty minutes or so, I will sketch the history of north Mississippi, which is Faulkner's "postage stamp of native soil." But before I do so, let me make a few observations.

In my study of Mississippi history, I am intrigued by the significance and irony of color. Red, for example. First there were the Redskins who hunted in the forests and tilled the land that destiny had determined would not be theirs. Bearing down hard on the "Trail of Tears" came the march of Southern civilization. Broadly and generally speaking, there were three columns in that march — the rednecks, the bluebloods, and the blacks. The rednecks were more like camp followers, scurrying on the outskirts of Southern civilization. The bluebloods, that small body of noble men, were the planters, engineers, the architects, and the generals. Blacks were the laborers, the builders of that society.

For some reason, which I do not fully understand, Southerners were possessed with a foreboding sense of destiny, a sense of history. Acclaimed historian Arnold J. Toynbee recognized this. "There is," he wrote, "a thing called history, but history is something unpleasant that happens to other people. If I had been a small boy in …. the Southern part of the United States, I should not have felt the same; I should have known …. that history had happened to my people in my part of the world." [Paraphrased]

History happened to Mississippi during the cataclysm we call the Civil War. History made museums of mansions and turned planters into insurance agents. Rednecks, the dormant majority, were aroused by the noise of that war. Rednecks and bluebloods eventually accommodated themselves to history and became red bloods who would insist that they are more American than most other Americans.

But what of blacks? History did not happen to them. There was a brief encounter during Reconstruction when blacks exercised political power commensurate with their numbers. But it proved to be illusory. Black is a color of extreme significance in the history of Mississippi and not without its own brand of irony. Black was, in the minds of some, and still is to some, a negative color denoting incapacity, incompetence, immortality. It is associated with the South's deepest anxieties: black rebellion, black domination, black power.

Notwithstanding the negative aspects of this color, one of Mississippi's major sources of income has been the production of black-gold. While I am on gold, or nearly on it, let me also point out that one of the most abundant minerals in Mississippi is pyrite, better known as "fool's gold." Several years ago the state legislature considered making pyrite the official state mineral. Had we adopted "fool's gold" as the state mineral, coupling it with the mockingbird, which is the state bird, the legislature would have achieved a level of irony the dimensions of which would have boggled the imagination. While on the mockingbird, let me note that its color is grey, a blend of black and white.

But white, by far, is Mississippi's favorite color. You have not really lived unless you have participated in that autumnal ritual when Mississippians gaze, ceremoniously, upon their fields "already white unto harvest."

White, more than any other color, is less an adjectival function, a mere part of speech. White is a decree conferring rank and status, a proclamation confirming inheritance and endowment. a bull intoning distinction and difference. White man, white supremacy, and white rule occupy the most conspicuous and illustrious positions on the value totem erected by white Mississippians as a monument to their glorious past.

Regarding our past, still another color forces itself upon our consideration. Many white Mississippians have always viewed their past through rose-colored glasses. Surely, then, it must come as no surprise to you that the present, when viewed through those same glasses, gives a predictable coloration or tint to those who would reconfigure the past or redirect the future, color the dissenter pink.

One more observation before we proceed with the historical sketch. Land is a word of primary importance in understanding Mississippi history. It has always had a social and political as well as economic significance. In one of my weaker moments, many years ago, I contemplated running for public office. When I revealed this dark secret to a friend, he replied, "Look, Dave, before you do that, you've gotta buy you some land." Let me add quickly, in the interest of my wife's peace of mind, that I have fully recovered my senses.

Anyone familiar with small, somnolent Mississippi towns has observed our attachment to the land. The lawyer, doctor, jeweler, grocer, merchant rarely funnels his profit back into his business; he siphons it off and puts it into land and enjoys restful sleep as he listens to his cotton grow. This ambition is indigenous to an agrarian people. An editorial in the Vicksburg Sun, dated April 9, 1860, reveals this ancient force at work in Mississippi:

A large plantation and negroes are the ultima thule of every Southern gentleman's ambition. For this the lawyer pores over his dusty tomes; the merchant measures his tape; the doctor rolls his pills. the

editor drives his quill, and the mechanic his plane — all, all who dare
aspire at all, look to this as the goal of their ambition.... The mind is
thus trained from infancy to think of and prepare for the attainment
of this end.

Let us now proceed with the historical sketch of north Mississippi, the land and the people Faulkner wrote about. The term north Mississippi for purposes of this discussion refers generally to the area south of the Tennessee border down to U.S. Highway 82, which extends from Greenville eastward through Indianola, Greenwood, Winona, and Starkville, to Columbus.

U.B. Phillips opened his classic study of *Life and Labor in the Old South* by suggesting, "Let us begin by discussing the weather." Average temperature extremes north of Highway 82 range from a low of 44 in January to a high of 81 in July. The average of 210 days without killing frost coupled with the relatively high degree of fertility in the various soil regions makes the area conducive to agriculture.

From west to east these soil regions include the Yazoo-Mississippi Delta, recognized as among the most fertile soil in the world. The Delta is a wedge of land about 200 miles long, from Memphis to Vicksburg, and 85 miles wide at its greatest extension eastward. Its alluvial deposits reach a depth of 35 feet. During the antebellum era, due to an absence of levies to protect the rich soil from annual flooding, Delta planters did not achieve the prestige and prominence enjoyed by their counterparts in the River Lowlands or the Old Natchez District. The Delta, as a geographic and political entity as we know it today, is largely a post-Civil War development.

Eastward from the Delta, the land rises suddenly into bluffs or hills that were formed by prehistoric dust storms that swept rich surface soil eastward across the flat Delta region. The Loess Bluffs, as this region is designated, varies in breadth from five to fifteen miles and extends the length of the state, paralleling the Mississippi River.

The Brown Loam Region, often called the Old Black Belt, is the only other soil type that extends the length of the state. It lies east of the Loess Bluffs and was at one time comparable to the Delta in fertility. The history of this region serves as a case study of soil abuse, exhaustion, and erosion. In the antebellum era it rivaled the Delta and the River Lowlands in south Mississippi in attracting land-hungry planters and was the scene of large and prosperous plantations. But after a century of abuse the soil was depleted of its fertility, and the Brown Loam Region became an area where the high concentration of farm tenancy was its most striking agricultural characteristic. Most of Lafayette County is in the Brown Loam Region.

East of the Brown Loam Region, soil regions occur with greater variety. They include the North Central Hills, which extend north of the Jackson Prairie northward through the eastern edge of Lafayette County and the western extreme of Union County, narrowing rapidly almost to a point on the Tennessee line. Before the Civil War, small farmers in these hills made feeble efforts to produce cotton, but the results were usually unsuccessful. The land was poor; the farms were small, and families were large. It was said that "nothing grows in those hills but trouble."

To the east of the North Central Hills are the Flatwoods, a long narrow strip of greyish soil of low fertility that produces little more than scrub oaks. On its southern border, the Flatwoods are bound on the east by the Tombigbee Prairie, a rich area of gently rolling terrain that extends into the southeast corner of Union County. Between the northern extremes of the Flatwoods and the Tombigbee Prairie is the Pontotoc Ridge, a region of rich sandy loam. The sandy hillsides of the Pontotoc Ridge were once the scene of Chickasaw farms; however, this area has suffered from erosion.

The remaining soil region in north Mississippi is labeled the Tennessee-Tombigbee Hills, which contain patches of rich bottom land. The rugged terrain, however, precludes large-scale agriculture. The residents of the Tennessee-Tombigbee Hills were more akin to the mountaineers of Tennessee than they were to other Mississippi farmers. This may explain why Union sentiment was stronger in this section than in any other part of Mississippi.

Coursing throughout north Mississippi are the almost numberless creeks and streams that form the state's major river systems. Their names bear eloquent testimony of those who first lived along those streams: the Tombigbee, Tilatobee, Tallahatchie, Lusascuna, Yalobusha, and Yockony Patawfa.

These rivers and many other Indian place names bespeak of those who were here before the white man came. There were at least sixteen tribes that occupied the territory that later became Mississippi. The major tribes included the Biloxi and Pascagoula on the coast, the Natchez in the southwest; the Tunica in the west central portion. the Choctaw in the central section. and the Chickasaw in the northern portion of Mississippi. Let me add, however, that these locations are approximate at best, and that all tribes ranged far into the territory of their neighbors. The most populous tribe was the Choctaws, who numbered about 20,000. The Chickasaws and Natchez numbered about 4,500 each.

The Choctaws and Chickasaws spoke virtually the same language, which was melodic. An early European traveler described it as "very agreeable to the ears, courteous, gentle, and musical .... the women in particular so fine and musical as to represent the singing of birds." None of the Mississippi tribes had a written language. Tribal folklore included a creation epic, a legendary migration epic from the "setting sun" to the "land of the great river," and a flood epic that described the use of rafts on which both men and animals escaped the relentless and rising tide. Tribal life was simple and close to nature. Virtually everything in the Indian universe was expressed in religious terms. The sun was an important manifestation of diety and was called the Great Holy Fire Above and was represented by a sacred fire in each household. Diety expressed itself in both good and evil spirts.

Tribal rites were elaborate both in life and in death. The Choctaws placed their dead on a scaffold where, at the appropriate time, bone pickers removed the flesh, and the remains were then buried amid lamentation and wailing. The Natchez often sacrificed wives and children as part of the burial rite. Chickasaws buried their dead beneath the floor of the household. The dead were placed in a sitting position facing west to enable the spirit to find its way into eternity.

Mississippi tribes developed a clan system of social organization. Clans were exogamic; members of the tribe would marry outside their clan, and descent was matrilineal and traced through the female. Most tribes also practiced both monogamy and polygamy. Essentially, most Mississippi Indians were town or village dwellers with a degree of local autonomy. The tribe was a confederation of towns or villages. Both the Choctaw and Chickasaw tribes developed a tribal council in which authority was shared and diffused. The Natchez were more autocratic. Tribal law followed custom and tradition, and in case of homicide, the victim's relatives had the right of vengeance. If the slayer escaped, his brother was deemed responsible under the right of retaliation.

Mississippi Indians were basically agrarian, and their commerce and industry remained primitive. The various tribes did, however, often engage in warfare. Second only to the consideration of territoriality, the chief benefit derived from these intertribal wars was the acquisition of slave labor. Prisoners taken in battle were reduced to bondage, and slaveholders would often sever the ankle nerves of their bondsmen, a simple technique to prevent escape without impairing the ability to work. Even if they had known the meaning of the word, most Mississippi Indians would probably not have considered their wilderness pristine. Nor could they have estimated the intoxicant effect that the lure of land would work on those strange-looking creatures walking through the woods during the winter of 1540 when Hernando DeSoto camped along the Pontotoc Ridge.

The white man came, and the Indians were caught in a three-way power struggle for empire among the Spanish, French, and English. Eventually, America would gain control of this territory, and Mississippi would become a political and geographic entity. In 1798 the Mississippi Territory was established under the same general provision as the Old Northwest Territory with one important exception. Slavery was permitted in the Mississippi Territory. Slavery had been practiced by the Indians; the French had recognized and regulated the institution of slavery in 1724 when Bienville published his Black Code; the British had allowed slavery, and the Mississippi economy presumed its continuation. By 1806 Mississippi's economic future was sealed. Cotton was rapidly becoming its chief money crop, and slavery was already an established institution. But Mississippi was not yet a closed society. Slavery had not yet become the acid test of Southern manhood, and cotton was the crown prince, but not yet king.

After almost twenty years as a territory, Mississippi was admitted to statehood in 1817. The invention of the cotton gin, the introduction of a cotton plant suitable for Mississippi's humid climate, and the development of the cotton press combined with the availability of millions of acres of land revolutionized Mississippi's economy. When Mississippi became a state, over two-thirds of its territory was Indian reserve and not accessible to white settlement. However, in rapid succession, this Indian territory was involuntarily sold to the United States under the Treaty of Doak's Stand in 1820, the Treaty of Dancing Rabbit Creek in 1830, and the Treaty of Pontotoc in 1832. The availability of this vast amount of fertile land generated a land rush of spectacular dimensions, and the effect was transformative. In a speech distinguished by its lack of exaggeration, a Mississippi politician proclaimed in 1830:

> *Already the feet of thousands press upon the borders of this new purchase… Kentucky's coming, Tennessee's coming, Alabama's coming, and they're all coming to join the joyous crowd of Mississippians.*

Unfortunately, land speculators, who have been described as the shock troops of empire, gobbled up over seventy-five percent of this new land. Prices skyrocketed from $1.25 an acre in 1830 to $40 an acre in 1835. Slave prices experienced a similar trend, and by the mid-1830s traders were asking and receiving $3,200 for a pair of young healthy slaves. The land rush was also accompanied by a population explosion. Mississippi's population increased about 200 percent from 1830 to 1840. Significantly, the census returns for 1840 indicate that Mississippi's slave population exceeded its white population, a rather simple notation for such alarming ramifications.

The 1830s were known as the "Flush Times" in Mississippi. During that exciting decade the "Crown Prince" became "King Cotton," and all public debate on slavery was closed. Let me trace the progress of that debate. In 1818 the Mississippi Supreme Court declared slavery to be an evil infesting the body politic. By 1831 Mississippi's premier orator, Sergeant Prentiss, still conceded that "slavery is a great evil…*but* a necessary one." By 1836 the debate had run its course, and Prentiss pronounced:

The people of the state of Mississippi look upon the institution of domestic slavery…not as a curse, but a blessing…a legitimate condition of the African race…and they hope to transmit this situation to their posterity as the best part of their inheritance.… We hold discussion upon this subject as equally impertinent with discussion upon our relations, wives, and children, and will allow no present change, or hope of future alteration in this matter.

This was not idle talk. In that same year, Governor John A. Quitman recommended legislation designed to prevent the dissemination of literature critical of slavery. The ultimate defense had been agreed upon. Slavery was declared a positive good. The burden of Southern history descended. The power structure would permit no further debate. In an 1836 speech before the United States Senate Mississippi's Robert J. Walker reiterated:

Our peculiar institutions will yield only at the point of the bayonet, and in a struggle for their defense we would be found invincible.

Walker's speech is remarkable because it revealed as early as 1836 the ultimate position Southerners would take in defense of slavery, and it also revealed over the next two decades the South's flawed assessment of its military prowess.

As cotton production became almost exclusively the basis of Mississippi's prosperity, the expansion of slavery became increasingly the basic issue in Mississippi politics and the test by which all public men were measured. If the great West were not opened to slave expansion, Mississippians reasoned, a surplus population would result in the devaluation of their capital investment in slaves. In 1860 the assessed valuation of Mississippi's 436,691 slaves was more than the combined valuation of its land and farm equipment.

Furthermore, if no new slave states were admitted from the new western territory acquired after the Mexican War in 1848, the balance of power in national politics would shift to the free states. That could lead to the eventual abolition of slavery. This was the rationale on which the advocates of secession pleaded their cause, which was so clearly enunciated in a *Vicksburg Sun* editorial on October 29, 1860:

> *We verily believe that the overthrow of the Union would not only perpetuate slavery where it now exists and establish it more firmly, but would necessarily lead to its widespread extension. The Southern states once constituted as an independent Republic, the acquisition of Mexico, Central America, Cuba, San Domingo, and other West India Islands would follow as a direct and necessary result. It would not be in the power of the North to prevent it, unless by an appeal to arms terminating in the subjugation of the South, and we presume that Abolition fanaticism would hardly venture upon such a Quixotic experiment as that. In possession of the Gulf of Mexico and our institutions established upon what is now the free soil of Mexico and the whole coast would be open to slave emigration, while the Northern and Western states would be completely cut off from our present possessions in that quarter. California would speedily become a slave state. The enormous wealth she is now pouring into the lap of the North would at once be withdrawn and become tributary to Southern prosperity and Southern power. While the Union lasts, it is in the power of the Northern majority to confine slavery to such territory as we already possess. She will exercise that power. Of course, no sane man believes that another slave state will ever be admitted into the Union. If they see proper the dominant majority in Congress — and this they would certainly do — can prevent the annexation of Mexico and Cuba, and other territories where slavery now exists and would be likely to go. Dissolve the Union, however, and the case is altered. The South would then be free to carry, without let or hindrance, her institution far beyond the limits to which they must be confined under our present form of government. In the Union the South cannot expand beyond her present limits; out of it she can extend her institutions over Mexico, Cuba, San Domingo, and other West India Islands and California, and thereby become the most powerful Republic that ever the sun shone upon.*

Every time I read this editorial, I more fully appreciate James L. Alcorn's assessment of the secession crisis. One of the state's wealthiest and largest slave owners in 1860 and a delegate to the Secession Convention, Alcorn said that "reason was dethroned; passions ruled, and Mississippi was hurled into the embrace of a causeless, cruel and bloody war." After that war, Alcorn joined the Republican Party, was elected governor in 1869 and was denigrated as a scalawag.

The Civil War, which was inaugurated in Mississippi with pageantry befitting a medieval joust, concluded in defeat, disillusionment, and bitter recriminations. Seventy-eight thousand young Mississippians were sent off not as soldiers to war, but as knight-crusaders in a holy and just cause. Almost half of them did not come home. Of those who did return, many came home as deserters before the war ended.

Mississippians conceded defeat, but only in battle. Their will to resist was weakened in war, but survived in peace. To most antebellum Mississippians, the world they lived in was flat; they saw only the danger but none of the adventure in that mysterious and treacherous sea of social change. Their ship of state sailed cautiously and in circles. I do not have the power to measure the magnitude of change in post-Civil War Mississippi. I will read a letter that does.

> *House of Representatives*
> *Jackson, Mississippi*
> *March 26, 1870*
> *To His Excellency Governor James L. Alcorn:*
> *Governor, I was a slave of Col. W. G. Henderson. Boys together as we were, he is the center of the tenderest associations of my life. Arrived at manhood's estate, I was still intimately connected with him.... When he was wounded at Upperville...he languished in the valley of Virginia...until it was my privilege to take him away, secretly, through the lines to his own people.*
> *My friend and loving master is a candidate for...Circuit Judge... and a good republican.*

> *Now Governor, I, by the mysterious providence of God, am a*
> *member of the Legislature…and I now place…my earnest prayer that*
> *you appoint to the Judgeship of the First District the playmate of my*
> *boyhood, the companion of my manhood, the generous friend of my*
> *whole life — my former master, Col. Henderson.*
> /s/ Ambrose Henderson

Governor Alcorn appointed Colonel Henderson to that judgeship, but Reconstruction was but an interim, a calamitous experiment, hesitantly adopted, hastily abandoned, by the white majority. Black suffrage was considered so injurious to good government that its elimination was justified by both fraud and violence. The legendary revolution of 1875 that restored a Democratic-conservative coalition to political power in Mississippi is without parallel in the history of election abuse. It was, however, in the vocabulary of Mississippi politics, an act of "redemption." Mississippi lost the war but won the peace.

As a basis for a permanent structure of peace, Mississippi redeemers, or Bourbons as they were called, forged a political organization from which there could be no dissent, which would tolerate no division on any issue, a party that, like the king, could do no wrong. The party's cardinal principle was white supremacy, its policy was color line voting. "The safety of Mississippi," LQC Lamar declared, "lies in the maintenance of the Democratic organization and its wise direction by conservative leaders."

Those conservative leaders were more than politicians; they were prophets who envisioned a "New South," an industrial, commercial, manufacturing, vibrant, and an energetic South. The energy and interests of those leaders were channeled in such a direction and were not without some success. The value of manufactured products in Mississippi rose more than 100 percent from 1870 to 1890. Railroad construction was Mississippi's most significant industrial enterprise. Mileage increased more than 108 percent from 1880 to 1890. In 1883 Mississippi laid more track than any other state in the country. The number of industrial jobs increased almost 300 percent from 1860 to 1890.

In contrast to industrial development, Mississippi agriculture declined. The total value of farm products rose only fractionally from 1870 to 1890. Mississippi farmers were caught in the cycle of declining prices and increasing production. Cotton prices dropped from 15 cents a pound in 1870 to 7.8 cents in 1890. But the crop lien system, under which a farmer mortgaged his crop against credit advances, induced the farmer to increase his cotton production to offset the falling prices. Such a system inevitably led to tenancy and sharecropping as the farmer became hopelessly indebted to his creditor. From year to year, the tenant farmed with reckless abandon in the hope of a bumper crop that could free him from debt. Under Mississippi's lien law, a tenant could not relocate until he was free and clear of debt. The relentless demands of the tenant system exhausted much of Mississippi's fertile land.

Farm tenancy and sharecropping in Faulkner's country was as fundamentally characteristic of post-Civil War agriculture as slavery had been in antebellum agriculture. In 1890, 60.27 percent of all Mississippi farmers were tenants or sharecroppers. Mississippi ranked number one nationally in the incidence of farm tenancy. In Lafayette County, over 55 percent of the farm families were tenants; in Union County, 50 percent; in the adjacent counties of Marshall and Panola the figures were 70 percent and 74 percent.

The economic disparity between poor whites and the white power structure in the 1880s generated political unrest among poor white farmers and laborers who vocalized their discontent through the Farmer's Alliance, an organization that also included some black members. Dirt farmers were confounded, however, by the accusations leveled against them by the ruling elite, who accused them of jeopardizing white supremacy by allowing blacks in their organization. Wilbur J. Cash described that confrontation:

> *When our common white…had come to this…the eyes of his old captains were ominous and accusing upon him. From hustings and from pulpits thousands of voices proclaimed him traitor and n…r-loving scoundrel; renegade to Southern Womanhood, the Confederate*

dead, and the God of his Fathers [and supporters] of the transforma-
tion of the white race into a mongrel breed.

The poor whites recoiled, but they were restless. An emerging leadership among poor whites both responded to and exploited that unrest. Their
strategy was to diminish the black vote by constitutional provisions such as
the poll tax and the literacy test that were included in the new state Constitution adopted in 1890. They would also exclude most blacks from political
activity by establishing the party primary system of nominating candidates
for public office. Because the Democratic Party did not allow blacks membership in the party, the nominating primary became known as the "lily
white primary." When blacks no longer posed a threat to white supremacy,
the poor whites, who became known as "rednecks," could then challenge
the Bourbons on political and economic issues, which they did in 1903.

James Kimble Vardaman, the White Chief and spokesman for the redneck farmer, was nominated for governor by the Democratic Party in the
first "lily white primary" and elected in 1903. Vardaman and his successors inaugurated their own brand of Southern progressivism. Among Vardaman's successors, and initially among his political allies, was Theodore
Gilmore Bilbo. Both Vardaman and Bilbo assailed corporate interests as the
enemies of reform and secured regulatory legislation to restrain their power.
Additionally, they promoted and achieved significant economic reform in
the interest of small farmers and laborers.

However, the upturn in Mississippi agriculture resulted largely from the
temporary increased demand for products caused by World War I. And the
changes in buying habits in postwar America activated a downward trend
that plunged Mississippi farmers, in common with the rest of the nation,
into abysmal depression during the 1920s.

Cotton, though still king in Mississippi, suffered humiliating assaults
against its prerogative. The lowly boll weevil drastically reduced production
just prior to and during the early 1920s. A flood in 1927 and a drought in
1930 added to the farmer's misery. Moreover, the plundering of Mississippi's
piney woods had run its course in the early twenties, and the forty thousand

workers formerly employed in timber production glutted the labor market. It is not difficult to see why Franklin D. Roosevelt would say, upon taking office in 1933, that the nation's number-one economic problem was the South.

As the depression deepened and revenues declined, the state treasury was exhausted. In his second term, Bilbo called the legislature into special session for the purpose of issuing bonds to meet the state's current obligations. But not enough legislators showed up to conduct business. In 1931, Bilbo issued another, more urgent, call. When the legislature did convene and authorized a bond issue, the state could find no purchasers for the bonds. Consequently, Mississippi's deficit increased to $12,000,000, a staggering amount at that time.

In the gubernatorial election of 1931, Martin Conner, a self-styled businessman-politician, promised to operate state government on a business-like basis. This meant rigid economy and a balanced budget. To achieve such ends, Governor Conner reduced the number of government employees and slashed government salaries and services and implemented a two percent sales tax, one of the first in the nation. When Connor left office in 1936, the state treasury showed a cash balance in excess of $3,000,000. Conner's businessman's approach to state government culminated in Governor Hugh L. White's Balance Agriculture with Industry program, established in 1936. The BAWI became an official, government policy of attracting industry into Mississippi through tax exemptions and low rental factories paid for by local bond issues.

The success of BAWI coupled with economic expansion prompted by World War II lifted Mississippi out of the doldrums of abject poverty, although Mississippi still ranks fiftieth in per capita income. Economic benefits notwithstanding, postwar conditions disquieted the issue of race in Mississippi. From 1931 to 1955 no governor in Mississippi owed his election exclusively to his position on race. But, as African Americans increasingly demanded the full political and social benefits of citizenship after World War II, a corresponding resistance among whites reactivated politicians who were willing to parley that resistance into political power and public office.

Mississippi politicians have more often been measured by eloquence than competence, not by their aspirations for the future, but by their devotion to the past, and not by their theories of government, but their theories of history. To most Mississippians history is not what happened, but what they wish had happened. Let me read an extract from an article written by Dunbar Rowland, who was for many years the director of the Mississippi Department of Archives and History. This article appeared in the official publication of the Mississippi Historical Society. Although it was written in 1900 it approximates what many Mississippians still believe about their past.

> *From 1817 to 1861 Mississippi was...a land of brave men, fair women, and eloquent statesmen.... The black toilers were happy in their work [and were] joyous and mirth-loving.*
>
> *The Mississippi planter was magnificent and great in everything, great in his strength and great in his weakness.... The grand and noble men and women of the "Old South" are rapidly passing away. Their memories, deeds, and virtues must be preserved by their sons and daughters. They must be preserved on the living pages of history... in story, poetry, song, in sculptured marble...so that they will endure forever and forever.*

Can you not now understand why many Mississippians revere Confederate statues and fly the Rebel flag? Can you now understand what Faulkner meant when he wrote, "The past is never dead, it's not even past?" Let me read from Faulkner's *Intruder in the Dust*:

> *It's all now you see. Yesterday won't be over until tomorrow and tomorrow began ten thousand years ago. For every Southern boy fourteen years old, not once but whenever he wants it, there is the instant when it's still not yet two o'clock on that July afternoon in 1863...it hasn't happened yet, it hasn't even begun yet, it not only hasn't begun yet but there is still time for it not to begin...yet it's going to begin, we all know that we have come too far with too much at stake and that moment*

doesn't even need a fourteen-year-old boy to think This time. Maybe this time with all this much to lose and all this must to gain: Pennsylvania, Maryland, the world, the golden dome and Washington itself to crown with desperate and unbelievable victory the desperate gamble.

If you would understand Mississippi, you must realize as Faulkner has said, we are haunted by a past that will not die. The past will not die because it is not past. Remember that we dreamed of empire, and when those dreams were laid waste on the fields of Antietam and Vicksburg and Gettysburg, we fantasized.

But like the land we live on, the woods we hunt in, and the streams we sit by, we are not unduly troubled by it all. We have this thing about being Mississippians. We accept, even if we do not understand, the purity of heart to will one thing: the duality of kindness and cruelty attendant in a single act, the plurality of forces at work in one man's nature. We are obsessed with our very being but are not baffled by it. We are, without reason, an incredibly happy people. We are, perhaps without the right, an incurably optimistic people. We have learned not even to ask the questions. We believe that we will not merely endure; we believe we will prevail.

William Faulkner

Richard Wright

Eudora Welty

John Grisham

Tennessee Williams

Natasha Trethewey

Willie Morris

Kathryn Stockett

3

MISSISSIPPI'S LITERARY TRADITION

A MARVEL IN THE WORLD OF LETTERS

Mississippi's literary tradition is a marvel in the world of letters and is the subject of numerous studies. The state's literary heritage emerged from its rich cultural and racial diversity, and the tradition of oral narratives, legends, and storytelling that are an integral part of Mississippi's history. Mildred Taylor explains that her books are literary enrichments of the stories she heard as a child. Mississippi writers are also influenced by a strong sense of place. Eudora Welty explained that "Mississippi is rich in resources for the writer [and] is forever astir, changing, reflecting, like the mind of man itself." Sterling Plump expressed a similar sentiment. "It dawned on me," he recalled, that "my rural upbringing in Mississippi [gave] me a sense of permanence, roots that are not easily dug up."

Literary scholars and historians also point to the state's preoccupation with the past, to conflict and to change, and to the burden of history. William Faulkner said, "The past is never dead. It's not even past." He also said that Mississippians do not study their past; they absorb it.

Among Mississippi's earliest women writers were Sarah Anne Dorsey, Eliza Ann Dupuy, and Catherine Ann Ware Warfield. In his biographical sketch of Sarah Dorsey on the *Mississippi History Now* website, Bertram Wyatt-Brown wrote that Sarah Anne Dorsey was "one of the most intellectually gifted women of Mississippi." In 1863-1864 she published her first novel in a literary magazine, and "like her other novels it was a barely disguised autobiography." Eliza Ann Dupuy, another writer of some renown, passed through Natchez during her lengthy literary career before moving on to New Orleans from her native Kentucky. Some of her best work during a long literary career was done during her sojourn in Natchez. While in Natchez she became a friend of Joseph Holt Ingraham. Her biographical sketch in James B. Lloyd's *Lives of Mississippi Authors* cites twenty-five publications. Another prominent early Mississippi writer was Catherine Ann Ware Warfield, one of those sentimental female writers whom Nathaniel Hawthorne described in 1855 as that 'damned mob of scribbling women.'"

One of Mississippi's most notable early writers was Joseph Holt Ingraham, who was born in Portland, Maine, in 1809 and died in Holly Springs, Mississippi, in 1860. After attending Yale College in 1829, he went to New Orleans and then to Natchez where he joined the faculty at Jefferson College in nearby Washington, Mississippi. In 1835 Ingraham published *The South-West, By a Yankee*. Throughout his remarkable career Ingraham published more than four hundred short, paper-bound novels, called "dime novels," and more than a hundred poems, articles, and letters. Ingraham's biblical novel, *Pillar of Fire, Israel in Bondage*, was a major source for the movie *The Ten Commandments*. In 1847 Joseph Holt Ingraham entered the ministry of the Protestant Episcopal Church. After serving various churches in Alabama and Tennessee, Ingraham took charge of Christ Church and St. Thomas School for Boys in Holly Springs in 1858. Ingraham's last publication was *The Sunny South* (1860), a defense of his adopted homeland in response to Harriet Beecher Stowe's *Uncle Tom's Cabin* (1850). Joseph Holt Ingraham died on December 18, 1860, as a result of an accidental self-inflicted gunshot wound. His biographer, Robert W. Weathersby, II, identified Ingraham as "One of the most popular and prolific authors of his time (but) one of the most obscure of ours." His son, Prentiss Ingraham, who was born in Natchez, was even more prolific than his illustrious father. Prentiss Ingraham (1843-1904) wrote six hundred dime novels and four hundred novelettes.

Ever since Andrew Marschalk brought the first printing press to Mississippi in 1798 and edited several newspapers during the territorial period, newsprint has been a powerful influence in Mississippi society and politics, and there have been many influential journalists during its often tumultuous history. The long-running feud between George Poindexter and Editor Marschalk is legendary in Mississippi history. On one occasion Judge Poindexter summoned Marschalk before the bar of justice and fined him for contempt of court. Marschalk said he would gladly pay the fine because that was just what he intended, contempt for Judge Poindexter. Until the beginning of radio transmission in the 1920s, newspapers were the primary source of news and information available to the American people.

Because Mississippians are so preoccupied with the past, it is only natural that the state would produce many distinguished historians. Among the state's earliest historians were John W. Monette, who published a two-volume *History of the Discovery and Settlement of the Valley of the Mississippi* in 1846, and J.F.H. Claiborne, the author of *Mississippi, as a Province, Territory and State*, which he published in 1880. J.F.H. Claiborne was the nephew of Governor W.C.C. Claiborne, the second governor of the Mississippi Territory.

Because we cannot discuss all of Mississippi's writers, we will focus on our state's major literary figures. Mississippi's most famous and widely acclaimed writers are William Faulkner, Richard Wright, Eudora Welty, and Tennessee Williams. They are literary giants in the world of letters, but they did not stifle creative writing in Mississippi. They inspired wave after wave of Mississippi writers.

William Faulkner (1897-1962)

William Faulkner grew up in Oxford, where his father was business manager at The University of Mississippi for several years. Most of Faulkner's novels and short stories take place in his fictional Yoknapatawpha County. Even though these people and places were created by this literary genius, they bear striking resemblance to real people in real towns, not only in Mississippi but around the world. The basic themes in Faulkner's novels are not local but universal, and include honor and greed, human dignity and depravity, the dissolution of families, class distinction and racial prejudice, love, hate, jealousy, and violence. These are mankind's deepest and innermost anxieties. Someone once asked Faulkner what he wrote about, and he said he wrote about the human heart in conflict with itself. The characters in his novels are Mississippians, but the struggles they faced are shared by men and women everywhere. His writings have been translated into many languages, and he is widely read in Europe and Asia.

William Faulkner won a Nobel Prize in Literature in 1949. The Nobel Prize is a prestigious award made by the Swedish Academy to a literary figure anywhere in the world. He also won a Pulitzer Prize in 1955 for *A Fable*, and in 1963 for *The Reivers*. Among Faulkner's most famous novels are *The Sound and the Fury* (1929), *As I Lay Dying* (1930), *Light in August* (1932), *Absalom, Absalom!* (1936), and *The Reivers* (1962).

Richard Wright (1908-1960)

Considered by many literary critics as America's major African American writer, Richard Wright was born a child of sharecroppers in Adams County, near Natchez. After his parents separated when he was five years old, Wright lived with various relatives in Mississippi, Arkansas, and Tennessee. In 1927, Wright joined the Great Migration and moved to Chicago to escape the racism and degradation in his native South. Throughout his youth, Wright developed an intense interest in literature and read most of America's major writers. Wright's first novel, *Uncle Tom's Children*, was published in 1938. The following year he received a Guggenheim Fellowship that made it possible for him to write *Native Son* (1940), which was an immediate success. It was a Book-of-the-Month selection and was translated into six languages. In 1945, Wright published an autobiographical novel titled *Black Boy*.

The basic theme in Wright's early novels is the black man's struggle to maintain dignity in a white man's world. Some critics describe Wright as an angry and bitter man because of the social and legal injustices blacks experienced in America. Disenchanted with his native country, Wright and his family moved to France in 1946, where he continued to write. None of his later works, however, equaled the quality and popularity of his earlier novels. The Natchez Literary and Cinema Celebration present annual Richard Wright Awards to outstanding Mississippi writers.

Eudora Welty (1909-2001)

Mississippi's distinguished woman of letters, Eudora Welty, was born in Jackson. Welty spent most of her life in Mississippi, which is the setting for most of her novels and short stories. Unlike Faulkner's Mississippi, which is "a place of violent men and desperate struggle," Welty's Mississippi is "a tidy, protected little world" where people live their lives in relative tranquility. This does not mean that Welty did not deal with the struggles and conflicts of the human heart. It means that Welty dealt with them in a different way. Her characters are set in more serene circumstances, and they respond to the human struggle in a more gentle and less desperate way. But, like Faulkner, Welty places great emphasis upon place and family in her novels and short stories.

Welty was a popular lecturer and held several visiting professorships at major universities in America and England. In addition to numerous other awards for her fiction, Welty received a Pulitzer Prize in 1973 for her novel *The Optimist's Daughter*.

Tennessee Williams (1910-1983)

One of America's most successful playwrights, Tennessee Williams was born in Columbus and spent much of his childhood visiting his grandparents in Clarksdale. Many of his most successful plays have Mississippi or Southern settings, and his characters speak a dialect and have manners that clearly reflect the Mississippi influence of his early youth.

A central theme in many of Williams's plays is the deceit and greed of mankind and the certainty of retribution for those weaknesses. Among his most successful Broadway hits are *The Glass Menagerie* (1945), *A Streetcar Named Desire* (1947), and *Cat on a Hot Tin Roof* (1955). Williams won both the New York Drama Critics' Circle Award and a Pulitzer Prize for two of his plays – *A Streetcar Named Desire* in 1948 and *Cat on a Hot Tin Roof* in 1955.

Tennessee Williams's given name was Thomas Lanier Williams. "Tennessee" was a college nickname that stuck with him for the rest of his life.

OTHER MAJOR WRITERS

It is difficult to determine who should be included on a list of Mississippi's other major writers. Literature is a matter of taste and preference, and the following names would be included on almost anyone's list of Mississippi writers. These biographical sketches are arranged alphabetically and are brief so more writers can be included on the list.

Margaret Walker Alexander (1915-1998)

This internationally renowned author spent most of her academic career at Jackson State University. She received the Yale Younger Poets prize, a Ford Fellowship, and a Houghton Mifflin Fellowship. She won wide acclaim for her book of poems, *For My People* (1942). Margaret Walker Alexander is best known for her novel, *Jubilee* (1966), the story of her great-grandmother; and for her book of essays, *On Being Female, Black, and Free* (1997). One of her major contributions to literary scholarship is her book, *Richard Wright, Daemonic Genius: A Portrait of the Man, a Critical Look at His Work* (1988). In 1968, at Jackson State University, she founded the Institute for the Study of the History, Life, and Culture of Black People. In 1989, the institute was renamed the Margaret Walker Alexander National Research Center.

William Attaway (1911-1986)

The Delta town of Greenville has produced many prominent writers and editors, including William Attaway. He was also a major figure in the Harlem Renaissance, a period of prolific writing, art, and music by African Americans in New York City in the 1920s and 1930s. His novels, *Let Me Breathe Thunder* (1939) and *Blood on the Forge* (1941), deal with the tribulations of segregation in the early twentieth century and the Great Migration of African Americans from the South.

Larry Brown (1951-2004)

Larry Brown was born in Oxford and grew up on the family farm in Lafayette County. His major works include the novels *Dirty Work* (1989); *Joe* (1991); *Father and Son* (1996), which won the Southern Book Award; and Faye (2000). He also wrote *On Fire* (1994), an account of his brief career as a fireman, and two volumes of short stories, *Facing the Music* (1988) and *Big Bad Love* (1990). Unfortunately, Larry Brown's remarkable literary career was ended by his untimely death at the age of fifty-one.

Will D. Campbell (1924-2013)

Will Campbell is known for many profound and outlandish statements. One of my favorites is "We are all bastards, but God loves us anyway." After Campbell received a BA in English from Wake Forest, he earned a divinity degree from Yale University in 1952. Will Campbell was among the early voices who spoke out for social equality and racial justice in a troubled world. When he was director of religious life at Ole Miss in the 1950s he was accused by the college board of playing ping pong with a "Negro" who worked on campus. During his illustrious life and literary career, Campbell published more than fifteen books including novels, biographies, and memoirs. His most famous book is *Brother to a Dragonfly* (1977). An edition was republished in 2000, with a foreword by President Jimmy Carter. Perhaps his most popular book was *Forty Acres, and a Goat: A Memoir* (1986).

David Cohn (1896-1960)

David Cohn was one of the Greenville writers who wrote books on a wide range of topics that included the influence of the automobile on American society; the technological revolution in American agriculture; and the mail-order sales technique of Sears, Roebuck and Co. He also wrote a humorous and perceptive account of life in the Delta titled *Where I Was Born and Raised* (1948). At the time of his death, Cohn left a seven-hundred-page autobiography, which has not been published. One of David Cohn's most popular quotes is "The Mississippi Delta begins in the lobby of the Peabody Hotel in Memphis and ends on Catfish Row in Vicksburg."

Ellen Douglas

This seventh-generation Mississippian was writing poetry and sketches at the age of nine. Ellen Douglas was born in Natchez but moved to Greenville after her marriage to Kenneth Haxton, Jr. Because of its more than sixty-four published authors, Greenville has been called the "Athens of the Delta." Douglas's novel, *A Family's Affairs* (1961), won the Houghton Mifflin Award and was listed as one of the five best novels in 1961 by *The New York Times*. Among her other works are *Black Cloud, White Cloud* (1963); *Apostles of Light* (1973); *The Rock Cried Out* (1979); *A Long Night* (1986); and two nonfiction books, *Truth: Four Stories I Am Finally Old Enough to Tell* (1998) and *Witnessing* (2004).

Richard Ford

A native of Jackson, Richard Ford attended Michigan State University and the University of California. Among his works are *A Piece of My Heart* (1987); *The Ultimate Good Luck* (1981); *The Sportswriter* (1986); *Rock Springs* (1987); and *Wildlife* (1990), a collection of short fiction. Ford won the 1996 Pulitzer Prize for *Independence Day*, a sequel to *The Sportswriter*. His most recent book, which ranks among his very best, is titled *Let Me Be Frank With You* and was published in 2014. As a child, Richard Ford lived across the street from Eudora Welty and went to the elementary school she had attended. He even had some of her same teachers, though there was a thirty-five year difference in their ages.

John Grisham

The Mississippi Writers Page refers to John Grisham as "an international phenomenon" and identifies him as "one of the world's best-selling novelists." There are approximately 300 million John Grisham books in print, and they have been translated into 42 languages. Grisham was born in Arkansas, but his family moved to Southaven when he was twelve years old. After earning a law degree at Ole Miss in 1981, Grisham practiced law and served in the Mississippi legislature. His first novel, *A Time to Kill* (1989), received good reviews but was not a best seller. His second novel, *The Firm*

(1991), was a runaway best seller, a popular motion picture, and launched one of the most remarkable literary careers in American history. Grisham has published more than thirty novels, most of which are best-selling legal thrillers. John Grisham has shared his good fortune with his fellow man. When he is not writing books, Grisham and his wife, Renee, devote their time and resources to serving mankind.

Barry Hannah (1942-2010)

Barry Hannah was one of Mississippi's most beloved writers. He grew up in Clinton and attended the creative writing program at the University of Arkansas. Hannah was catapulted into fame for his first book, *Geronimo Rex* (1972), which won the William Faulkner Prize. Some critics think it is his finest work. Among his other books are *Night-Watchmen* (1973), *Ray* (1980), *The Tennis Handsome* (1983), *Hey Jack!* (1987), *Boomerang* (1989), *Never Die* (1991), *Men Without Ties* (1995), *High Lonesome* (1996), and *Yonder Stands Your Orphan* (2001). His collections of short fiction include *Airships* (1978), *Captain Maximus* (1985), and *Bats Out of Hell* (1993). He was writer in residence at The University of Mississippi when he died.

Beth Henley

Beth Henley's *Crimes of the Heart* (1978) is a play about three awkward and ill-at-ease sisters in Hazlehurst. The play was a remarkable success and won several awards, including the New York Drama Critics' Circle Award and the Pulitzer Prize, both in 1981. Her two-act play, *The Miss Firecracker Contest* (1985), was also a huge success. Both plays were made into popular movies. Among her other works are *Impossible Marriage*, which premiered in New York in 1998; *Family Week* (2000); and *Ridiculous Fraud* (2006).

Greg Iles

Best known for his thrillers, which have won rave reviews, Greg Iles was born in Germany at the height of the Cold War when his father was stationed at the American Embassy. Iles graduated from The University of Mississippi in 1983 and published *Spandau Phoenix* in 1993. His second novel, *Black Cross*, appeared two years later. Since then, Iles has published several novels in rapid succession. Among his works are *24 Hours* (2000), which was made into a movie called *Trapped* in 2002; T*he Footprints of God: A Novel* (2003); *Turning Angel* (2005); and *The Devil's Punchbowl* (2009). His novels have been translated into twenty languages and published in thirty-five countries.

Anne Moody (1940-2015)

Anne Moody won fame and acclaim for her autobiography *Coming of Age in Mississippi* (1968). *Coming of Age* is a compelling story of a young black woman, a child of sharecroppers, growing up in rural Mississippi during the Civil Rights Movement. Moody became an active member of the NAACP, CORE, and SNCC. Her autobiography was required reading in colleges all across the country. *Coming of Age in Mississippi* won the Brotherhood Award from the National Council of Christians and Jews, the Best Book of the Year Award from the National Library Association, and the International PEN/Faulkner Award. Anne Moody eventually moved to New York City.

Willie Morris (1934-1999)

When Willie Morris graduated from Yazoo City High School, his father advised him to leave Mississippi to seek greener pastures and broaden his horizons. Willie Morris went to the University of Texas and edited the *Daily Texan*, the largest student newspaper in America at that time. After graduating, he moved to New York City and soon became the youngest editor of *Harper's*, one of America's oldest and most prestigious magazines. Morris chronicled these early years of his life in *North Toward Home* (1967), a popular memoir and an American classic. In 1980, he came back home as writer-in-residence at The University of Mississippi and taught in the School of Journalism. He wrote about coming home in the book *Homecomings*, which was illustrated by William Dunlap, a celebrated Mississippi artist. Among Morris's many popular books are *Yazoo: Integration in a Deep-Southern Town* (1971); *Terrains of the Heart* (1981); *The Courting of*

Marcus Dupree (1983); *Faulkner's Mississippi* (1990); *New York Days* (1993); *My Dog Skip* (1995), which was made into a popular movie; and *The Ghosts of Medgar Evers* (1999).

Walker Percy (1916-1990)

Born in Alabama, Walker Percy moved to Greenville after his parents died. He grew up in the home of his cousin, William Alexander Percy. Walker Percy earned a medical degree, but bad health prevented his practice of medicine and he became a successful and highly acclaimed writer. In 1962, Percy received a National Book Award for his novel *The Moviegoer*. Walker Percy also wrote *The Last Gentleman* (1966), *Love in the Ruins* (1971), *Message in the Bottle* (1975), *Lancelot* (1977), *The Second Coming* (1980), and *The Thanatos Syndrome* (1987).

William Alexander Percy (1885-1942)

This distinguished Greenville writer is best known for his classic autobiography, *Lanterns on the Levee* (1941). William Alexander Percy chronicled life in the Mississippi Delta in the 1920s and wrote of his father's resistance to the racial violence of the Ku Klux Klan. His father was LeRoy Percy, a Delta planter and politician who served in the United States Senate from 1910 to 1913. William Alexander Percy also published several volumes of poetry, including *Sappho in Levkas, and Other Poems* (1915) and *In April Once* (1920).

Sterling Plumpp

As a small boy Sterling Plumpp, while living with his grandparents, worked in the cotton fields near Clinton. When he was fifteen years old, he moved to Jackson, where he completed his high school education. He was valedictorian of his class in 1960. After two years in the U.S. Army, Plumpp enrolled at Roosevelt University and graduated in 1968. Although he is best known as a poet, Plumpp has written several books, including *Portable Soul* (1969); *Half Black, Half Blacker* (1970); *Clinton* (1976); *The Mojo Hands Call, I Must Go* (1982); *Blues: The Story Always Untold* (1989); *Harriet Tub-*

man (1996); *Ornate With Smoke* (1997); and *Paul Robeson* (1998). His 2013 book of poems, *Home/Bass*, won the 2014 American Book Award for Poetry.

Elizabeth Spencer

Born in Carrollton and educated at Belhaven College and Vanderbilt University, Elizabeth Spencer published her first major novel when she was twenty-seven years old. *Fire in the Morning* (1948) was listed in the book review section of *The New York Times* as one of the three best novels of 1948. While serving on the faculty at The University of Mississippi, Spencer published *This Crooked Way* in 1952. She received a Guggenheim Fellowship in 1953 and spent two years in Italy researching her novel, *The Light in the Piazza* (1960). Her novel, *The Voice at the Back Door* (1956), won the Rosenthal Award of the National Institute of Arts and Letters, which is now known as the American Academy of Arts and Letters. In 2013, at the age of ninety-two, Elizabeth Spencer published *Starting Over*, her thirteenth book.

Kathryn Stockett

Seldom in the history of American literature has a first book achieved so much acclaim as Kathryn Stockett's 2009 novel, *The Help*. It might be added, rarely has a first novel sold 1.9 million copies. The setting is Jackson during the Civil Rights Movement. The major characters are two African American maids and a young white woman who recently graduated from Ole Miss. *The Help* was made into a blockbuster movie in 2011.

James Street (1903-1954)

James Street's novel *Tap Roots* (1942) was about the legendary "Free State of Jones" and was made into a popular movie. In his later years, Street wrote two religious novels, *The Gauntlet* (1945) and T*he High Calling* (1951).

Donna Tartt

Donna Tartt took the literary world by storm in 1992 when she published *The Secret History*, which is a story of murder and intrigue at a small, fictional Vermont college. Donna Tartt wrote her first poem at five years of age and published her first sonnet in a literary review at thirteen. At Ole Miss, she took Barry Hannah's graduate course in short stories in her freshman year. She began writing *The Secret History* during her sophomore year at Bennington College in Vermont. The initial printing of *The Secret History* was 750,000 copies, a remarkable number for a first novel. Since her fabulous debut, Donna Tartt has published two more novels, *The Little Friend* in 2002, and *The Goldfinch* in 2013, which won the 2014 Pulitzer Prize.

Clifton Taulbert

A successful author, lecturer, and entrepreneur, Clifton Taulbert came of age during the early days of the Civil Rights Movement in Glen Allan, a small community in the Mississippi Delta. His first book, *Once Upon a Time When We Were Colored* (1989), is a compelling account of his childhood. Rather than focusing on the barriers between blacks and whites, Taulbert writes about the bonds that held his extended family together during those days of conflict and change. His second book, *The Last Train North* (1992), chronicles his decision to leave Mississippi and join the U.S. Air Force. Among Taulbert's other works are *Watching Our Crops Come In* (1997); *Eight Habits of the Heart: The Timeless Values That Build Strong Communities* (1997); *The Journey Home: A Father's Gift to His Son* (2002); and three children's books. Taulbert was awarded the 27th annual NAACP Image Award for Literature and the Mississippi Arts and Letters Award for Nonfiction. Time magazine has named Taulbert one of America's outstanding entrepreneurs.

Mildred D. Taylor

When Mildred D. Taylor was three months old, her family joined the Great Migration and moved from Mississippi to Ohio. In the early years of her childhood, her father often brought the family back to visit their relatives in Mississippi. During those visits, storytelling was a regular feature of Mildred Taylor's homecoming. The stories she heard about the dignity and survival of her people living in a hostile and segregated society left a lasting impression on her. The characters and events in her novels are drawn largely from her memory of those family stories. Her first novel, *Song of the Trees* (1975), won the Council on Interracial Books for Children Award. Her second novel, *Roll of Thunder, Hear My Cry* (1976), won the Newberry Award from the American Library Association and was made into a popular motion picture. The Newberry Medal is awarded each year for the most distinguished American children's book published the previous year. In 2001 Mildred Taylor received the Corretta Scott King Author Award, and in 2004 Mississippi celebrated Mildred D. Taylor Day, and she presented a well-attended public address at Ole Miss.

Natasha Trethewey

Trethewey was born in Gulfport but grew up in Decatur, Georgia. During her early childhood, she spent the summers with her grandmother in Mississippi and New Orleans. She has often written about her life growing up in the South, the child of a white father and a black mother. Among her books are *Domestic Work* (2000), *Bellocq's Ophelia* (2002), *Beyond Katrina: A Meditation on the Mississippi Gulf Coast* (2010), and *Thrall* (2012). Among her many awards are the 2008 Mississippi Governor's Award for Excellence in Poetry and the 2009 Richard Wright Award, presented annually by the Natchez Literary and Cinema Celebration. Natasha Trethewey won a Pulitzer Prize in 2007 for her book of poems *Native Guard*. She has served as poet laureate of Mississippi and has twice been named America's poet laureate. Natasha Trethewey is the Robert W. Woodruff professor of English and creative writing at Emory University in Atlanta, Georgia.

Jesmyn Ward

In 2017 Jesmyn Ward won her second National Book Award for *Sing, Unburied, Sing*, which won critical acclaim and was compared to works by William Faulkner and Toni Morrison. She won her first National Book Award in 2011 for *Salvage the Bones*.

Ida B. Wells (1862-1931)

A journalist, teacher, and social activist, Ida B. Wells was a pioneer in the Civil Rights and Women's Suffrage Movements. She was born into slavery in Holly Springs in 1862. After her emancipation, she devoted her life to the elevation of blacks and women to full citizenship. She was active in the Niagara Movement, which evolved into the NAACP. The story of her life is told in *Crusade for Justice: The Autobiography of Ida B. Wells* (1970), which was edited by her daughter.

Ben Ames Williams (1889-1953)

Born in Macon, Mississippi, Ben Ames Williams wrote his first major novel, *All the Brothers Were Valiant* (1919), about a seafaring family in New England. It became a major motion picture. In later years, he wrote several Civil War novels. His *House Divided* (1947) ranks with Stark Young's *So Red the Rose* (1934) and Margaret Mitchell's *Gone With the Wind* (1936) as America's best and most popular Civil War novels.

Al Young

Born in Ocean Springs in 1939, Al Young majored in Spanish at the University of California. His interest in language and music are evident in his writing, which includes fiction, poetry, and films. Among his major works are the novels *Who Is Angelina?* (1975), *Sitting Pretty* (1976), *Ask Me Now* (1980), and *Seduction by Light* (1992). His collections of poems include *Dancing* (1969), *The Song Turning Back Into Itself* (1971), *Geography of the Near Past* (1976), *The Blues Don't Change* (1982), and *Heaven* (1988). Young has been writer-in-residence at the University of Michigan and the University of Arkansas. From 2005 to 2008, Al Young was the poet laureate of California. He was appointed by California's governor to spread the art of poetry across the state and inspire a new generation of poets.

Stark Young (1881-1963)

The sudden appearance of numerous Southern writers in the 1920s and 1930s is identified as the Southern Renaissance by literary scholar Louis

Rubin. Stark Young of Como is considered one of the most important of those writers. *So Red the Rose*, which Young published in 1934, is considered, along with *Gone With the Wind* and *House Divided*, as one of the best Civil War novels in American fiction. For many years, Stark Young was also one of America's foremost literary critics. At various times during his long career, he wrote for *Theatre Arts Monthly*, *The New Republic*, and *The New York Times*.

The Oxford Literati

Since the founding of Square Books in 1979 by Richard and Lisa Howorth, and the appointment of Willie Morris to the Ole Miss faculty in 1980, and Barry Hannah's taking residence in Oxford, and especially after the establishment of the John and Renee Grisham Writer in Residence at Ole Miss, Oxford has become the locus of a literati of some distinction. Among the prominent writers who currently live in Oxford are Curtis Wilkie, Neil White, Megan Abbott, Beth Ann Fennelly, Ace Atkins, Tom Franklin, Julie Cantrell, Ann Fisher-Wirth, and Larry Wells.

JOURNALISTS AND HISTORIANS

In addition to Mississippi's tradition of creative writing, the state has also produced many famous journalists and historians. But like Mississippi's writers, there are so many renowned journalists and historians that only some of them can be discussed.

JOURNALISTS

Turner Catledge (1901-1983)

Among Mississippi's most famous and prestigious journalists was Turner Catledge, the editor of *The New York Times*. A native of Choctaw County and a graduate of Mississippi State University, Catledge began his career in journalism as a fourteen-year-old part-time printer at the *Neshoba Democrat* in Philadelphia. Catledge later became editor of the *Tunica Times*, where he wrote several editorials condemning the Ku Klux Klan. After serving briefly as editor of the *Tupelo Journal*, Catledge joined the staff at *The New York Times* in 1929. In 1943, Catledge was promoted to editor of one of the world's great newspapers. A year after he retired in 1970, Catledge published a popular autobiography, *My Life and The Times* (1971).

Lerone Bennett Jr. (1928-2018)

One of Mississippi's most prominent African American writers, Lerone Bennett, Jr., was born in Clarksdale in 1928. Bennett was a journalist, historian, and essayist. He is best known as editor of *Ebony* magazine, where he was senior editor from 1958 to 1987. In 1998 Bennett received the Silver Em Award for Outstanding Journalism from Ole Miss. Among his major works are *Before the Mayflower: A History of the Negro in America* (1962), *What Manner of Man: A Biography of Martin Luther King, Jr.* (1964), and *Forced into Glory: Abraham Lincoln's White Dream* (2007).

Hodding Carter II (1907-1972)

Although Hodding Carter II was not born in Mississippi, he spent most of his adult life in Greenville, where he edited the *Delta Democrat Times*. Carter was an influential journalist who frequently criticized Mississippi's long tradition of racial discrimination. For his editorials condemning the violence of the Ku Klux Klan, Carter was awarded the Pulitzer Prize for journalism in 1946. In addition to his editorial achievements, Carter won recognition for his other publications including *The Lower Mississippi* (1942); *Man and the River* (1970); and his popular memoir, *Where Main Street Meets the River* (1953). In 1968 Hodding Carter received the prestigious Silver Em Award for outstanding journalism from the University of Mississippi.

William Raspberry (1935-2012)

William Raspberry was one of America's most distinguished journalists. He was born in Okolona and spent most of his career as a columnist with *The Washington Post*. During the 1970s and 1980s, his column appeared on *The Post's* editorial page and in more than two hundred newspapers across the country. Raspberry won the Silver Em Award from Ole Miss in 1976 and a Pulitzer Prize for Distinguished Commentary in 1994. From 1995 until his retirement in 2008, Raspberry was a professor of journalism and public policy at Duke University.

Charles Overby

In 1967 Charles Overby began his career in journalism at the University of Mississippi as editor of the *Daily Mississippian*. After serving briefly as press secretary for Senator John C. Stennis, Overby returned to Jackson in 1982 as editor of *The Clarion-Ledger*, Mississippi's largest newspaper. Under Overby's leadership, *The Clarion-Ledger* won a Pulitzer Prize in 1983 for its coverage of Governor William Winter's 1982 Education Reform Act. Two years later he received the Silver Em Award from Ole Miss. In 2008, the Overby Center for Southern Journalism and Politics was established at the University of Mississippi and named in honor of Charles Overby.

Craig Claiborne (1920-2000)

One of Mississippi's most widely read journalists was Craig Claiborne, the food editor of *The New York Times* from 1957 to 1986. Before he became the newspaper's food editor, he was editor of *Gourmet* magazine. As the food editor at *The New York Times*, Claiborne is credited with introducing America to Asian and Latin cuisines. Claiborne also published more than twenty cookbooks and wrote a syndicated column that appeared in papers throughout the country.

Ira Harkey (1918-2006)

In 1948, Ira Harkey purchased the *Pascagoula Chronicle-Star*, and this young editor almost immediately became embroiled in a war of words with Mississippi's white power structure. He supported the 1954 *Brown* decision and James Meredith's admission to Ole Miss in 1962. For his courageous editorials, Ira Harkey won a Pulitzer Prize in 1963. In 1967, Harkey published a memoir titled *The Smell of Burning Crosses*. Harkey was awarded the prestigious Silver Em Award by the University of Mississippi in 2002.

Hazel Brannon Smith (1914-1994)

Hazel Brannon Smith was a young Mississippi editor who championed the cause of racial and social justice. As editor of the *Lexington Advertiser* in Holmes County, Smith supported the *Brown* decision, advocated the repeal of Mississippi laws that discriminated against black citizens, and endorsed Robert Clark, an African American, in his successful campaign for the Mississippi legislature in 1967. Hazel Brannon Smith won a Pulitzer Prize in 1964. A boycott of her newspaper eventually forced her to file for bankruptcy, and she moved to Tennessee. In 1984 Hazel Brannon Smith received the Silver Em Award from the University of Mississippi.

Oliver Emmerich (1896-1978) and George McLean (1904-1983)

Among the lesser known Mississippi journalists who were positive voices during Mississippi's volatile Civil Rights Era were Oliver Emmerich, editor of the *McComb Enterprise-Journal*, and George McLean, editor of the *Tupelo Daily Journal*.

Percy Greene (1897-1977)

In 1938 Percy Greene founded the *Jackson Advocate*, which is the state's oldest African American newspaper. From 1948 to 1973, the *Jackson Advocate's* circulation increased from 3,000 to 10,000. Percy Greene was editor of the *Advocate* from its founding until his death in 1977, and he was often a controversial figure. Some of his critics complained that he was too conservative and that he was too friendly with the State Sovereignty Commission.

Charles Tisdale (1926-2007)

After Percy Greene's death, Charles Tisdale became the owner and editor of the *Jackson Advocate*. During his long tenure, Tisdale was an ardent supporter of civil rights and was an outspoken critic of both black and white leaders who failed to meet his high standards. Tisdale often received death threats, and his office was firebombed twice. After Tisdale's death in 2007, his wife, Alice, assumed the role of editor. The current circulation of the *Advocate* is approximately 8,000.

Ronnie Agnew

A son of sharecroppers, Ronnie Agnew grew up in Saltillo. After graduating from the University of Mississippi in 1984, Agnew began his journalism career as a reporter for the *Greenwood Commonwealth*. In 1986, he joined the *Cincinnati Enquirer*, where he was assistant city editor, and in 1993, he was named managing editor of the *Hattiesburg American*. In 2001 Agnew was afforded his dream job; he was named managing editor of *The Clarion-Ledger*. After editing *The Clarion-Ledger* for ten years, Ronnie Agnew was named executive director of Mississippi Public Broadcasting. Agnew received the Silver Em Award from Ole Miss in 2008.

Bill Minor (1922-2017)

From 1946 to 1976 Bill Minor was the Jackson Bureau chief of the New Orleans *Times-Picayune* in Jackson, and much of the world learned what was going on in that place called Mississippi from his immensely popular columns. After the *Times-Picayune* closed its Jackson office, Minor launched very successful career as a syndicated columnist. Among his many awards are the 1966 Louis Lyons Award from the Nieman Foundation at Harvard; the 1977 John Chancellor Award from the Annenberg School for Communications of Pennsylvania; the 2001 Richard Wright Award by the Natchez Literary Celebration; and the Silver Em Award presented by The University of Mississippi. After his retirement Minor published a book of memoirs in 2001 titled *Eyes on Mississippi: A Fifty Year Chronicle of Change*.

Jerry Mitchell

Jerry Mitchell is an award-winning investigative journalist for *The Clarion-Ledger*. Information uncovered by Mitchell has led to the trial and conviction of several members of the Ku Klux Klan for murders of civil rights workers in the 1960s. He received the Silver Em Award from Ole Miss in 2000. In 2005 Mitchell became the youngest journalist to win Columbia University's John Chancellor Award for Excellence in Journalism. Mitchell was awarded the Richard Wright Award in 2016 by the Natchez Literary Celebration.

L to R: Willie Morris, Barry Hannah, Larry Brown, John Grisham
and Josephine Haxton, aka Ellen Douglas, at
Chancellor Robert Khayat investiture.

L to R: Curtis Wilkie, Neil White, Meg Abbott, Beth Ann Fennelley, Ace
Atkins, Tom Franklin, Julie Cantrell, Ann Fisher-Wirth, Lawrence Wells

Rick Cleveland

The most awarded sportswriter in Mississippi history, ten-time winner of the Mississippi Sportswriter of the Year Award, the 2011 recipient of the prestigious Richard Wright Award, Rick Cleveland started writing professionally at the age of 11. He is the former sports editor of the Jackson *Clarion-Ledger* and the former director of the Mississippi Sports Hall of Fame. Rick Cleveland is currently a member of the staff of *Mississippi Today*, "a nonpartisan, nonprofit digital news and information resource that aggressively and objectively covers state and local government and community issues." *Mississippi Today* was established in 2014.

Billy Watkins

A popular writer with *The Clarion-Ledger*, Billy Watkins was born in Noxubee County and has been writing about people and places, sports and politics in Mississippi for more than thirty years. He has won many prestigious awards and is the author of three books. In 2018 he received the Richard Wright Award, presented by the Natchez Literary Celebration.

HISTORIANS

Dunbar Rowland (1864-1937)

In 1902 the legislature established the Mississippi Department of Archives and History, and the Board of Directors appointed Dunbar Rowland its first director. Rowland received a BS degree from Mississippi A&M College in 1886 and a law degree from the University of Mississippi in 1888. He was awarded an LL.D. from Ole Miss in 1906. Dunbar Rowland served as director of the MDAH from his appointment in 1904 until his death in 1937 and published a quadrennial *Official and Statistical Register of the State of Mississippi* from 1904 until 1928. Included among his many publications were *Mississippi: Comprising Sketches of Counties, Towns, Events, Institutions, and Persons, Arranged in Cyclopedic Form* (3 vols, 1907); *History of Mississippi: The Heart of the South* (4 vols, 1925); and *Courts, Judges, and Lawyers of Mississippi, 1798-1935* (1935).

Shelby Foote (1916-2005)

After publishing several novels, Shelby Foote began his masterpiece three-volume history of the Civil War. He spent twenty years researching and writing *The Civil War: A Narrative* (1958-1974). Foote was a consultant and commentator on Ken Burns's 1992 award-winning PBS series on the Civil War. His frequent appearances on this popular series made him a popular national figure.

David Donald (1920-2009)

David Donald, a native of Goodman and a graduate of Millsaps College, received two Pulitzer Prizes, the first in 1961 for his biography of the Massachusetts abolitionist Charles Sumner. He won a second Pulitzer Prize in 1988 for his biography of the great Southern writer Thomas Wolfe.

Dumas Malone (1892-1986)

Dumas Malone is from a distinguished family of writers from DeSoto County. He won a 1975 Pulitzer Prize for his biography of Thomas Jefferson.

James W. Silver (1907-1988)

A professor of history at Ole Miss from 1936 to 1964, and a confidant of William Faulkner, James W. Silver was the author of *Mississippi, The Closed Society* (1963, Reprint, 2012). Many historians link the publication of that book with the beginning of the opening of Mississippi's closed society that was predicated on racial segregation and white supremacy. As the state legislature was contemplating the dismissal of Professor Silver, he accepted an appointment as visiting professor at Notre Dame, where he remained until 1969, when he accepted a position at the University of South Florida. On September 30, 2011, the Silver Pond on the Ole Miss campus was dedicated and named in honor of Professor James Silver.

Winthrop Jordan (1931-2007)

A professor of history at Ole Miss from 1982 until his retirement in 2004, Professor Winthrop Jordan won a National Book Award in 1968 for

White Over Black, American Attitudes Toward the Negro. In 1993 Professor Jordan won a Bancroft Prize for *Tumult and Silence at Second Creek: An Inquiry Into a Civil War Slave Conspiracy*.

William Kauffman Scarborough

Few historians write books that become classics, but Professor William Scarborough, who joined the University of Southern Mississippi faculty in 1964, and is now professor emeritus, has written two American classics. His first was *The Overseer: Plantation Management in the Old South* (1966); his second was *Masters of the Big House, Elite Slaveholders of the Mid-Nineteenth-Century South* (2003). In addition to being a celebrated writer, Professor Scarborough was also a distinguished teacher.

John F. Marszalek

Among Mississippi's most prolific historians, John Marszalek has published 14 books and more than 300 articles. Professor Marszalek joined the Mississippi State University faculty in 1973, was named W.L. Giles Distinguished Professor of History in 1994. In 2002 Marszalek received the Richard Wright Award, and in 2004 the Mississippi Historical Society presented him its highest award, the B.L.C. Wailes Award. Although he is regaled for his extensive bibliography, he is even more renowned for his successful effort to relocate the Ulysses S. Grant Presidential Library from Chicago to a new 21,000-square-foot addition to the Mississippi State University Library. The new Grant Presidential Library was formally dedicated on November 30, 2017, and will be under the direction of John Marszalek and Frances N. Coleman, MSU Dean of Libraries.

WEBSITES AND ANTHOLOGIES

There are several websites, but two in particular, that provide significant information about Mississippi writers. Those two sites are The Mississippi Writer's Page, maintained by The University of Mississippi; and Mississippi Writers and Musicians Project, which originated at Starkville High School but is currently maintained by Kathy Jacobs. In addition to these websites there are several anthologies of Mississippi writers, which include Robert L. Phillips, (ed), *Antebellum Mississippi Stories* (1976); Noel Polk and James R. Scafidel, (eds), *An Anthology of Mississippi Writers* (1979); James B. Lloyd, (ed), *Lives of Mississippi Authors, 1817-1967* (1981); Dorothy Abbott (ed), *Mississippi Writers: Reflections of Childhood and Youth* (1985, 4 vols.) and *Mississippi Writers, An Anthology* (1991); Marion Barnwell, *A Place Called Mississippi: Collected Narratives* (1997); and Lorie Watkins (ed), *A Literary History of Mississippi* (2017). Interviews with some of Mississippi's famous writers are available online at University Press of Mississippi, Literary Conversation Series.One of the marvels of Mississippi is that it has the highest rate of illiteracy in America, but The Other Mississippi has perhaps the richest literary tradition of any state in the country.

First Capitol 1822

4

Centennial Celebration of the New Capitol

1903-2003

As we gather here today to commemorate the centennial of the New Capitol, we can also celebrate a New Mississippi. And just as we honor the architects and craftsmen who built this majestic building a century ago, I want to recognize the architects and craftsmen of the New Mississippi. Many of them are in this audience today, and some are on this platform.

At the dedication of this building in 1903 Bishop Charles Galloway said, "My ardent ambition for [Mississippi] is that she will not sit forever on the opposition benches, but develop a generation of... creative and constructive [leaders] and I... insist that the Negro should have equal opportunity with every American... to fulfill in himself the highest purposes of an all-wise and beneficent Providence."

We have taken too long, far too long, but I believe Bishop Galloway's "ardent ambition" has at last been fulfilled.

Mississippians now sit in the highest councils of government, business, education, and arts and letters.

And any Mississippian can fulfill his or her loftiest aspirations. If they can dream it, they can do it.

When we dedicated this building one hundred years ago, there were two men living in Mississippi whose lives are worthy of note.

Second Capitol 1839

One you have probably never heard of; the other is one of Mississippi's favorite sons.

One was a black man, born in obscurity deep in the piney woods of South Mississippi.

The other was a white man, born on the northern edge of the Pontotoc Ridge, the son and grandson of prominent men.

The black man, Thelma Andrews, was a cook in a college cafeteria. At least that's how he started. He later became the director of food services at Perkinston Junior College. He was a man of quiet dignity; there was something noble about him in his simple devotion to duty and in his goodness. [Several of Mr. Andrews's family members were introduced and applauded.]

In the 1960s after Perkinston was integrated, he was a role model and mentor to students and faculty alike, and in his own way he was as much a teacher as I was.

Mr. Andrews, as far as I have been able to ascertain, was the first African American for whom a building was named on one of our traditionally white college campuses.

The white man, William Faulkner, has been acclaimed throughout the world for his literary genius. Faulkner produced some of the world's magnificent literature and has won every important literary award.

Thelma Andrews and William Faulkner did not know each other, yet their lives were ineradicably linked in that seamless flow of time we call history, and they, with many others like them, built the New Mississippi.

Andrews and Faulkner are typical of the goodness and the genius of our people.Mississippians are an intriguing and almost baffling blend of goodness and genius.

Someone asked Faulkner once what he wrote about, and he said, "I write about the human heart in conflict with itself."

Mississippi, like the human heart, is often in conflict with itself.

Our hospitality is legendary, but so too is our hostility to outsiders.

We have a high rate of illiteracy, but there are more Pulitzer Prize winners per square mile in Mississippi than in any other state.

Third Capitol 1903

Mississippi is a sad and lonely place; it was here the blues were born, and we gave the world B.B. King.

But we are also happy and exuberant, and we gave the world Elvis Presley, the Boy Wonder of Rock and Roll.

For every trait that is typical of Mississippi, there seems to be a correspondingly opposite trait that is equally typical.

Perhaps that is why people are so fascinated with us. Mississippians are amused by the attention we get when we visit other parts of the country, especially "up North."

People seem somehow intrigued to find a real live Mississippian outside its natural habitat.

To be a Mississippian is an existential predicament, and it may be that there is just no other place in America quite like Mississippi.

Just as there is a blend of goodness and genius in Mississippi, there is also a blend of good and bad. There will be time enough to speak of the bad. Today, we will talk only of the good. And there is much to say.

In the century since the dedication of this New Capitol there has been a sea change, a seismic shift in Mississippi.

One of the most enduring changes came in 1920 with the passage of the Nineteenth Amendment, extending the franchise to women. With their newly won right to vote our mothers and grandmothers, aunts, wives, and sisters refreshed American democracy and brought an earnestness to politics and public policy that the Republic had not known before.

This was the prelude to the New Mississippi.

Perhaps the fount from which almost all of the other changes flowed were the economic forces that industrialized and urbanized Mississippi. Early in the twentieth century the legislature, meeting in this spanking new building, passed laws encouraging industry to move to Mississippi, but the embrace of industry by a rural people was slow and halting. The Great Depression of the 1930s, however, called for a bold and innovative remedy to the deepening poverty that held a nation in its grip.

The Balance Agriculture With Industry, the BAWI program, was Mississippi's gift to the South and to the nation. The benefits of attracting industry to the rural South were obvious and widespread, but the strategy for achieving that goal was conceived and implemented by Mississippi's political, business and educational leadership.

In the election of 1935 Mississippians gave Hugh White a mandate to inaugurate the BAWI program. Thirty years later in March 1965 in a quiet ceremony in his office, in this building, Governor Paul Johnson, Jr., announced that industrial employment exceeded agricultural employment for the first time in the state's history.

Now, 38 years later, many of the world's greatest performing artists who use high-tech acoustical equipment, buy instruments and sound systems made in Mississippi by Mississippians.

Last week, here in the heartland of Mississippi, was dedicated one of the largest automobile assembly plants in the world. Almost two thousand cars a day will roll off an assembly line in Canton.

Economic development and opportunity have brought an ethnic diversity to Mississippi that is quite remarkable. In the hotel where I stayed last night the safety instructions on the elevator were recorded in seven languages.

And those instructions did not include the language of Native Americans that can still be heard in parts of our state. The Mississippi Band of Choctaws are virtually a sovereign nation within our midst, and under the leadership of Chief Phillip Martin they have produced a model social and economic development program that enables them to live in independence and dignity on their ancestral land.

Industrialization and urbanization have also produced a transportation revolution that will take us from dusty country roads to the far reaches of outer space. The Stennis Space Center in Hancock County has long been an important site in America's space program.

And how proud we all are that William Parsons, a Mississippian, is now in command of NASA's shuttle program.

For decades an out-migration deprived Mississippi of the energy and intellect of some of our best and brightest. But we have stemmed the "brain drain" and have reversed the "black exodus."

We accomplished this because we have transformed public education from K through 12, and I want to salute Mississippi's classroom teachers, in both the public and private schools.

They are the foot soldiers in the army of the New Mississippi. And they, perhaps more than anyone else, have built the New Mississippi.

We have also developed a system of higher education that compares favorably with those in other parts of the country.

And there are many prestigious and valuable scholarships, generously funded by Mississippians, that make it attractive for our best and brightest to stay at home for their collegiate education. If they don't go away, we don't have to worry about them coming back.

Since 1955 the University of Mississippi Medical Center has provided superior medical education to Mississippi students who formerly went out of state for their training. Many of them never came back.

It would be almost impossible for me to overestimate the contribution that the medical center has made to the health and well-being of Mississippi.

In our medical center one of the first human organ transplants was performed.

All of these marvelous achievements occurred during a cultural flourishing that I call the Mississippi Renaissance.

In the century since the dedication of this New Capitol we have taught the world to sing.

Three major genres of American music have their roots in Mississippi.

The blues were born here. Howlin' Wolfe, Bo Diddley, Muddy Waters, Big Bill Broonzy, John Lee Hooker, Robert Johnson, Son Thomas, Mississippi John Hurt, and B.B. King are from Mississippi, and they first made their music here.

Country music, the most popular singing style in America, was raised to an art form by Mississippi's Jimmie Rodgers, the first singer inducted into the Country Music Hall of Fame. His progeny is numberless, and I can mention only two of our own: Charley Pride, who has won virtually every award given by the industry; and Marty Stuart, an artist of international renown and one of the great pickers of all time.

And who does not know that rock and roll began here in Mississippi with "Heartbreak Hotel," and that Elvis was "King" and that he changed the style of American music?

But let us not forget, Mississippi's Grand Lady of Opera, Leontyne Price who, in her 1961 Metropolitan Opera debut, received a 42-minute standing ovation.

We may not have taught the world to dance, but every four years the world of dance comes to Mississippi when the International Ballet Competition showcases the world's most talented young dancers.

In the performing arts Mississippians have reached the heights in perhaps the most competitive industry in America. Our stars are too numerous even to list, so I will note only four who can represent the many: Gerald McRaney and Morgan Freeman, two of the nation's premier actors; and Oprah Winfrey, one of the most influential women in America; and Jim Henson, who created the Muppets who live on Sesame Street.

During the Mississippi Renaissance some of America's great writers found their voice. Among them were Richard Wright, William Faulkner, Tennessee Williams, and Eudora Welty.

Inaugurated by these four great writers, Mississippi's literary tradition is a marvel in the world of letters.

A partial list of Mississippi writers would include Margaret Walker, Shelby Foote, William Alexander Percy, Hodding Carter, Ira Harkey, Hazel Brannon Smith, Turner Catledge, Lerone Bennett, Jr., Dumas Malone, David Donald, Willie Morris, Ellen Douglas, Elizabeth Spencer, Beth Henley, Richard Ford, Barry Hannah, Sterling Plumpp, Larry Brown, Clifton Taulbot, Thomas Harris, Greg Iles, Nevada Barr, Natasha Trethewey, and John Grisham.

In 1903 local newspapers estimated the attendance at the dedication of the New Capitol at 20,000. One report said that everyone in Brandon attended the ceremony, except the constable. The state's population was only about a million and a half, which means that more than one out of every ten Mississippians attended the dedication. That says something rather remarkable about that generation.

Mississippians had suffered and were still suffering from the devastation of Civil War and the lingering depression of the 1890s.

But amid that gloom there was a brief, shining moment when Mississippi paused to dedicate this grand and towering structure, which was unexcelled by any state capitol between Richmond, Virginia, and Austin, Texas.

In that moment of pride Mississippians caught a glimpse of what could be, of what might be, and the New Mississippi was aborning.

Like Bishop Galloway, I, too, have an ardent ambition for Mississippi.

Not in my wildest flights of fantasy can I imagine what Mississippi will be like in 2103.

But I know this: the future belongs to those who prepare for it.

Too many white Mississippians still celebrate the past and remember what was.

Too many black Mississippians will not forgive or forget the sins of our fathers.

William Faulkner said we cannot get beyond the reach of our past. That may be true, but we can break its hold on us.

We cannot rewrite the past, but we can chart our future.

My most ardent ambition for Mississippi is that we will let go of yesterday so we can take hold of tomorrow.

The future is ours; it is our Promised Land. And I can see it with my heart, if not my eyes. It is over there, just beyond the rise. Come, and go with me.

Thank you, and God Bless Mississippi.

The author wishes to thank Paul Breazeale, Bernard Cotton, Robert Khayat, Aubrey Lucas, Jack McLarty, Andrew Mullins, Charles Sallis, and William Winter for their assistance in the preparation of this address.

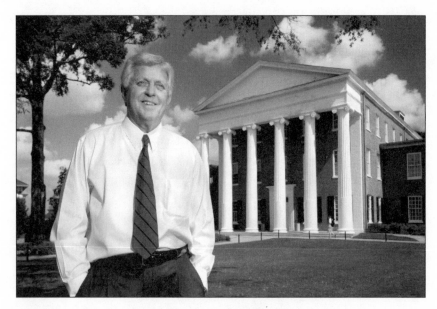

Chancellor Emiritus Robert Khayat

Robert C. Khayat Law Center

Great Laws and Lawyers
A Celebration of the
American Legal System

A wise old sage once said, "Give me the songs of the people, and I care not who writes their laws."

Now isn't that a dumb thing for a wise old sage to say?

That's like saying Elvis Presley's "You Ain't Nothing But a Hound Dog," is more important than Mr. Jefferson's "Virginia Statute of Religious Liberty."

But, let us measure the sage's wisdom.

I Googled two of America's most popular songsters, Michael Jackson and Britney Spears, and found more than 10 million citations to them and to their work on the World Wide Web.

In all their vast repertoire I did not find one refrain as beautiful as "no person shall be deprived of life, liberty, or property without due process of law."

I did not find one jingle to match "the accused shall enjoy the right to a speedy and public trial by an impartial jury."

And I did not find one line as lyrical as "Ours is a government of laws, not men."

Man's greatest achievement is not "Jingle Bells."

Mankind's greatest achievement was not even the invention of the wheel.

Man's greatest achievement was the discovery of the force and power of law.

For without law, we would still be riding around in circles; there would be no yellow line down the middle of the highway; there would be no speed limits and no stop signs.

There would be time; there would be night and day, but without law there would be no yesterday, today, or tomorrow.

Men would live in proximity, but without law they could not live in peace.

One of the climactic moments in human history was the transfer of revenge from the clan to the community. The ending of the blood-feud was the beginning of law and order.

The law cannot create paradise, but it can prevent pandemonium, and, like the rhythm of the seasons, law makes life predictable.

Now wait a minute, if the law is so wonderful, how come lawyers have such a bad name?

Well, before we go any further, I want to say up front that some of my best friends are lawyers. In fact, I have a son and a daughter-in-law who are attorneys. Sometimes I joke that if I were charged with a heinous crime and was innocent, I would let my son defend me. But if I were guilty I would want my daughter-in-law to defend me. She thinks that's hilarious, but my son sits there with a knowing smile, as if the joke is really on me.

Speaking of jokes and lawyers, I Googled the topic and found that cyberspace is an expanding universe of denigrating anecdotes about the second-oldest profession.

For "Laws and Lawyer Jokes" I found more than one hundred thousand citations.

Among my favorites were lawhaha.com, and lawpsided.com. One site says that laughing at lawyers is good for you and offered a Lawyer Joke of the Day.

There is also a website devoted to laughable lawsuits. I think the law can sometimes be funny, but I don't think a lawsuit is a laughing matter. Getting hit with a laughable lawsuit is like being shot by friendly fire.

Writers and scholars cannot resist the lure of legal comedy. Some of my favorite book titles include, *It Ought to Be a Law, But It's Not*, and its companion volume, *It's a Law, But it Shouldn't Be*. Other titles include *Laughable Laws and Courtroom Capers*; *Looney Laws and Curious Cases*; *Lawyers and Vampires*; and my absolute favorite, *Habeas Codfish, Reflections on Food and Law*.

I was somewhat surprised to learn how ancient is the scorn for lawyers. Puns and putdowns have followed them all the days of their history, from ancient Egypt, through the glory of Greece and Rome, through Chaucer, Scott, Dickens, and Shakespeare.

In ancient Egypt only written pleadings were allowed, for fear that oral arguments by a cleaver advocate might "befuddle the... judges."

The portrayal of lawyers in Roman comedy is replete with bitter satire.

In Sir Thomas More's Utopia there were no lawyers. Someone has said there will be no need for lawyers in heaven. Someone else has said, that's good, because there won't be any up there.

And who has not heard Shakespeare say, "The first thing we do is kill all the lawyers."

Carl Sandburg, America's laureate, once asked, "Why does a hearse horse snicker when he carries a lawyer away?"

I think the vein of scorn is not deep, but it is wide and is rooted in the common complaint:

You just wait and see; some smart lawyer will get him off, scot free.

Whatever may have been its public image, the bench and bar was America's first aristocracy. Before the rise of the great planters of the Old South, and long before the emergence of the captains of industry and the paragons of medicine, lawyers enjoyed a place of prominence in American society.

And it is no wonder, for young America was a land made for lawyers, with its receding frontier, an expanding population, millions of small farmers and entrepreneurs all needing deeds and contracts.

It is not crime nor injury, but the omnipotent contract that is a lawyer's best friend.

As America came of age, she became a rich and powerful nation and a litigious society.

How could it be otherwise, for there are approximately 50 million laws, codes, rules, and regulations in force across America.

"The Mother of American Law," I believe, is Mr. Jefferson's Virginia Statute of Religious Liberty.

In the early morning of man's existence, the world was a place of wonder, mystery, and chaos. In his hunt for an answer to the mystery, man found religion, and in his quest for order, he discovered the law.

Religion and law are not siblings of a common search; in fact, they are not even distant cousins.

Religion is a system of beliefs. Law is a system of dictates.

The function of religion is to solve the mystery of who we are and how we got here.

The function of law is to determine what we can and cannot do, now that we are here.

The overlap of religion and law is one of those entangling alliances the Founding Fathers warned us about. There is more than mere contention between church and state; there is a direct contradiction.

The premise of religion is that man is born in sin and is by nature corrupt.

The premise of American law is that man is good and noble by birth and capable of self-rule.

So how do we reconcile this contradiction?

We don't. We don't even try.

We accommodate the contradiction.

The genius of the American mind is that we can accept simultaneously two mutually exclusive concepts.

We believe in a free market. So, we regulate the market to keep it free.

We believe that man is basically good AND that man is basically bad.

This accommodation is possible, because in a state of liberty as envisioned by Mr. Jefferson, it is not a man's belief but his conduct, not his thoughts but his actions, that are subject to the rule of law.

This accommodation is possible because law is pragmatic, not speculative.

Law is fact not opinion. That's why judges write long opinions telling us what the facts are.

And that's why we give juries the power to declare a man guilty or innocent.

As much as I admire the bald eagle and love to watch him soar, the enduring symbol of America is the public square, built around the courthouse, not a church house, a synagogue, a temple, or a mosque.

It may be a stretch to rate Mr. Jefferson up there with Hammurabi, Moses, and Justinian, but no more than I am being paid for this lecture, I can say just about anything I want to.

Among America's many great laws is an antebellum statute that embodied all the pathos and all the promise of this great country. The 1839 Mississippi Married Women's Property Act was the first law to recognize a woman's right to own private property in the United States.

Known as the Betsy Love Allen law, the married women's property statute was a result of Mississippi Supreme Court Justice William Sharkey's opinion giving this Chickasaw Indian woman the right to protect her slave property from her husband's creditors.

I call this remarkable legislation the "red, white, and black law." A red-skinned woman was accorded the right to own a black-skinned person by a white-skinned judge.

However bizarre this case may seem to us now, the Betsy Love Allen law was an early expression of America's effort to get it right in an increasingly complex world, though, of course, there was much more to do.

The GI Bill surely qualifies as one of the great laws in American legal history. It did more than any other law in the twentieth century to change, alter, remake, restyle, and remodel America and infused this nation with the will and the way to build a bold, new world upon the ruins of that war that changed everything.

For millions of young Americans the GI Bill was the yellow brick road to the American dream.

In 1951, as one of nine children, at the age of seventeen, with a waiver signed by my parents, I joined the army so I could get the GI Bill and go to college. In 1976 I bought a house with a VA loan. I was one of those millions. I am sure some of you are also in that number.

It was inevitable, I suppose, that a nation of laws would become a nation of lawyers. To wit, there are approximately one million lawyers who have been admitted to the American bar.

In our purview of the lives and legacies of great American lawyers where better to begin than with The Philadelphia Lawyer himself?

In 1735 John Peter Zenger, the editor of a small weekly newspaper, was arrested for criticizing the colonial governor of New York. The local attorneys who agreed to represent Zenger were summarily disbarred. Zenger then asked Andrew Hamilton of Philadelphia, the most renowned attorney in colonial America, to take his case.

The Philadelphia Lawyer agreed to represent Zenger in what one historian has called "a case of transcendent importance." Another has called it "the morning star of [American] liberty." The Philadelphia Lawyer's closing in the Zenger case is an American classic. "I hope to be pardoned, Sir," he addressed the court, "for my zeal upon this occasion. ...You see that I labor under the weight of many years. ...Yet, old and weak as I am, I... think it my duty...to go to the utmost part of the land... to [challenge] the arbitrary [acts] of men in power."

He then turned to the jury and, as all great lawyers do, he elevated and enlarged the issue before them. "The question before you... gentlemen of the jury... is not the cause of one poor printer. ... It is the cause of liberty... which nature and the laws of our country have given us."

Who in young America, on the brink of revolution, would not strike a blow for liberty?

In defiance of the governor and English legal tradition, those twelve men, good and true, found John Peter Zenger not guilty.

Can you imagine what it must be like to be in a case of transcendent importance?

Most of us are more apt to experience the trouble a young lawyer had with his first witness in his first case. It went something like this:

Mr. Benefield, would you please state your name and address?

My name is Jimmie Benefield, and I'm 22 years old.

And your address, Mr. Benefield?

I don't have an address.

Where were you living at the time of the accident at the factory?

I was living in the back seat of my car.

Do you still live in the back seat of your car?

No, sir, I moved.

Oh, okay, well where did you move to?

To the front seat.

Mr. Benefield, why did you move to the front seat?

My wife said it was too crowded in the back seat.

You are married, Mr. Benefield. To whom are you married?

To my wife.

Okay, that's fine; let's move on. Mr. Benefield, what do you do?

What do I do when?

When you work?

Well, I work.

I know. But what do you work at?

I work at a bench.

I know, I know, but WHERE do you work at a bench?

In a factory.

Good. Now, what kind of factory is it?

A brick factory.

Okay, now we're getting somewhere. The factory makes bricks, right?

No, the factory is made of bricks.

Mr. Benefield, will you please tell the court what you MAKE at the factory?

I make about forty dollars a week.

No, no, what does the factory make?

I don't know, they make a lot of money, I guess.

Now, look, Mr. Benefield, what kind of products does the factory make?

Oh, we make real good products.

But what kind of good products?

Oh, I think the best kind there is.
Your honor, I have no further questions of this witness.

In 1854 when Jacob Thompson pleaded with the legislature to found a school of law at the University of Mississippi, he reminded the lawmakers, "It is well known that for a thousand years the bar has been the road to the titles [and] the power of the politician."

No American honored that thousand-year tradition with greater fidelity then Abraham Lincoln. He was a lawyer's lawyer and was heralded for his use of language. One historian said Lincoln won the Civil War with metaphors. Listen to his letter to Mrs. Bixley, who lost her five sons on the field of battle:

> *I feel how weak and fruitless must be any word of mine which should attempt to beguile you from the grief of a loss so overwhelming. But I cannot refrain from tendering to you the consolation that may be found in the thanks of the republic they died to save. I pray that our heavenly Father may assuage the anguish of your bereavement and leave you only the cherished memory of the loved and lost. And the solemn pride that must be yours to have laid so costly a sacrifice upon the alter of freedom.*

The Southern bench and bar actually enjoyed a higher social standing than their counterparts above the Mason-Dixon.

If you were bright and ambitious but not a son of the gentry, you found your calling in law and politics, and it is not surprising that most of the great Southern lawyers were also prominent politicians.

High on the list of Southern luminaries is Lucius Quintus Cincinnatus Lamar. LQC Lamar is distinguished for many reasons.

As a professor of law at the University of Mississippi immediately after the Civil War, Lamar was one of the pioneers of the new method of studying case law, which was just then making its debut in law schools across the country.

Lamar was one of the few American statesmen whose career spanned the great divide of Civil War. He drafted Mississippi's Ordinance of Secession in 1861, but as a Congressman in 1874 he eulogized Massachusetts Senator Charles Sumner, the most hated Yankee in all the South. In that speech, Lamar urged both sections to forgo the past and join together to build a new and stronger America.

Some historians cite that speech as the beginning of the reconciliation of the North and the South, and John F. Kennedy featured Lamar in his Pulitzer Prize-winning book, *Profiles of Courage*.

Lamar is also one of only a handful of Americans to serve in all three branches of the federal government. He served in the Congress, both the House and the Senate, in the executive branch as secretary of the interior, and was a justice of the United States Supreme Court.

If the illustrious Lamar is found on one end of the list of great Southern lawyer-statesmen, Theodore G. Bilbo can be found on the far opposite end.

Although Bilbo was kicked out of Vanderbilt Law School, he read law and was admitted to the bar, twice elected governor, and three times elected to the U.S. Senate.

Known by friend and foe alike as "The Man," Bilbo was only five feet two, but he was ten feet tall on the stump. Although he was short, bald, and ugly, he was involved in several sex scandals.

I never heard him speak, but I interviewed Mrs. Bilbo when she was 99 years and four months old. She was charming and vivacious and had a mind full of vivid memories.

Her son told me before the interview not to bring up the rumors of Bilbo's infidelity. I didn't, but she did.

"You know, Mr. Bilbo loved the women," she said, "and the women loved Mr. Bilbo." As tempting as it was, I did not pursue the matter.

The honor roll of great American lawyer-statesmen would include Governor William Winter, whose distinguished half-century of service to Mississippi and the nation has won him the laurels and the accolades of those he served.

I consider William Winter the Abraham Lincoln of Mississippi, and so high is my regard for Governor Winter that if I ever found myself on the other side of an issue from him, I would immediately reevaluate my position.

I'm not sure what it means, but two of the three most famous Southern lawyers, Atticus Finch and Gavin Stevens, are fictional characters, and the third most famous Southern lawyer, John Grisham, is known more for his fiction than his legal career.

You may recall that Atticus Finch and Gavin Stevens are the central characters of Harper Lee's *To Kill A Mockingbird* and William Faulkner's *Intruder in the Dust.*

It was Lawyer Gavin Stevens who spoke Mr. Faulkner's most frequently quoted line: "The past is never dead. It's not even past." (*Requiem For A Nun*)

You may also know that John Grisham is one of the most widely read authors in the English language.

Just out of curiosity I Googled John Wayne and found that he made 142 movies. But, as best as I could determine, John Wayne never played a lawyer.

There is much to celebrate about the American legal system, and two of its greatest dividends are coalescence and continuity.

First, coalescence. Of all the luminaries of American legal history, the single most important name is John Doe; he is the everyman of American law.

Before the bar of justice, we are all John Doe.

Now, in deference to the times, I should add the name Jane Doe and tell you that after diligent research, I have concluded that Jane Doe is John Doe's double first cousin.

There are those who say that the interstate has brought the four corners of this disparate country together and that the familiar, reassuring signs of McDonald's and Walmart symbolize American unity and cohesion.

Now, that's even dumber than what that wise old sage said earlier.

We are not bound together by highways and hamburgers and bargains.

Law is the tie that binds us.

From America's teeming cities to its quiet little country towns, from the industrial North to the rural South, from the high rollers of Beverly Hills to the holy rollers of the Bible Belt, from the church to the synagogue to the mosque and the non-believer's bench, only the rule of law could bridge such deep and wide cultural divides.

Religion and class and ethnicity stir the melting pot.

Law is the ingredient that blends all the different flavors.

Law is what makes us all Americans.

The other great dividend of the rule of law is continuity, the peaceful transfer of power.

In 1800, a tie vote in the electoral college threw the presidential election into the House of Representatives. After thirty-six ballots, Thomas Jefferson succeeded John Adams. And for the first time in history, the party in power peacefully transferred its authority to an elected successor.

Two centuries later, in a bold, new world unimaginable even to Mr. Jefferson, another presidential election was contested.

Although we could not foresee its outcome, we knew exactly how to resolve the issue.

After six weeks of legal maneuvering, a handful of lawyers and five judges decided who would become the most powerful man on earth.

And a nation, conditioned by its history to live by the rule of law, accepted their decision.

Whatever you may think of Al Gore, at a crucial moment in American history, he validated the hope and promise of a nation conceived in liberty and dedicated to the rule of law.

A thousand years from now in some remote and distant corner of the cosmos, a professor will tell his students about a tiny speck in the universe called the planet Earth and will speak fondly of a nation state called America.

He will tell his students that the flaws and failures of mankind, that the greed for earthly goods, the discord of contending faiths, the dissonance of cultural diversity, and the strife of rival factions were all modulated by the American legal system.

The professor will regale Americans for many reasons, but most of all for their devotion to the rule of law and their near naive belief that in the end, after all is said and done, justice would be served.

General Robert E. Lee said that "the sublimest word in the English language is duty."

Who am I to differ with Mr. Lee, but I believe the sublimest word in the English language is "justice."

And you, great lawyers of America, are the guardians of the gate of justice.

Do your duty, and a grateful nation will not forget you.

6

FLAGS OVER MISSISSIPPI

Emblems, banners, standards, and flags are an ancient tradition that date from the early Roman Empire. Flags are powerful symbols that express personal and political allegiance to a state or nation. Flags also stir deep emotions and sometimes controversy. The Beauregard battle flag, the banner under which thousands of Confederate soldiers marched into battle during America's Civil War, is a symbol that has been swept up in the passions of modern politics and racial discord. In recent years the battle flag has flown over several state capitols and is currently displayed in the state flag of Mississippi. This flag is now the focus of public discourse.[1]

The current controversy over the Mississippi state flag began in 1988 when a bill was introduced in the legislature to remove the Beauregard battle flag from the state emblem. In response to that bill, which was an indication of an increasing sentiment to change the flag, a Committee to Preserve the State Flag was established on January 9, 1988. Since that time the debate over the state flag has continued and has recently intensified.

After its establishment as an American territory in 1798, Mississippi did not officially adopt a state flag until 1861, when it seceded from the United States and joined the Confederate States of America. Before that time, several flags had flown over the geographic area that became the state of Mississippi on December 10, 1817.[2]

In 1540 Hernando De Soto's expedition into Mississippi carried an emblem known as the Castile and Leon flag, depicting the golden castles of Castile and the red lions of Leon, the two dominant provinces of Spain.

Bonnie Blue Flag

Christopher Columbus had displayed this same standard from the mastheads of his tiny flotilla when he landed in the new world in 1492.[3]

At various times during the colonial period, the British Union flag and the British Red Ensign flew over the area that became the state of Mississippi.[4] While England held little more than an empty claim to the area that later became Mississippi, French explorers under Robert Rene Cavalier, Sieur de La Salle, laid formal claim and took possession of the lower Mississippi Valley on April 9, 1682, and named it Louisiana in honor of the Bourbon King Louis XIV. The Bourbon Flag of France was the flag of dominion over Mississippi from 1682 until 1763.[5]

Under the provisions of the Treaty of Paris of 1763, France ceded its territory east of the Mississippi River to England, and its territory west of the River, along with New Orleans, to Spain. Under the Treaty of Paris, Spain also ceded Florida to England. Because of the transfer of this territory, Mississippi again came under British control and under the dominion of another flag. The new colors raised at Natchez in 1763 were the British Red Ensign.[6]

During the early months of the American Revolution an unofficial flag known as the Cambridge Flag was raised by George Washington at his headquarters in Cambridge, Massachusetts. The field of the Cambridge Flag, also known as the Grand Union Flag, included seven red stripes and six white stripes. The British union was in the canton corner, which is the upper quarter of a flag next to the pole. The Cambridge flag was superseded on June 14, 1777, when the Continental Congress adopted the Stars and Stripes. America's first official national flag included seven red and six white stripes. In the canton were thirteen white five-pointed stars arranged in a circle on a ground of blue.[7]

When Mississippi became a territory in 1798, the thirteen stars and thirteen stripes had increased to fifteen. With the prospects of many more states being added to the Union, it was decided that each new state would be represented by an additional star in the canton, and the number of stripes would remain at thirteen, one for each of the original thirteen states.

The northern and southern boundaries of the Mississippi Territory in 1798 were the thirty-two twenty-eight parallel, just above Vicksburg, and

Magnolia Flag

the thirty-first parallel, just below Natchez. The area above Vicksburg was Indian territory, and most of the area between Natchez and the Mississippi Gulf Coast was Spanish territory known as West Florida. Spain had regained this territory from Great Britain during the American Revolution. The Spanish flag, known as the Spanish Bars of Aragon, flew over the Mississippi Gulf Coast until 1810.[8]

In 1810 a small group of Americans living below the thirty-first parallel in Spanish Florida rebelled against Spain and established the Republic of West Florida. The flag adopted by that short-lived republic was a field of blue with one white star, an emblem that would later be heralded in song and verse as "The Bonnie Blue Flag." The Republic of West Florida was eventually annexed by the United States, and its territory was divided between Mississippi and Louisiana.

Twenty-six years after the West Florida rebellion, Texas won its independence from Mexico. Many of the Florida rebels had moved on to Texas and were prominent players in its revolution. Known as the "Lone Star Republic," the state of Texas adopted the Bonnie Blue Flag as its official standard. When Texas was admitted to the Union in 1845, its new state flag included the Bonnie Blue star along with one red and one white bar.

The Bonnie Blue Flag resurfaced in Mississippi in 1861 when the state seceded from the Union and declared itself a sovereign and independent state. When the Secession Convention, which was meeting in the House chamber in the state capitol, approved the Ordinance of Secession on January 9, 1861, spectators in the balcony handed a Bonnie Blue Flag down to the delegates on the floor. The appearance of that famous banner prompted a tumultuous response. Later that night residents of Jackson paraded through the streets under the blue banner bearing a single white star. Harry McCarthy, who observed the parade, was inspired to write "The Bonnie Blue Flag," which, after "Dixie," became the most popular song in the Confederacy.[9]

From January 9, 1861, to March 30, 1861, the Bonnie Blue Flag was the unofficial emblem of the sovereign state of Mississippi. On January 26, the last day of the first session of the 1861 convention, the delegates approved the report of a special committee that had been appointed to design

Current Mississippi Flag

a coat of arms and "a suitable flag." The committee's recommendation for an official flag was "A Flag of white ground, a Magnolia tree in the centre, a blue field in the upper left-hand corner with a white star in the centre, the Flag to be finished with a red border and a red fringe at the extremity of the Flag." This emblem became known as the Magnolia Flag.[10]

Under the pressure of time and the urgency of raising the "means for the defense of the state," the delegates forgot to adopt an ordinance formalizing the flag committee's report. When the delegates reassembled in March, however, that oversight was corrected. On March 27 the secession convention authorized the governor "to have a Confederate flag [the Stars and Bars] made and hoisted" and on March 30, again on the last day of the session, the delegates officially adopted the Magnolia Flag as the state flag.[11]

After its ratification of the Confederate constitution on March 29, 1861, Mississippi became one of the eleven states of the Confederate States of America. Although Kentucky and Missouri sent delegates to the Confederate congress and supplied troops to the Rebel army and are represented in the thirteen stars in various Confederate flags, they were not officially members of the Confederacy.

The first national flag of the Confederacy, known as the Stars and Bars, was displayed widely in Mississippi and flew over government buildings as well as Confederate troops. Although the second national flag, known as the Stainless Banner, was adopted on May 1, 1863, almost two years before the war ended, it is unlikely that it was used to any extent in Mississippi. The Stars and Bars was still flying above the Confederate fortress of Vicksburg when it fell on July 4, 1863. By then, the lower Mississippi Valley, including Memphis, Vicksburg, Natchez, Baton Rouge, New Orleans and much of the Mississippi Gulf Coast, was under federal control, and the second national flag was rarely if ever displayed in this area. Since the third national flag was adopted barely a month before the surrender at Appomattox, it probably did not fly over any government agencies or troops anywhere in the Confederacy. Regardless of the extent of their use in Mississippi, all three national flags represent a period of the Confederacy, and they all have a place in the history of flags over Mississippi.[12]

The Beauregard battle flag was not adopted as a national flag or as the official battle flag of the Confederate army, but it was used by Mississippi troops, especially during the time that General Beauregard commanded Rebel forces at Shiloh and Corinth in the spring of 1862. The Mississippi regiments under General Robert E. Lee's command also fought under the Beauregard flag after its adoption as the flag of the Army of Northern Virginia. Many other Mississippi regiments, however, designed their own distinctive battle flags that bore no resemblance to any of the national flags or to the Beauregard battle flag.[13]

Although it was not widely used or displayed during the Civil War, the Magnolia Flag remained the official state flag of Mississippi until August 22, 1865. In the aftermath of the Civil War a constitutional convention assembled in Jackson on August 14, 1864, to revoke and repeal many of the actions taken by the Secession Convention of 1861. On August 22 the convention declared the Ordinance of Secession null and void and repealed several other ordinances. Among those repealed was the ordinance adopting a coat of arms and a state flag. This action left Mississippi without an official flag.[14]

Almost thirty years later, on January 22, 1894, Governor John Marshall Stone sent a written message to the legislature calling its attention to the fact that Mississippi did not have a state flag or a coat of arms and urged the lawmakers to adopt an official state emblem and a coat of arms. The legislature responded quickly to Governor Stone's suggestion and sent him a bill creating a state flag on February 6, 1894.[15]

According to the best information available, Senator E.N. Scudder of Mayersville, a member of the Joint Legislative Committee for a State Flag, designed Mississippi's new standard. In 1924 Mrs. Fayssoux Scudder Corneil, Senator Scudder's daughter, stated in an address to the annual convention of the Mississippi Division, United Daughters of the Confederacy, that her father designed the flag and included the Beauregard battle flag in the canton corner to honor the Confederate soldier. Mrs. Corneil recalled:

My father loved the memory of the valor and courage of those brave men who wore the grey. ... He told me that it was a simple matter for him to design the flag because he wanted to perpetuate in a legal and lasting way that dear battle flag under which so many of our people had so gloriously fought.[16]

On February 7, 1894, Governor Stone, a Confederate veteran and former colonel of the Second Mississippi Infantry Regiment, signed into law the bill creating the state flag. With its bold lines and bright colors, the battle flag in the canton, the field fringed in gold, the new state flag was a compelling symbol.[17]

The emblem adopted in 1894 remained the official state flag only until 1906 when a legal oversight resulted in the repeal of the law establishing it. In 1906 Mississippi adopted a revised code that included a provision that repealed all general laws that were not reenacted by the legislature or brought forward in the new code. For some reason, which contemporary records do not reveal, the compilers of the new code did not bring forward the law that created an official state flag and a coat of arms. Because of this oversight, which must have been inadvertent, the state of Mississippi did not have an official state flag for several years.[18]

The 1906 unintended repeal of the law establishing a state flag was an oversight that completely escaped the notice of Dunbar Rowland, the director of the Mississippi Department of Archives and History, and editor of the *Official and Statistical Register of the State of Mississippi*. The *Official Register*, which is published every four years, is now edited by the secretary of state and is known as the Blue Book. In the 1908 edition of the *Official Register*, Rowland included a full-page, four-color picture of the "State Flag of Mississippi," which technically did not exist.

This oversight also escaped the state legislature, which passed a flag desecration statute on April 8, 1916, making it illegal to deface or disfigure "the flag… of the United States or of the State of Mississippi, or confederate [sic] flag." A year later when *The Annotated Mississippi Code Showing the General Statutes In Force August 1, 1917*, was adopted, William Hemingway, a Jackson attorney who compiled the code, did not include the 1894 statute establishing the flag, but he did include a reference to the flag in Section

903 entitled: "Flags — Desecration of the nation and state prohibited."[19]

Even though Mississippi did not legally have an official state flag after 1906, no one seemed to have known it, and practically everyone who was interested in such things presumed that it did and continued to fly the flag. Whether it was the flag by law or custom, the Mississippi state flag with its prominent display of the Beauregard battle flag eventually became a symbol that stirred the deep passions and power of memory. When the Beauregard battle flag, which is identified in the public mind as the Rebel or Confederate flag, resurfaced as a southern symbol of resistance to the Civil Rights Movement in the 1960s, the passions that gave it life in the 1860s were rekindled.

Although America is not yet a race-neutral society, and full racial justice is still a goal and not a fact, the Civil Rights Movement was one of America's great legal, social, and cultural successes. The Movement overturned virtually all of the nation's racially discriminatory laws and opened up new avenues of power and influence to African Americans. After achieving a fundamental and substantive change in American race relations, many African Americans eventually turned their attention to the symbols and icons of racial discord, which are the vestiges and residue of Southern resistance to racial equality.

In the 1970s, following the desegregation of Mississippi's public schools and the integration of intercollegiate athletics, the prominence of the Confederate battle flag at high school and college sporting events prompted a discomfort and eventually a deep resentment among African Americans whose recent memory identified that flag with the KKK, the white Citizens' Council, and various hate groups that perpetrated violent crimes against blacks and hoisted the Rebel flag as a symbol of their belief and commitment to white supremacy. As the Beauregard battle flag became increasingly associated with the advocates of white supremacy, historical organizations and Southern heritage groups were unable to separate or distinguish the historical character of that flag or insulate it from the political agenda of its modern bearers.

The simmering public controversy over the Rebel flag exploded at the University of Mississippi in 1983 when John Hawkins, the first African

American cheerleader, announced that he would not wave or distribute Rebel flags at Ole Miss football games. Friends and foes of the flag engaged in an ongoing public discourse on Southern history and heritage, on slavery and racial suppression, and on the alleged and actual causes of the Civil War. That impassioned discourse produced far more heat than light.[20]

Amidst this tumult, Aaron Henry, a member of the state legislature and president of the Mississippi Conference of the NAACP, introduced a bill at the beginning of the 1988 legislative session to remove the battle flag from the state flag. Neither that bill, nor any of the others he introduced in 1990, 1992, and 1993, were ever brought to the floor for a vote.

Following the failure of these bills, the Mississippi NAACP filed a lawsuit on April 19, 1993, in the Hinds County Chancery Court seeking "an injunction against any future purchases, displays, maintenance or expenditures of state funds on the State Flag" on the grounds that its display violated the "constitutional rights [of African Americans] to free speech and expression, due process and equal protection as guaranteed by the Mississippi Constitution."[21]

After the Chancery Court dismissed the suit, the NAACP appealed to the Mississippi Supreme Court. While adjudicating this case the court discovered the inadvertent repeal of the law establishing an official state flag. Notwithstanding the fact that the state had no official flag, the Supreme Court upheld the lower court's dismissal of the suit. The Supreme Court further declared that the display of the flag, however offensive it might be to some citizens, "does not deprive any citizen of any constitutionally protected right." The court further ruled that a dispute over the adoption and display of a state flag is a political issue that must be resolved by the legislative and executive branches of state government and not the judiciary.[22]

Following this ruling, handed down on May 4, 2000, Governor Ronnie Musgrove, Lieutenant Governor Amy Tuck, and Speaker of the House of Representatives Tim Ford appointed a seventeen-member commission to consider the issue of an official state flag. After the Flag Commission designed a new flag and submitted the issue to the public on April, 17, 2001, the people of Mississippi voted 65 percent to 35 percent to keep the 1894 emblem.

Endnotes

1   For newspaper clippings detailing this debate, see "Mississippi State Flag," Subject File, Mississippi Department of Archives and History.

2   See House Bill 208 and the statement announcing the establishment of the Committee to Preserve the State Flag in ibid.

3   See Cyril E. Cain, *Flags Over Mississippi* (n.p., 1954). Much of the information on the European flags over Mississippi comes from this early study of state flags. See also Myrtle Garrison, *Stars and Stripes* (Caxton Printers Ltd, 1941); Whitney Smith, *The Flag Book of the United States* (William Morrow & Co., 1970), and *Flags Through the Ages and Across the World* (McGraw-Hill, 1975).

4   Cain, *Flags Over Mississippi*, 11.

5   Ibid, 13.

6   Ibid, 15.

7   Ibid, 17, 18.

8   Ibid, 21.

9   Ibid, 22; Devereaux D. Cannon, Jr., *The Flags of the Confederacy, An Illustrated History* (St. Lukes Press, 1988), 31-33.

10   *Journal of the State Convention... January 1861*, (E. Barksdale, 1861), 89-90.

11   Ibid, 27, 35, 42, 43, 77, 86.

12   For details on the adoption of the various Confederate flags, see Mrs. Lucile Lange Dufner, "The Flags of the Confederate States of America," (MA Thesis, University of Texas, 1944); E. Merton Coulter, "The Flags of the Confederacy," *Georgia Historical Quarterly*, vol. 37 (1953), 187-199; Cannon, *Flags of the Confederacy*; Howard M. Madaus and Robert D. Needham, *The Battle Flags of the Confederate Army of the Tennessee* (Milwaukee Public Museum, 1976); Richard Rollins, (ed.), *The Returned Battle Flags* (Rank and File Publications, Redondo Beach, CA edition, 1995); Alan K. Sumrall, *Battle Flags of Texans in the Confederacy* (Eakin Press, Austin Texas, 1995); and Smith, *Flag Book of the United States*, and *Flags Through the Ages*.

13   See Madaus and Needham, *Battle Flags*, 41.

14   *Journal of the Constitutional Convention...August 1865* (E.M. Yerger, State Printer, 1865), 214, 221-222

15   *House Journal, 1894* (Clarion-Ledger Publishing Co., 1894), 193-194, 350-351.

16   See a copy of Mrs. Corneil's address in the State Flag Subject File, MDAH. This file includes a wealth of information on the state flag compiled by Anne Lipscomb Webster, Head of Reference Services, Archives and Library Division, MDAH.

17   *Laws of Mississippi, 1894* (Clarion-Ledger Publishing Co., 1894), 33.

18   See Section 13, *Mississippi Code 1906* (Brandon Printing Co., 1905).

19   *Laws of Mississippi, 1916* (E. H. Clarke and Bro., 1916), 177; *The Annotated Mississippi Code...1917* (Dobbs-Merrill Co., n.d.), 902.

20   For a discussion of the Rebel flag controversy at Ole Miss, see David G. Sansing, *The University of Mississippi, A Sesquicentennial History* (University Press of Mississippi, 1999), 281-314, 321-342.

21   See copies of Representative Henry's bill and the Mississippi Supreme Court ruling, NO.94-CA-00615-SCT, in State Flag Subject File, MDAH.

22   See a copy of the Supreme Court ruling in ibid.

7

THE EVOLVING DEFENSE OF
SLAVERY IN MISSISSIPPI

In 1798 the United States Congress established the Mississippi Territory and legalized slavery in the new Territory. That geographic area had previously been under the dominion of Native Americans, Spain, France, and England, and slavery had existed under their dominion. There were approximately 2,000 slaves in the Mississippi Territory when it was established.

Three years after its establishment, Territorial Governor Winthrop Sargent noted the rapid increase in the number of slaves and issued a dire warning: "That we deprive slaves of the sacred boon of liberty is a crime they can never forgive [and] they might be irresistibly stimulated to vengeance." In 1802 Governor William C.C. Claiborne expressed a similar concern about the "alarming" increase in the slave population, which he said "will (sooner or later) prove a source of much distress." According to some historical accounts, cotton production was so profitable that a field hand could pay for himself in one year.

In June 1818 the Mississippi Supreme Court declared that "Slavery is condemned by reason and the laws of nature." In that same year Mississippi Congressman George Poindexter, a future governor, addressed the dilemma that Mississippi was facing:

It is not with us a matter of choice whether we will have slaves among us or not: we found them here, and we are obliged to maintain and employ them. It would be a blessing, could we get rid of them; but the wisest and best men among us have not been able to devise a plan for doing so.

A statement by Seargent S. Prentiss in 1831 illustrates the evolving defense of slavery from an evil to a necessary evil:

> *That slavery is a great evil, there can be no doubt, and it is an unfortunate circumstance that it was ever introduced into this, or any other country. At present, however, it is a necessary evil, and I do not think admits of a remedy.*

After the Indian land cessions of the 1830s added millions of acres of fertile soil, and the cotton fields "whitened the earth," Mississippi's ruling elite dramatically changed their assessment of the institution of slavery from a necessary evil to a positive good.

Joseph Ingraham, a professor at Jefferson College in Natchez, described the situation in 1835:

> *A plantation well stocked with hands, is the [goal] of every man's ambition who resides in the south.... As soon as a young lawyer acquires... lands and a few slaves, he quits his profession...and turns cotton planter.... Physicians make more money more rapidly than lawyers, and sooner retire from practice.... Even editors have an eye that way.*

The appearance of William Lloyd Garrison's abolitionist newspaper, *The Liberator*, and the increasing abolitionist rhetoric in the late 1830s, which not only condemned slavery as an evil system but also condemned slave owners as evil men, angered Southerners and "crystallized" their defense of slavery. In 1836 Governor John Quitman condemned the "orations, tracts and even school books emanating from the non-slave-holding states." After noting the rise of abolition societies in the North, Quitman said:

It is enough that we, the people of Mississippi, professing to be actuated by as high regard for the precepts of religion and morality as the citizens of other states, and claiming to be more competent judges of our own substantial interests, have chosen to adopt into our political system, and still choose to retain, the institution of domestic slavery.

Even Southern moderates like Seargent S. Prentiss would shift the premise of their defense. In 1836 Prentiss introduced a resolution in the Mississippi legislature that enunciated the new Southern position:

Resolved, That the people of... Mississippi look upon the institution of domestic slavery, as it exists among them, not as a curse, but a blessing, as the legitimate condition of the African race, as authorized both by the laws of God and the dictates of reason and philanthropy; and that they hope to transmit this institution to their posterity, as the best part of their inheritance.... We hold discussion upon this subject as equally impertinent with discussion upon our relations, wives and children, and will allow no present change, or hope of future alteration in this matter.

Another prominent Mississippian, Senator Robert J. Walker, went even further than Prentiss in excoriating abolitionists and Northern politicians who attacked the institution of slavery. In 1836 on the floor of the United States Senate he proclaimed bombastically and prophetically:

They may publish document after document, and print after print, but it will all be in vain and nugatory. They will not have made the slightest approach towards the grand object of all their efforts. No; our peculiar institutions will yield only at the point of a bayonet.

Over the next decade Southerners would defend slavery not as an evil, not even as a necessary evil, but as a positive good. Whites justified slavery not only in economic terms, but in religious, philosophical, and racial terms. Ministers and politicians pointed out that slavery had existed in previous civilizations and that the Apostle Paul seemed to have condoned slavery when he instructed Onesimus to return to his master Philemon. Teachers, editors, and other white leaders also justified slavery on the grounds that black Africans were not as advanced in civilization and culture as white Americans. Although those views were accepted to a greater or lesser degree throughout much of the western world in the early nineteenth century, the American Revolution had popularized the belief in natural rights, a theory that holds that all men, everywhere, are endowed by God and nature with the rights of life, liberty, and property. After the American Revolution, and later the French Revolution in 1789, this belief in natural rights gradually led to a worldwide movement for the abolition of slavery.

During and just after the American Revolution, most Northern states abolished slavery. But in the agricultural South slavery survived and eventually became the symbol, or focus, of the many differences between the Northern and Southern states. The mounting political controversy over slavery did not stem exclusively from the continuation of the institution, but also from the South's determination to expand the institution into the new western territories added to the United States after the war with Mexico.

Southerners argued that the restriction of slavery to the South would result in a greater majority of slaves in proportion to whites. In the event of a race war, which many white Southerners feared would some day occur, the minority of whites would be at a great disadvantage. Southern whites also feared that a large slave surplus would drive the price of slaves down and that they would lose their investment in slaves. In 1860 the value of Mississippi's 436,631 slaves was $349,344,800, more than all the land, farm equipment, and livestock combined.

Most white Mississippians were convinced that only by guaranteeing the right of slave owners to expand into the new western territories could they protect their economic investment, provide for the safety and security of their families, and maintain the Southern way of life.

When the Mexican War began in 1846, Mexico included the Southwestern portion of the present United States, including the present states of New Mexico, Arizona, Utah, Colorado, Nevada, and California. The war, coming as it did during the era of America's Manifest Destiny, was designed to establish American control of that area. However, Northern and Midwestern free states realized the potential power that would accrue to Southern states if slavery were made legal in the new states created by the acquisition of that territory. Consequently, David Wilmot, a congressman from Pennsylvania, attached a proviso to a military appropriation bill. The Wilmot Proviso of 1846 stipulated that slavery would not be legal in any land acquired from the war with Mexico then in progress. The House, which was controlled by the more heavily populated free states, passed the proviso, but it was defeated in the Senate, where slave states had a slight majority. Although the proviso was defeated, it further agitated the slave issue and became the point of departure from which both free and slave states would develop their postwar policies.

While both sections were formulating a rationale for or against slave expansion, the California gold strike of 1848 and its attendant population explosion pressed the country to an immediate decision. By 1849 California had a population of over 60,000, which made it eligible for statehood. Once again the policy of maintaining a balance between free and slave states was threatened. In 1849 there were fifteen free and fifteen slave states. California's admission under any circumstances, free or slave, would alter that balance.

In March 1849 an informal convention of Mississippi Democrats and Whigs was held in Jackson. Both parties were united on the right of Southern states to expand their "peculiar institution" into the western territories. That convention issued a call for a state convention to consider "the threatening relations between the North and South." The state convention was held at Jackson in October 1849. William L. Sharkey, chief justice of the Mississippi Supreme Court, presided over the convention. He argued, and the delegates agreed, that because Mississippi had provided soldiers and resources in acquiring the new western territory, it should enjoy its benefits. The Mississippi convention recommended that a Southern Convention be held at Nashville to develop a unified Southern strategy.

Nine Southern states sent representatives to the convention at Nashville in June 1850. Both Whig and Democrats attended the Nashville Convention and elected William L. Sharkey presiding officer. The convention was dominated by moderates, who adjourned to wait Congressional action concerning the compromise measures that had just been introduced by Henry Clay.

The admission of California as a free state was only one of several problems that jeopardized the precarious truce between slave and free states in 1850. Additionally, there was in the national capital the unsightly slave market, which many Americans wanted to abolish. Abolitionists argued that it was derogatory of America's image as the land of the free. Southerners also complained of the loose enforcement of the fugitive slave laws. But the major issue was the status of slavery in the new western territories, New Mexico and Utah, that had been recently established in the Mexican Cession. Henry Clay perceived the dangerous and disruptive potential of these and other problems. He therefore proposed a series of bills that became known collectively as the Great Compromise of 1850. The Compromise temporarily settled the divisive issues by allowing the state of California to be admitted as a free state. In the two new territories, a referendum known by Stephen A. Douglas's term, "popular sovereignty," would decide the question of slavery. Because the territories were west of slave states along the same parallel, it was anticipated that they would become slave states. Finally, the Compromise abolished the slave market in Washington, D.C., and it also tightened enforcement of the fugitive slave law.

A smaller and more radical group of Southern States Rights' delegates, who were dissatisfied with Clay's Compromise, reconvened the Nashville Convention on November 11. They rejected the Compromise measures and passed a series of resolutions stating the Southern position that included the following:

> recognized the right of secession and recommended relations with the
> North be suspended;
> recommended a boycott of national parties until slave expansion was
> guaranteed;

recommended the prevention of abolitionist literature and sentiment
in the South;

recommended publications in defense of slavery and secession.

Following the Nashville Convention and the adoption of these resolutions, the South was in the unenviable position of having to defend slavery as a positive good and secession as a constitutional right. The defense of slavery as a positive good was based on John C. Calhoun's theory that men were not endowed with inalienable rights, but had only those rights granted to them by the government under which they lived.

The divisive issue of slavery that had disrupted the United States for so long eventually caused most slave states to secede from the Union, which caused the Civil War. The Mississippi Ordinance of Secession was drafted by LQC Lamar and adopted by the Mississippi Secession Convention on January 9, 1861. The ordinance was a brief document that did not include any explanation or reason justifying secession from the Union. On January 26, the last day of the convention, the delegates adopted "A Declaration of the Immediate Causes Which Induce and Justify the Secession of the State of Mississippi From the Federal Union" that declared:

> *Our position is thoroughly identified with the institution of slavery... the greatest material interest of the world. ... There was no choice left us but submission to the mandates of abolition, or a dissolution of the Union.*

Mississippi and ten other slave states seceded from the Union so they could establish a new nation in which slavery would be legal.

When that cause was lost, after the surrender of Gettysburg and Vicksburg in 1863, desertion among Confederate troops increased dramatically, and many Confederate leaders advocated a negotiated settlement. But Mississippi Governor Charles Clark, a wounded Confederate general, castigated that notion and offered a bizarre alternative in an 1863 message to the legislature:

> *There may be those who delude themselves with visions of a re-constructed Union. ... If such there be, let them awake from their dreaming! Let the last of our young men die upon the field of battle, and when none are left to wield the blade or uphold the banner, then let the old men, our women and our children, like the remnant of the Pascagoulas, when their braves were slain, join hands together, march into the sea and perish beneath its waters.*

According to folklore, the Pascagoula Tribe, men, women, and children walked into the Pascagoula River, and then into the waters of the Gulf of Mexico, singing and holding hands, in preference to surrendering to Spanish Conquistadors. The Pascagoula River is also known as the Singing River. Fortunately, our forebears did not heed Governor Clark's admonition.

In 1900, in the first year of the New Century of Change and Progress, Andrew H. Longino was the first governor of Mississippi elected after the Civil War who was not a Confederate veteran, and he offered Mississippians an opportunity to illuminate that long, dark shadow cast by human bondage. In his inaugural address, Governor Longino beseeched Mississippians to embrace the dawning age of technology and admonished the legislature that "capitalists... will be slow to go where life and property are not... protected by the courts." He then presented a resume of mob rule in Mississippi and suggested a means of preventing racial violence that must have startled his listeners:

> *I would therefore recommend... a law giving the family of anyone who may be hereafter lynched a right to recover in the chancery court a fixed sum in damages. ... I [further] commend... that the office of sheriff or constable shall become vacant, ipso facto, whenever any prisoner is taken from the jail... and mobbed. In my judgement the time and occasion are here for some such stringent measure, and it is to be hoped the Legislature will prove itself equal thereto.*

Unfortunately, the legislature was not "equal thereto," and Mississippians postponed their day of reckoning.

8

ELIZABETH TAYLOR GREENFIELD

THE BLACK SWAN

Prejudice must sink before the sublime gift which nature has bestowed upon her.

Albany Evening Journal, January 19, 1852

Elizabeth Taylor Greenfield was born in bondage and obscurity in Natchez, Mississippi. She died free and famous in Philadelphia, the City of Brotherly Love. One year after her sensational debut in 1852, a contemporary historian wrote, "Miss Eliza Greenfield, the Black Swan, is among the most extraordinary persons of the present century." The flight of the Black Swan, out of slavery into world celebrity, a sojourn that took her from Cherokee Mansion along the banks of the Mississippi River to the River Thames, and into Buckingham Palace, is one of the most remarkable individual achievements of the nineteenth century.

The Black Swan was born in Natchez and was owned by Elizabeth Greenfield Roach. According to the most reliable sources, Elizabeth Taylor Greenfield's father was a native-born African and her mother was a Seminole Indian. Her father may have been a free man of color because several sources identify him by the surname of Taylor, a name that the Black Swan kept throughout her life.

In the early to mid-1820s Elizabeth Greenfield Roach, a Quaker from Philadelphia, freed her slaves, including Elizabeth's mother, Anna, provided for their passage to Liberia, and divorced her second husband, Benjamin Roach. That divorce mercifully ended an unhappy marriage. According to the Methodist divine William Winans, who was a frequent guest in their home, Benjamin Roach was "a dashing and handsome young man of thirty" and Elizabeth Greenfield was a woman in her sixties who was endowed by nature with "few charms." Winans recalled in his diary that Roach boasted that he would "marry a woman a hundred years old, provided she has as many thousand dollars."

After the divorce, Mrs. Greenfield resumed the surname of her first husband, Jessie Greenfield, and provided a substantial endowment for Elizabeth Female Academy in Washington, the County Seat of Adams County. Elizabeth Female Academy was the first college in America to grant collegiate degrees to women. When Mrs. Greenfield returned to Philadelphia, she took Elizabeth, who was still a child, with her. Elizabeth remained in Mrs. Greenfield's home on Arch Street until her early teens. Elizabeth returned to Mrs. Greenfield's household to nurse her during her declining years.

Elizabeth Taylor Greenfield's great gift was discovered inadvertently by the daughter of a physician who lived near the Greenfield home on Arch Street. That propitious moment in the Black Swan's majestic flight into fame has been artfully described in *The Black Swan, at Home and Abroad*, or *A Biographical Sketch of Elizabeth Taylor Greenfield*. This book was published in 1855 by an unnamed author:

> *Miss Price listened with delighted surprise to [Miss Greenfield's] songs [and] offered to accompany her on the guitar. This was a concurrence of circumstances which formed the era of her life. Her pulses quickened as she watched the fingers of her young patroness run over the key board of a full-toned piano-forte. She sang and before she had finished she was surrounded by the astonished inmates of the house who [were] attracted by the remarkable compass and sweetness of her voice.*

The applause which followed the first trial before this small audience gratified as much as it embarrassed her. The progress of genius is not like that of common minds. It is needless to say that her improvement was very rapid.

The records are largely silent for the years between that first parlor performance and the professional debut of the Black Swan, and little is known of those years. But Elizabeth Taylor Greenfield was surely aware, and she may have been a member, of that fabulous ensemble of black musicians in antebellum Philadelphia that included Captain Frank Johnson, Joseph G. Anderson, Andrew Cooper, William Appo, and the Bowers family. A brief but fascinating biography of Elizabeth Taylor Greenfield was published in 1969 by Arthur R. La Brew, titled *Elizabeth T. Greenfield, The Black Swan*.

In the fall of 1851 Miss Greenfield traveled from Philadelphia to Buffalo to visit some friends she had met in Philadelphia. Mrs. M.P.L. Thompson, a prominent citizen of Buffalo, had heard Eliza sing in Philadelphia and may have invited her to Buffalo in October 1851 for a special reason. Both Jenny Lind and Teresa Parodi, two of the great divas of that age, were performing in Buffalo in October, and Miss Greenfield likely went to Buffalo to hear them. Martin R. Delany, in his book, *The Condition, Elevation, Emigration, and Destiny of the Coloured People of the United States*, published at Philadelphia in 1852, wrote: "we have it from her own lips, that not until after the arrival of Jenny Lind and Parodi in this country" did Miss Greenfield understand the majesty and wonder of her gift.

During that long, slow train ride through western New York, Mrs. Heman Potter, another prominent citizen of Buffalo, heard Miss Greenfield sing. Like everyone else, she was astonished at the compass and sweetness of Miss Greenfield's voice. Mrs. Potter later arranged for several private concerts in Buffalo where Miss Greenfield quickly became a sensation. In its October 10, 1851, announcement of her coming professional debut, the *Buffalo Commercial Advertiser* gave Miss Greenfield the stage name that followed her the rest of her life:

A Black Swan!

Among the musical novelties of the day, the public are soon to be astonished by the debut of a young lady of African extraction, by the name of Eliza Greenfield. We had the pleasure last evening in company with a party of Musical Amateurs, of listening to her performance and must confess we were completely surprised and delighted.

Miss Greenfield possesses a voice of great purity and flexibility, and of extraordinary compass: singing the notes in alto, with brilliancy and sweetness, and descending to the bass notes with a power and volume perfectly astonishing. She sang among other pieces "Like the gloom of night retiring," with a degree of artistic finish that many of our celebrated Prima Donnas might envy.

We learn that measures are in progress to give our citizens an opportunity of hearing this new musical wonder, and we can safely vouch there will be no disappointment.

Miss Greenfield made her debut in Buffalo on October 22, 1851, only days after both Jenny Lind and Teresa Parodi had performed in that city. The program was in two parts. In the first part she sang "Salut a la France" from the opera "La Fille du Regiment," and "Make me no gaudy Chaplets," from "Lucrezia Borgia," by Donizetti, and "On the Banks of Guadalquiver," from "Linda di chamounix." During the second part she sang "Like the Gloom of Night Retiring" and "Sweetly O'er My Senses Stealing."

The musical critic for the *Buffalo Express* raved:

The Black Swan Concert, (we are sorry that the worthy Miss Greenfield has been so named, but it cannot now be remedied), occurred last evening, and it certainly was a remarkable event. On Monday, Parodi in all her splendor sang at Townsend Hall to half a house. Last night Miss Greenfield sang at the same place to a crowded house of the respectable, cultivated and fashionable people of the city. Jenny Lind has never drawn a better house as to character, than that which listened with evident satisfaction to this unheralded and almost un-

known African Nightingale. Curiosity did something for her but not all. She has merit, very great merit, and with cultivation (instruction) she will rank among the very first vocalists of the age.

She has a voice of great sweetness and power, with a wider range from the lower to highest notes than we have ever listened to, flexibility is not wanting, and her control of it is beyond example for a new and untaught vocalist. May we not hope that her music may tend to soften the hearts of the free and lighten the shackles of her race enslaved.

Miss Greenfield would have many cognomens during her illustrious career: the Black Diva, Ebony Angel, Sable Cantatrice, African Nightingale, and the Black Swan. There is some indication that she actually preferred Black Swan, and it became her stage name.

Following her triumph in Buffalo, the Black Swan went on a whirlwind tour north of the Mason-Dixon line that took her to most of the free states. The success of that tour is reflected in several reviews of her concerts: The *Rochester Daily American* wrote:

This astonishing songstress has made her appearance in Rochester, and will sing again this evening in Corinthian Hall, the most commodious building in western New York. She ought to have as large a house, and as brilliant, as any that thronged to hear the Swedish Nightingale.

We heard the "Black Swan" more than two years ago in Philadelphia and New York, in rooms little adapted to give effect to her performances: but we were, even then, struck with the astounding compass, power, and clearness of her voice.

We understand that since that time, she has applied herself with praiseworthy perseverance and assiduity to the cultivation of her extraordinary powers, and has attained great proficiency in the art, which is evidently the bent of her genius. By her own energy, and unassisted, she has made herself mistress of the harp, guitar and piano.

We are informed that the proceeds of the entertainment this eve-

Elizabeth Taylor Greenfield

ning, are to be wholly appropriated to the completion of her musical education in Paris, under the world-famed Garcia. We predict for Miss Greenfield a successful and brilliant future.

The *Lockport Journal* musical critic wrote:

Much has been said and written of this personage since she was introduced to the public as a musical prodigy. All sorts of surmises and conjectures have been indulged in, respecting the claim put forth of her merit, and generally the impression seemed to prevail that the novelty of "colour" and idle curiosity, accounted more for the excitement raised, than her musical powers.

Well, she has visited our place, and given our citizens an opportunity of judging for themselves.

We are ignorant of music, and unqualified to criticize, but a large audience were in attendance at Ringueberg Hall last evening — among those present were our musical amateurs — and we heard but one expression in regard to the new vocalist, and that was, wonder and astonishment at the extraordinary power and compass of voice, and the ease with which she passed from the highest to the lowest notes seemed without an effort. Her first notes of "Where are now the hopes?" startled the whole audience, and the interchange of glances succeeded by thunders of applause, at the end of the first verse, showed that her success was complete. She was loudly encored, and in response sung the barytone, "When stars are in the quiet sky," which took down the whole house.

The *Albany Evening Journal* of January 19, 1852 had this report:

The programme, too, was a difficult one. Here was a favorite song of Jenny Lind's, there a master-piece of Catharine Hayes, here a piece from a sacred opera, and there a merry Scotch ballad. Success in such a varied field certainly could hardly be anticipated, yet success the "Black Swan" certainly had.

The compass of her voice embraces twenty-seven notes, ranging from a bass, seldom or never before reached by a female voice, to a few notes higher than Jenny Lind's. It is as remarkable for its power and sweetness as for its compass, though it doubtless lacks something in these, as well as in flexibility, which will be supplied by cultivation, the advantages of which she has not yet enjoyed, to any great extent. She sings with the same absence of effort that is so remarkable in Jenny Lind. Add to this a courteous desire to oblige, and a perfectly composed and refined demeanor.

A second notice in the *Albany Evening Journal* read:

The "Black Swan" achieved a complete triumph on Saturday evening. In spite of the drawbacks of prejudice, enthusiasm of a large, fashionable and discriminating audience. She deserves to be ranked next to Jenny Lind. Her slight artistic defects are forgotten in the wonderful compass and sweetness of her voice, and in the general good taste with which she executes the most difficult passages of music. She deserves success and she will have it. Prejudice must sink before the sublime gift which nature has bestowed upon her. Let those who doubt go and hear her to-night, and do justice to real merit.

In New Bedford, Massachusetts, the *Mercury* declared on February 10, 1852:

Rara Avis. The Black Swan.
This wonderful vocalist, who seems to be asserting for the African race a position in the musical world, a good deal above the "Dandy Jim" and "Lucy Long" school, gives a concert tomorrow evening. She is a remarkable instance of natural talent, and her voice is said to be the most remarkable part of the whole matter, possessing as it does a compass and quality in certain of its notes, absolutely unique.

The Lowell, Massachusetts, *Mercury* wrote:

> *The Black Swan sounds twenty-eight full notes, a qualification accorded to no one before her. ... Every piece was rapturously encored.*

Sometimes racism reared its ugly head on this otherwise triumphant tour. In Cincinnati and Columbus, Ohio, free blacks were not allowed to attend her concerts, and a Cincinnati critic referred to Miss Greenfield derisively as the "African Crow."

Many of the critics who lauded the Black Swan's great talent marveled at her control of such a powerful but untrained voice. Some predicted that with training she could become the diva of that age.

The *Ohio State Journal*, on March 3, 1852, wrote:

> *We know the natural prejudice that we all have against her color, and it is very difficult to divest one's self entirely of them, and criticize fairly and justly in such a case.*
>
> *When it is considered that our celebrated singers — our Linds and Parodis — have had long years of toilsome, severe training, under the best teachers of the world, and then reflect that this woman has had the advantage of none of these, but displays only her natural powers and capacities, we may well ask the question whether the veritable Queen of Song herself has the natural gift, and powers and capacities in more lavish abundance than this person.*

The *Daily Capital City Fact* wrote on March 3, 1852:

> *She is indeed a remarkable swan. Although coloured as dark as Ethiopia, she utters notes as pure as if uttered in the words of the Adriatic.*
>
> *The magnificent quality of her voice, its great power, flexibility, and compass, her self-taught genius, energy, and perseverance, combine to render Miss Greenfield an object of uncommon interest to musicians.*
>
> *We have been spell-bound by the ravishing tones of Patti, Sontag,*

Malibran, and Grisi; we have heard the wondrous warblings of "the Nightingale;" and we have listened with delight to the sweet melodies of the fair daughter of Erin; but we hesitate not to assert that, with one year's tuition from the world-famed Emanuel Garcia, Miss Greenfield would not only compare favorably, with any of the distinguished artists above named, but incomparably excel them all.

The *Toronto Globe* of May 13, 1852 agreed:

Her present defects will be removed by the tuition of Garcea (sic) the instructor of Jenny Lind, under whom she is soon to be placed.

Miss Greenfield and her manager, Colonel J. H. Wood, decided to make a European tour that would also allow the Black Swan to study with Manuel Garcia, the famous Parisian master. Just before sailing for England, Miss Greenfield held a concert in New York City.

That concert was marred by threats of riot by some whites who objected to the public celebration of Negro talent and threatened to set fire to the concert hall if the Black Swan was permitted to sing. In an apparent compromise to minimize the danger of riots, the managers of the music hall agreed not to allow free blacks to attend the concert, a decision that angered New York's large free black population, many of whom wanted to attend the concert. A group of local black ministers petitioned her to cancel the concert. In response to their objections, the Black Swan offered to give a benefit concert for blacks in New York City. "I will," she said, "with pleasure sing for the benefit of any charity that will elevate the condition of my coloured brethren." There is no indication that she actually held a concert exclusively for blacks in New York.

Frederick Douglass, perhaps antebellum America's best known free man of color, was critical of the Black Swan for performing at a concert from which her own race was excluded. Petitions and threats notwithstanding, the concert was eventually held under heavy police security without incident on March 31, 1853, in a sold-out Metropolitan Hall.

The raucous and discourteous crowd was estimated at 4,000. The reviews were generally bad, and it may have been the most unpleasant performance of her career. One reviewer even criticized her for singing in the lower octaves:

> *The idea of a woman's voice is a feminine tone; anything below that is disgusting; it is as bad as a bride with a beard on her chin and an oath in her mouth.*
>
> *We hear a great deal about Woman's sphere. That sphere exists in Music, and it is the soprano region of the voice.*

The *National Anti-Slavery Standard*, published in New York City, carried a detailed account of the Black Swan's farewell concert and predicted a triumphant European tour. The *Standard* also predicted that Miss Greenfield would be received graciously by the European community as "one of Uncle Tom's daughters."

When the Black Swan arrived in England, she found to her dismay that her manager, who was a close relative of P.T. Barnum, Jenny Lind's American manager, had abandoned her. She was alone in London without funds or friends. The *National Anti-Slavery Standard's* prophecy that Miss Greenfield would be accepted as "one of Uncle Tom's daughters" was fulfilled in a most intriguing manner. Harriet Beecher Stowe, the author of *Uncle Tom's Cabin*, was visiting London at that time and heard of her misfortune.

In a diary of her London visit, titled *Sunny Memories of Foreign Lands*, which she published in 1854, Mrs. Stowe described her first meeting with the Black Swan:

> *May 6 (1854) A good many calls today. Among others came Miss Greenfield the (so called) Black Swan. She appears to be a gentle, amiable, and interesting young person.... She has an astonishing voice. C. sat down at the piano and played, while she sung.... While she was there, Mrs. S.C. Hall, of the Irish Sketches, was announced.... I told her of Miss Greenfield, and she took great interest in her, and requested*

her to sing something…she sang "Old Folks at Home," first in a sopra-
no voice, and then in a tenor or baritone. Mrs. Hall was amazed and
delighted, and entered at once into her cause.

Mrs. Hall, later that same day, took Miss Greenfield to meet Sir George
Smart, "the head of the Queen's musical establishment, and of course, the
acknowledged leader of London musical judgement." Miss Stowe wrote that
Sir George was "astonished and charmed at the wonderful weight, compass,
and power of her voice." He even agreed to rehearse her if she had an opportunity for a public performance. Miss Stowe added, "Mrs. Hall says this
is a great deal for him, whose hours are all marked with gold."

Over the next several weeks Mrs. Stowe arranged for several private
concerts for the African American Nightingale. One of the most celebrated of those concerts was held at Stafford House, the home of the Duke
and Duchess of Sutherland. Among the airs she sang were "Home Sweet
Home," and a new song, "I am Free," which was composed especially for
her by Charles Glover. Harriet Beecher Stowe described the Black Swan's
triumph before London's high society:

The concert room was the brilliant and picturesque hall I have be-
fore described to you. It looked more picture-like and dreamy than ever.
The piano was on the flat stairway just below the broad central land-
ing. It was a grand piano. … Sir George Smart presided. The choicest
of the elite were there. Miss Greenfield…is not handsome, but looked
very well. She has a pleasing dark face. … A certain gentleness of man-
ner and self-possession, the result of the universal kindness shown her,
sat well upon her. Chevalier Bunsen, the Prussian ambassador, sat by
me. He looked at her with much interest. "Are the race often as good
looking?" he said. I said, "She is not handsome, compared with many,
though I confess she looks uncommonly well to-day."

Miss Greenfield's turn for singing now came, and there was pro-
found attention. Her voice, with its keen, searching fire, its penetrating
vibrant quality, its "timbre," as the French have it, cut its way like a

Damascus blade to the heart.

She sang the ballad, "Old folks at home," giving one verse in the soprano, and another in the tenor voice.

As she stood partially concealed by the piano, Chevalier Bunsen thought that the tenor part was performed by one of the gentlemen. He was perfectly astonished when he discovered that it was by her. This was rapturously encored. Between the parts Sir George took her to the piano, and tried her voice by skips, striking notes here and there at random, without connection, from D in alt to A first space in bass clef: she followed with unerring precision, striking the sound nearly at the same instant his finger touched the key. This brought out a burst of applause.

After several highly successful concerts in Brighton, Dublin, Hammersmith, and London, for which she received rave reviews, Queen Victoria commanded a personal performance by the American sensation on May 10, 1854. The Queen was so moved by her performance that she directed Sir George to give her private lessons for a small remuneration.

Elizabeth Taylor Greenfield remained in England for just over a year, but there is no indication that she toured the continent, visited Paris, or that she studied under Garcia. In the summer of 1854 the Black Swan returned to the United States.

After her return to America she conducted several more successful tours. During an 1855 tour she sang in Baltimore, Maryland, which may have been her only performance in a slave state. Her great gift and her singular achievement could not be obscured even by the dark shadows of slavery itself. A correspondent for the Provincial Freeman, of Ontario, filed this report of her Baltimore concert:

The Black Swan (Miss Elizabeth T. Greenfield), the celebrated artiste, gave four concerts last week in the City of Baltimore; on which occasion she succeeded triumphantly, and gave great satisfaction and delight to her large and fashionable audiences, and was frequently encored. The tone of the Baltimore Press relative to her performances —

Pro-Slavery as they are — manifested towards here, however, quite a respectful attitude, and not a few gentlemen and ladies "conquered their prejudices" and made "calls" upon the gifted vocalist during the few days in their midst.

Miss Greenfield's activities during the Civil War are not known, but she did resurface immediately after the war. In 1865 she appeared on a program with Frederick Douglass in Philadelphia where he lectured on "Equality Before the Law." Two years later she was again singing in Buffalo for the Freedmen's Aid Society. During her visit she was interviewed by a Buffalo reporter, and a lengthy article recalling her long and happy association with Buffalo appeared in a local newspaper.

In the last years of her life, Miss Greenfield lived in Philadelphia and gave private voice lessons to some of that city's most promising young African American vocalists. Among her students was Thomas J. Bowers, America's premier black male vocalist, who was often and favorably compared to the Italian Mario. In fact, Bowers was often billed, against his own wishes, as the "African Mario."

Miss Elizabeth Taylor executed her last will and testament in 1866. In that legal document she resumed the surname of her father rather than using the name of her former owner. My mind wonders about the process of her mind that caused her to resume that name, the surname of her father.

The Black Swan's graceful and noble flight ended on May 2, 1876. Her passing was noted in a lengthy obituary in the *New York Times*.

It is unfortunate that the remarkable achievements of this gifted person are submerged in that vast wasteland of neglect during the nineteenth century when black history was disregarded by some as unworthy of record. But her achievements and her contributions to American culture, like those of many other African Americans, are now being rediscovered. Hopefully, the work being done on the Black Swan will rescue her from obscurity, place her in the pantheon of great Americans, and enrich our cultural memory.

9

Sallie Eola Reneau

Universal love to all mankind.

Sallie Reneau

On January 9, 1856, Governor John J. McRae presented to the Mississippi legislature a remarkable recommendation from an exceptional young woman named Sallie Eola Reneau. Governor McRae described Sallie Reneau as "a young lady of accomplishment, intelligence, and talent, educated in this state, a resident of Grenada, engaged in the business of female instruction, and devoted to the intellectual advancement of her sex." Governor McRae, who was himself a man of learning and letters, endorsed Reneau's proposal for a state-supported female college and passed along to the legislature an erudite and sophisticated document that she had drafted detailing an organizational plan for the institution. When Reneau presented her proposal to the legislature there were no state-supported female colleges in the United States.[1]

"The present era is propitious to woman," she wrote. "Our state... is rapidly advancing on the great road of human progress" and the "time has arrived when daughters and sisters may claim the right to have their minds as fully enlightened as sons and brothers; and when man shall cheerfully concede that his own interest and the welfare of the whole human family are promoted by the... intellectual improvement of woman." She added, "History attests, and everyday observation confirms, that woman is capable of receiving the highest order of intellectual culture" and "wielding a powerful influence in the 'republic of letters.'"[2]

Sallie Reneau did not envision a female college just for the Southern elite. A significant benefit derived from a public female college, she said, would be that both "the indigent and the opulent" could receive from this institution "the imperishable riches of a well cultivated mind."[3]

She assured the Mississippi lawmakers that a state female college would be a worthy and enduring legacy. And then she appealed to their pride of place and their sense of destiny:

> *If you now charter and liberally endow the proposed College, the enlightened public sentiment at home and abroad will hail your action, with pleasure and pride, and your noble example will soon be followed throughout the South and West.*[4]

Sallie Reneau was eighteen years old and a graduate of Holly Springs Female Academy when she wrote this seminal document that "sent an influence upward to the higher social strata and downward to the lowest." This remarkable young woman was born May 21, 1837, in Somerville, Tennessee. Her family moved to Mississippi when she was about five years old.[5]

Born into the Southern white middle class, she was among the 74 percent of white Southerners in 1860 who did not live in slave-owning families. In Mississippi slightly more than 50 percent of the white population in 1860, which included Sallie's family, did not belong to the slave-holding class. In 1860 her father was not a slave holder, nor was the uncle she lived with, or uncle her younger brother lived with. Her father was an entrepreneur of varied interests that would include merchandising, railroading, and silver mining. In 1860 her brother William Edward Reneau was a store clerk, and Sallie was a school teacher.[6]

Teaching was an old and honored tradition among Sallie Reneau's forebears. In the late 1790s her great grandfather was "one of the 'schoolmasters' of Hughes School in the Sinking Creek Community in what is now Carter County, Tennessee. Her father's brother, Isaac Tipton Reneau, also taught and was considered by some as "the best English scholar in Southern Kentucky" in the early 1830s. For a while he "boarded at the home of John M. Clemens, the father of Samuel L. Clemens," better known as Mark Twain. Isaac Reneau later "became one of the foremost preachers in that part of the country."[7]

Sallie Reneau's mother, Eliza Darwin Rawlings, was born in North Carolina January 27, 1819. Eliza Reneau died in Grenada on January 19, 1841, soon after giving birth to her second child, William Edward Reneau. Sallie and her younger brother were semi-orphans and mostly fended for themselves, living with various relatives, because their father was often gone in search of his fortune.[8]

According to the 1850 census, William Edward Reneau lived in Panola County with an aunt, Mrs. Anderson D. Patton, who was his mother's sister. Sallie does not appear in the 1850 census, but in 1860 she also lived in Panola County with another aunt, Mrs. Lawson G. Taylor.[9]

Sallie's father was the adventuresome Nathaniel Smith Reneau, a veteran of both the Mexican War and the Civil War. Nathaniel Reneau is interred in the American Cemetery in Mexico City. Born in Kentucky in 1814, he moved, by way of Tennessee to Grenada, Mississippi, before 1840, where he engaged in some business enterprise. He is listed in the 1850 census in Marshall County as a thirty-two-year-old merchant, born in Kentucky. In 1856 he was back in Grenada but does not appear in any Mississippi census records after 1850. He did, however, maintain his residence in Mississippi. He was named a trustee of the State Female College in Yalobusha County, and later a trustee of Reneau Female University of Mississippi at Oxford.[10]

In 1856 the Mississippi legislature endorsed Sallie Reneau's proposal and established the State Female College in Yalobusha County, which then included the town of Grenada, where Reneau was teaching. The law founding the college also named an eighteen-member board of trustees to organize and oversee the state's newest collegiate institution. Among the board members were Governor McRae, future governor John J. Pettus, and Reneau's father, Nathaniel S. Reneau.[11]

Unfortunately, the lawmakers did not appropriate any funds for the institution. After the legislature again failed to allocate funds to the women's college at its 1858 session, Sallie Reneau drafted a memorial to the United States Congress asking that an additional land grant be dedicated to the State Female College. Several other Mississippi collegiate institutions including Jefferson College, Mississippi College, the University of Mississippi, and later Alcorn University and Mississippi State University were beneficiaries of federal land grants. Even though it was a reasonable request, and the state of Mississippi was actually due another land grant that the University of Mississippi finally received in the 1890s, the United States Congress was preoccupied with the impending civil war and did not approve Sallie Reneau's request. Consequently, the establishment of a state collegiate institution for women was postponed until Salle Reneau brought the idea back to life during Reconstruction immediately after the Civil War.[12]

Although Sallie must have been disappointed that her dream for a state female college did not materialize in 1856, she was not dismayed, and in the great crisis that soon engulfed the nation she would be found in the front lines of public service. In the spring of 1861 her father and her younger brother, like thousands of other Southern men and boys, were imbued with the romantic notion of war and rushed off to the front. According to a history of Panola County, her brother William Reneau, died during the Civil War, and other records indicate that her father was captured and later released from Fort Lafayette in New York Harbor in 1862.[13]

Immune to any romantic notion of war, Sallie organized a group of ladies in Panola County and wrote to Governor John. J. Pettus offering their services as "Mississippi Nightingales... to go around to the various camps... to nurse the sick and wounded soldiers and to sew for those who might need it." To protect themselves in the lawless environment that always parallels a state of war, she asked the governor for some "small arms... that we could carry conveniently," and for the sake of quick and easy identification, she asked that he supply them with uniforms.

"If you will provide for us as we request," she concluded her letter, "we will endeavor to organize a Mississippi Volunteer Relief Association... to go around to the camps to distribute to the [soldiers] such necessities as the Association may furnish them, and to nurse the sick as best we can." Sallie's effort to establish a wartime Volunteer Relief Association predated the establishment of the International Red Cross by several years.[14]

Sallie's plan to establish a volunteer relief association in June 1861 was a rare anticipation of the bloody conflict that followed. In January 1861 Governor Pettus declined an opportunity to import firearms from a Brussels manufacturer because he did not believe there would be any war. As late as March 14, 1861, the editor of Sallie Reneau's hometown newspaper, the *Panola Star*, predicted that there would be no war and that Lincoln would pursue a policy of peace.[15]

Mississippi State University Professor John K. Bettersworth was probably the first Civil War historian to cite Sallie's letter to Governor Pettus. In a 1973 history of Mississippi he wrote of her "spectacular zeal" and highlighted the fact that her "Mississippi Nightingales" would be armed, uniformed, and would receive pay equal to soldiers. Subsequent historians who cited Bettersworth, but apparently did not read Sallie Reneau's letter, also focused on the side arms, uniforms, and soldiers' pay.[16]

The popular and highly respected *Encyclopedia of the Confederacy*, edited by the renowned historian Richard Current, includes the following statement: "Girls, too, were eager to help. Sallie Eola Reneau attempted to form a company of 'Mississippi Nightingales,' complete with uniforms and sidearms."[17]

Karen Zeinert, in *Those Courageous Women of the Civil War*, writes, "Sallie Reneau of Mississippi offered to raise a company of women to be armed, uniformed, and paid like soldiers to defend the home front." It is evident from these two examples that historians who have cited Sallie Reneau as an advocate of female militarism have not read her letter to Governor Pettus and have read too much into her request for military accouterments.[18]

Sallie Reneau's plea for equal pay for the women volunteers was also an early expression of one of the founding principles of feminism.

Governor Pettus did not fund Sallie's "Mississippi Nightingales," and the Volunteer Relief Association was not formed. But Sallie Reneau did not allow that defeat to deter her from her larger goal. She organized the ladies of Panola County, established the Society of Sisters, and conducted on a

Sallie Reneau

smaller scale the volunteer relief program that she had envisioned in her letter to Governor Pettus. Sallie was the corresponding secretary of the society, and the local newspaper carried several articles about the society's effort to provide relief and aid to Panola County soldiers.[19]

A December 9, 1861, article in the local newspaper reported that the Society of Sisters had provided Panola County troops with 90 pairs of socks, 50 over shirts, 17 under shirts, and 62 pairs of "drawers." Sallie expressed her appreciation to all the ladies for their "carding, spinning, and knitting" and to all the others who had made a contribution to the Society of Sisters.[20]

As the Civil War divided the nation into North and South, so it divided the Reneau family into blue and grey. While Nathaniel Reneau supported the Confederacy, two of his brothers sided with the Union. By all accounts, "Berry Jordan Reneau's Unionism is legendary." It was said, perhaps in jest, that he would not allow his girls to wear anything but blue dresses, and he named one of his sons Ulysses S. Grant Reneau. Nathaniel Reneau's oldest brother, Isaac Tipton Reneau, was also an ardent Unionist. And while Sallie's brother, William, served in the Confederate army, her first cousin Thomas Reneau was a sergeant in the Union cavalry.[21]

When the war finally ended Sallie Reneau went back into the classroom at the Batesville Academy, and she openly and publicly embraced the new age of opportunity for women engendered by the Civil War. In a local newspaper article announcing a gala musical program and the crowning of a May Queen by her students, Sallie invited the general public to attend the concert and announced, "Ladies can exercise the customary right of escorting each other, or going alone." In that time and place women were not supposed to go out at night alone, especially to an event that lasted until well after midnight, as that one did.[22]

Most white Mississippians were psychologically unprepared for military defeat and the emancipation of the state's 436,000 slaves, but circumstances beyond their control forced them to accept the "world remade by the Civil War." Sallie Reneau, however, welcomed that bold new world with open arms and renewed her effort to establish a state female collegiate institution.[23]

On April 5, 1872, the Reconstruction legislature, which for the first time in the state's history included African Americans and Republicans, established a state-supported female college and named the institution in honor of Sallie Reneau. The state's second Republican governor, Ridgely C. Powers, signed the bill into law. Governor James L. Alcorn, Mississippi's first Republican governor, and for whom Alcorn University was named, had been elevated to the United States Senate. Powers was then lieutenant governor and succeeded Alcorn as governor.[24]

The Reneau Female University of Mississippi was established as a co-equal branch of the University of Mississippi at Oxford to provide college-level courses for women "on the same and equal privileges that the males have been and are now being taught." The statute named Sallie Reneau principal of Reneau Female University and vice president of the faculty of the University of Mississippi at Oxford. A nine-member board of trustees included James M. Howry, an original member of the University of Mississippi Board of Trustees; Absalom M. West, a railroad owner and one of the state's most successful businessmen; Joshua S. Morris, the Republican Attorney General; Governor Ridgely C. Powers;, and Sallie's father, Nathaniel S. Reneau.[25]

A special feature of Reneau Female University of Mississippi was its commitment to Mississippi's increasingly important teacher corps. In 1870 Mississippi established a state system of public education. To staff that system with qualified and well-trained teachers, Sallie Reneau proposed and the legislature agreed to provide a four-year college education, including tuition, room, and board, to female orphans who would agree to teach in the public schools for two years after their graduation.[26]

Again, Sallie Reneau's hopes and dreams were dashed when the legislature did not appropriate any funds to Reneau Female University of Mississippi. Defeated but undeterred, she again appealed to the United States Congress for a land grant to fund a Mississippi university for women, but no land grant was appropriated.

In 1872 the state of Mississippi was funding the University of Mississippi; Alcorn University, a public university for African Americans; the

State Normal School, a public coeducational teachers' college for African Americans in Holly Springs; and the normal department at Tougaloo, a private co-educational college for African Americans in Jackson. White women were the only segment of Mississippi's population that did not reap the benefits of state-supported higher education.[27]

After the United States Congress declined to make another land grant to Mississippi, the legislature in 1873 repealed the act establishing Reneau Female University as a branch of the University of Mississippi.[28]

But Sallie Reneau would just not give up on her vision for a women's college, where "the indigent and the opulent" could acquire "the imperishable riches of a well cultivated mind." Apparently under the spell of her persuasive power, on February 20, 1873, the Mississippi legislature established the Reneau Female University of Mississippi at Sardis. To accomplish the goal she had first conceived in 1855 as an eighteen-year-old teacher in a girls' school, she enlisted the support of her long-time friends in Panola County. According to J.F. Lavender, whose reminiscences appeared in the Panola County *Southern Reporter* on February 12, 1903, he and several other prominent citizens of Sardis were eager to have the Reneau Female University located at Sardis and agreed to help Reneau. Lavender even located twenty acres of property that would be suitable for the college. Their machinations also included getting Nathaniel Reneau elected to the legislature, "and through his influence secure the college." Nathaniel Reneau was not elected to the legislature, but Sallie and her Sardis allies were successful in getting the Reneau University established at Sardis in 1873. The university's fifteen-member board of trustees included Governor Powers and Nathaniel Reneau, but there was no appropriation for the institution, and the founding and funding of a Mississippi state college for women was postponed again.[29]

Reneau's crusade for the education and elevation of women was a remarkable story, and what she had long envisioned was at last achieved in 1884 with the founding of the Industrial Institute and College at Columbus, largely through the efforts of Annie Coleman Peyton and Olivia Valentine Hastings.[30]

In his 1903 reminiscences, J.F. Lavender recalled that Sallie Reneau was teaching in the "Stark School at Holly Springs" in 1873 when the legislature established but did not fund Reneau University at Sardis. In 1877, or early 1878, "a group of civic-minded citizens" of Germantown, Tennessee, wrote to Sallie Reneau asking her to help them organize a school. Sallie went to Germantown, "where she lived in the home of Postmaster and Mrs. Miller. The school was planned and organized, and pupils were enrolled, and Sallie then returned to her home in Mississippi in July 1878."[31]

During the Yellow Fever epidemic in the late summer of 1878 Sallie Reneau went back to Germantown, where she organized a small group of ladies to care for those who were sick and dying from that scourge that swept across the lower Mississippi valley. On September 28, 1878, Sallie Reneau wrote to her father, who was then in Washington, D.C. :

> *My dear Father, I sent you a postal card and six papers today, and I do not know that I could say more in a letter than I have said in the card and the papers. ... I am very anxious to see frost and be rid of all this dreadful excitement. I am tired. ... It has been two months of continual fear and excitement, which is as much as human nerves can stand. ... There have been ten thousand deaths from this disease... and it has scattered gloom and distress all over the land. ... I have never felt so entirely helpless as now. Who is there to look to but God? God help us! And send us frost. ... I am low spirited, distressed. After all, I had rather be here than at Batesville, I had rather die here. I am glad that I came. I will write again as soon as I can. Write. God bless you! Good night. Your affectionate child, S.E. Reneau.[32]*

Two weeks after she wrote this letter, Sallie Eola Reneau fell victim to that dreaded disease. Her obituary in the October 20, 1878, issue of the *Memphis Daily Appeal* speaks eloquently of this truly remarkable woman:

> *The deceased leaves a large circle of friends throughout the Union who will mourn her loss. A woman of great mental endowments and*

rare intellectual attainments, she leaves her impress upon the minds and hearts of those who were favored in being her pupils, as well as upon her associates and friends. The motto of her life was "Universal love to all mankind," and like many others at this hour, she laid down her life for her neighbors and friends. Verily, Death loves a shining mark."

When Mississippi's United States Senator James L. Alcorn learned of Sallie Reneau's death he declared, "The state of Mississippi, at the earliest session of her legislature, should erect over her remains some monument... worthy of this great scholar of the state of which she was proud to have been a daughter."[33]

But no state monument has been erected.

In 2009 there was widespread discussion about renaming Mississippi University for Women because it had become a coeducational institution in 1984 and was no longer a women's college. During that discussion, I prepared this paper on the life of Sallie Eola Reneau for MUW President Claudia Limbert. She recommended that the name of Mississippi University for Women be changed to Reneau University in honor of Sallie Reneau. But after President Limbert's retirement in June, 2010, the discussion about renaming the institution declined, and no action has been taken on renaming MUW.

Endnotes

1 Mississippi House of Representatives, *Journal 1856*, p 22-23; 282-288; the House *Journal* is hereafter cited as *Journal* and date; see also Bridget Smith Pieschel and Stephen Robert Pieschel, *Loyal Daughters: One Hundred Years at Mississippi University for Women* for a history of the founding and evolution of MUW; see page 4 for a picture of Sallie Reneau.

2 Journal 1856, p 22-23

3 Ibid.

4 Ibid.

5 Pieschel, Loyal Daughters, p 4; Sheldon Scott Kohn, T*he Literary and Intellectual Impact of Mississippi's Industrial Institute and College*, [Electronic Edition] p 63; see also the biographical sketch of Reneau in the Sallie Eola Reneau Subject File in the Mississippi Department of Archives and History in Jackson. Some documents indicate that Sallie Reneau was born in August 1836.

6 Alan Brinkley, Frank Freidel, Richard Current and T. Harry Williams, *A Survey of American History* (1991) states on page 331, "But even with all members of slave-holding families included in the figures, those owning slaves still amounted to perhaps no more than one quarter of the [Southern] white population." In *Mississippi History* (1930) Charles Sydnor and Claude Bennett state on page 173, "If the families of slave owners are considered, we find that less than one-half of the white people of the state were members of slave-holding families." William Edward Reneau stated on his enlistment papers that he was a store clerk.

7 See references to Charles Reno, Sallie's great-great grandfather, and her uncle Isaac Tipton Reneau, in Steven G. Fancy and Sue Reneau Damewood, *Genealogy of the Reno/Reneau Family in America, 1600-1930* [Electronic Edition], cited hereafter as the *Reno/Reneau Genealogy.*

8 See references to Eliza Reneau and William Edward Reneau in the Reno/Reneau Genealogy. In some other Reneau family genealogical records the date of their births and deaths differ slightly.

9 See Xerox copies of census records.

10 See references in *Reno/Reneau Genealogy*; see also *Laws of Mississippi, 1856* p 383; *Laws 1872*, p 125; *Laws 1873*, p442.

11 *Laws 1856*, 383-384.

12 See David G. Sansing, *Making Haste Slowly, The Troubled History of Higher Education in Mississippi* for references to various institutions receiving federal land grants.

13 Panola County Historical and Genealogical Society, *History of Panola County*, T23 and T27; for the release of Nathaniel Reneau, see Richmond, Virginia, *The Daily Dispatch*, February 2, 1862 [Electronic Resource].

14 See Sallie Reneau's June 7, 1861, letter to Governor John J. Pettus. The original letter was located and transcribed by the Mississippi Department of Archives's renowned Civil War historian H. Grady Howell, Jr., and I wish to express my appreciation to Mr. Howell for his assistance in finding and transcribing Reneau's letter.

15 For Governor Pettus's refusal to import Belgium rifles, see David G. Sansing and Carroll Waller, *A History of the Mississippi Governor's Mansion*, p 48.

16 John K. Bettersworth, "The Home Front, 1861-1865," vol. 1, Chapter 16, pp 492- 517, Richard A. McLemore (ed.), *A History of Mississippi*; see p 517 for Reneau's letter.

17 Richard N. Current (ed.), *Encyclopedia of the Confederacy*, vol.2, p 516.

18   Karen Zeinert, *Those Courageous Women of the Civil War*, [Electronic Edition] p 25.

19   *Panola Star*, December 9, 1861. The files of the *Panola Star* cited here are located in the Panola County Courthouse in Sardis.

20   Ibid.

21   See references to Berry Jordan Reneau, Isaac Tipton Reneau, and Thomas Reneau, in the *Reno/Reneau Genealogy*.

22   *Panola Star*, April 27, 1872 and May 4, 1872.

23   *Laws 1872*, 125-128.

24   Ibid.

25   Ibid.

26   Ibid.

27   See Sansing, *Making Haste Slowly*, for the various state supported colleges.

28   *Laws 1873*, p 113-114.

29   *Laws 1873*, 443-444; James T. Lavender was named to the board of trustees of the Reneau Female University at Sardis. He could have been the J.F. Lavender who wrote about founding the Reneau University in the 1903 Panola County *Southern Reporter*.

30   See Pieschel, *Loyal Daughters* and Kohn, *The Impact of Mississippi's Industrial Institute and College*, for the founding of the Industrial Institute and College at Columbus.

31   Information about Sallie's organizing a school at Germantown was graciously provided by Anita Reneau Daniels of Vancouver, Washington, and first appeared in the *Reneau Book of Memories Through the Years, October 2004*.

32   Ibid.

33   Senator Alcorn's statement is found in a clipping from an unidentified Mississippi newspaper in the Sallie Eola Reneau Subject File in the Mississippi Department of Archives and History.

Professor B.L.C. Wailes

10

PROFESSOR B. L. C. WAILES

A Forgotten Man of the Old South

On The Occasion Of Unveiling His Portrait In The Mississippi Hall of Fame

"The common sin of procrastination together with current duties not to be postponed has caused all preparation for this occasion to be deferred until the eleventh hour. I admit this to be no legitimate excuse, yet it may serve to account for, if it does not extenuate, some of the shortcomings for which I thus make myself accountable." With those words Benjamin Leonard Covington Wailes opened his presidential address to the first meeting of the Mississippi Historical Society in 1859.[1]

B.L.C. Wailes was a busy man, in great demand, and a man of humility as most great men are, and he almost never declined an invitation to deliver a speech. As president of the Agricultural, Horticultural and Botanical Society of Jefferson College, Wailes was obliged to deliver the society's 1841 annual address. He opened that address by saying, "It is with diffidence that I attempt to comply [for] I greatly distrust my ability to interest you on a subject upon which many of my auditors are much better informed, both theoretically and practically, than I know myself to be. To such, I can expect to impart no new facts [or] principles... connected with my subject. In my hands the attempt can prove but a hackneyed reiteration... feebly expressed and tamely delivered."[2]

But toward the end of that address Wailes must surely have captivated his audience with a brilliant and beautiful tribute to the gardener's art:

> *A universal passion for flowers pervades the human breast.... Prized by the peasant, cherished by the peer, they entwine themselves in the lattice of the humble cottage and cling around the marble columns of the statelier pile.... As agriculture has been accounted the first step in the march of civilization, so Horticulture may be said to be the first in the career of refinement.... The calm repose of nature is... congenial to the silent workings of the contemplative mind.[3]*

B.L.C. Wailes was born on August 1, 1797, in Columbia County, Georgia, the son of Levin Wailes and Eleanor Davis, both of Prince Georges County, Maryland. Through various marriages the Wailes family was closely allied to the Covingtons and the Magruders. The fifth of six sons and a surveyor by trade, Levin was lured to Mississippi by the rills and hills of a virgin land along America's receding frontier with its boundless promise of prosperity. When his family moved to the Mississippi Territory in 1807, Benjamin was ten years old.[4]

While his father was surveying the northern boundary of the second Choctaw cession under the Treaty of Mount Dexter in 1805, and other federal lands in the newly acquired territory of Louisiana, young Benjamin was growing up in Washington, the Mississippi territorial capital. In those halcyon days Washington was a tiny intellectual clearing in the dense Mississippi wilderness, which included Natchez, the cultural center of the Old Southwest. There were two institutions of higher learning in the Mississippi Territory, Elizabeth Female Academy and Jefferson College. In 1803 the Mississippi Society for the Acquirement and Dissemination of Useful Knowledge was established in Washington, and William Dunbar, a scientist of some renown, a member of the American Philosophical Society, and correspondent with Mr. Jefferson, imported a large and powerful telescope to Washington. Dunbar, incindentally, was scolded by a local evangelical minister for invading the privacy of the Almighty. In addition to Dunbar and Wailes, Washington's other notable residents included John and Lucy Audubon, Joseph Holt Ingraham, John Wesley Monette, David Ker, John F. H. Claiborne, Andrew Marschalk, and, on occasion, the famous circuit rider, Lorenzo Dow.[5]

In that sophisticated village the territorial assembly and later the state legislature met; Mississippi's first constitution was drafted; the federal land office was located, and Andrew Marschalk kept a reading room where the gentlemen of Washington could browse through the latest gazettes, new books and maps, and engage in friendly disputation. At times the disputations were lively and not so friendly. A Washington literary society known as the Lyceum published a learned journal, the *South-western Journal*, which included articles by Lyceum members and members of the Jefferson College faculty.[6]

In this stimulating environment young Benjamin Wailes spent his formative years. He enrolled at Jefferson College, probably in 1814. During his attendance he formed a deep attachment to that institution and remained loyal to his alma mater throughout his life. From 1824 until his death he was a member of the Jefferson College Board of Trustees and for several years he served as the financial secretary of that often financially troubled institution. His most valuable service to Jefferson College was rendered in 1832 when he persuaded the U.S. Congress to exchange the institution's 1803 land grant, which had proved to be of little value, for a more lucrative grant in the new Choctaw cession lands in north Mississippi.[7]

Benjamin interrupted his education to accept a job in a surveyor's office in Washington, the territorial capital. Following a brief period during which he worked for his father in Louisiana, he was appointed assistant postmaster in the Choctaw Agency, and he moved to the agency headquarters located on the Natchez Trace seven miles north of Le Fleur's Bluff, which is now Jackson. Soon thereafter he was appointed secretary to a commission that was negotiating another land cession with the Choctaws. During those negotiations at the Old Fort Confederation on the Tombigbee River, he met

Pushmataha and Mushulatubee. When the cession treaty was signed at Do-aks Stand in 1820, Wailes was there, and he met Andrew Jackson.[8]

After the treaty ceremony Wailes made his first journey to Washington City. While he was in the nation's capital he was invited to a levee given by President James Monroe and had the pleasure of meeting the president.

In that same year, 1820, Wailes married his cousin, Rebecca Susanna Magruder Covington. Rebecca's father, General Leonard Covington, was the military commander of Fort Dearborn, located in Adams County. General Covington, who was later killed in the War of 1812, built a home near the fort, which he called Propinquity. Benjamin and Rebecca would live there for a short time with her widowed mother. In 1823 Rebecca received her share of her father's considerable estate, and in 1828 she received another bequest during a second division following the death of her mother. Following that division, the Wailes family moved into Meadvilla, the former home of Governor Cowles Mead, which they purchased with Rebecca's inheritance. Through Rebecca's family, they would later inherit Fonsylvania, a plantation in Warren County, and two other plantations and over one hundred slaves.[9]

Wailes' advantageous marriage freed him from the necessity of employment and allowed him to pursue his scientific and intellectual interests. Although he was a man of many talents and varied interests, he found affairs of state not to his liking. In 1825 and 1826 Wailes represented Adams County in the State House of Representatives. During the legislative session of 1826 the designation of Jackson as the state capital rather than Columbia in Marion County, the relocation of the State Supreme Court from Natchez to Jackson, and the reapportionment of the legislature, in favor of the recently established northern and eastern counties, were achieved through the most arduous political machinations, which disappointed and disgusted Wailes, and he abandoned his budding political career.[10]

It was the mysteries of nature, not the machinations of politics, that Wailes found compelling and interesting. At his home in Washington Wailes began exploring those mysteries, collecting specimens of flora and fauna, artifacts, relics, and keeping his copious notes, which eventually formed a thirty-six-volume diary.

By 1824 he was already known for his flock of sheep, on which he lavished the greatest care. His flock was descended from a ram from the celebrated flock owned by Chancellor R.R. Livingston of New York. At Meadvilla his orchard included eighteen varieties of fruit trees. Among them were peaches, pears, apples, pomegranates, quince, and figs, which were his favorite. In his diary he carefully noted when he picked the first and last fig of each season. Above all else, however, Wailes was a collector. His collection of geological and archeological specimens and Indian artifacts, grew so large that Meadvilla could not contain them. He deposited the overflow in cabinets at Jefferson College and soon filled them to capacity. Eventually he added two wings to Meadvilla to store his ever-expanding collection.[11]

During his lifetime Benjamin Wailes shared his scientific interests with some of America's most prominent men of science. As a member and president of Adams Athenaeum, a scientific and literary society in Natchez, he was closely associated with historian John W. Monette. He was also an intimate friend of both John James Audubon and Joseph Holt Ingraham. He also met and shared his field research with Professor Louis Agassiz of Harvard and M.W. Dickerson, one of America's best-known naturalists; he collected specimens for Spencer F. Baird and Joseph Henry of the Smithsonian Institution, and he often made sketches of specimens and geological formations he could not collect.[12]

Wailes' major work, and his most significant contribution to science, was his geological survey of Mississippi, published in 1854. That survey took him into virtually every corner and across every quadrant of Mississippi. More often than not, those field trips were taken alone and under the most arduous conditions. His diary of that famous trip through south Mississippi in 1852, with its vivid descriptions of that pristine wilderness, has been published by John Hebron Moore in the 1955 edition of the *Journal of Mississippi History*. It is delightful reading.[13]

The geological survey itself has an interesting history. As early as 1838 the Washington Lyceum had suggested the need for a soil survey of Mississippi. The legislature, however, did not authorize the survey until 1850. The enabling legislation directed the professor of geology at the University of

Mississippi to conduct the field work. But there was no professor of geology at the university, and the university faculty declared that such a survey was not properly the function of a classical university. In the 1850s the perpetuation of knowledge derived from the ancient classics and the disciplining of the mind, not investigation and the accumulation of new knowledge, were the primary purpose of American collegiate institutions. Nevertheless, the legislature appropriated funds for a geology professor and ordered the survey, and Benjamin Wailes immediately applied for the position. But the university's board of trustees did not create the new position. Instead, the board allocated the additional funds to Professor John Millington, who held the chair of chemistry, and directed him to conduct a survey. Millington hired an assistant, who stayed only one year and accomplished very little. Wailes was then named assistant professor of chemistry. He was to conduct the actual survey and send samples of soil, water, and minerals to Millington, who would then analyze the samples and would eventually draft a report to the legislature. This arrangement, which worked quite well, was dissolved by the resignation of Professor Millington, who was succeeded by Lewis Harper. Soon after his appointment, Harper and Wailes became embroiled in an intense disagreement that threatened the success of the survey. Eventually, Harper was reassigned, and Wailes was allowed to complete the survey and draft the final report in 1854, which consisted of four hundred pages of text and many illustrations.[14]

That was an enormous accomplishment. Without the benefit of any clerical assistance and before the invention of the typewriter, Wailes meticulously penned the text and made all the sketches and illustrations himself. But that was not the end of the story. The cost of publishing Wailes' four-hundred-page manuscript would greatly exceed the legislative appropriation for that purpose. After a great deal of finagling, and with the assistance of his friend Stephen Baird, Wailes was finally able to publish his manuscript.[15]

After the publication of his survey, Wailes turned his attention to managing his plantation interests and to the preservation of the archives and historical records of Mississippi. To promote that important work Wailes and several others organized the Mississippi Historical Society on November 9, 1858. Benjamin Wailes was elected president, and the Reverend William Carey Crane, a Baptist minister and college president, was elected vice president. From then until his death, Wailes devoted much of his effort and energy to collecting historical documents, public records, newspapers, private manuscripts, ledgers, and other written material.[16]

Throughout most of his life Wailes was conservative in matters of politics. He strenuously opposed an elective judiciary, and he was extremely distrustful of Democrats, and long after the party had ceased to exist, he continued to identify himself as a Whig. Like most other large planters and slave owners, Wailes was a Unionist and not surprisingly, he placed the blame for the disruptive debate over states' right and sectional agitation squarely and solely on the Democrats. As the sectional crisis deepened, Wailes increasingly despaired for the Union and he denounced the demagogues. In March 1860 he described Mississippi's governor, John J. Pettus, as "a bigoted prejudiced 'nincompoop,'" and he was alarmed that Pettus might "by some hasty and intemperate action seek to precipitate the State into Secession." He was equally despairing of President James Buchanan. "What a poor imbecile blundering incompetent executive this Union has been cursed with," he wrote. The name of James Buchanan, he continued, "will forever be linked to the wreck of this glorious Republic."[17]

The Civil War, as he and many other Unionists had predicted, was devastating to the Southern economy. His own considerable holdings had become liabilities, and Union troops confiscated and burned several hundred bails of his cotton. When his oldest son, Leonard, wrote from Corinth on April 10, 1862, that he had typhoid fever and was too ill to remain with his regiment, and pleaded with his father to send someone to care for him, Wailes did not have sufficient funds to send for him immediately. Later, after Leonard had come home and his health had been restored, Wailes had to borrow the money to send him back to his unit.[18]

Over the next few months Wailes' own health began to decline, and by the fall of the year he was gravely ill. On November 5, 1862, he made the last entry in his diary. Eleven days later he died.[19]

B.L.C. Wailes was eminently a man of the Old South, a man of the nineteenth century. Yet he had much in common with the eighteenth-century enlightenment and its belief in the advancement of mankind. He also had much in common with the ecologists of the twentieth century and their sense of stewardship over the environment. Wailes was a man of science and letters and learning. He lived in the nineteenth century, but he would have been at home in any age or era. His contemporary, J.F.H. Claiborne, said of him: "In literature and science he was the foremost man in the state, and would have achieved the greatest eminence had his life been spared." In 1938 Charles Sydnor called him "a forgotten man of the Old South."[20]

But fame hovers over those who are worthy of its reflection. An account of Wailes' life in a Jackson newspaper in 1978 correctly called him a renaissance man. And his recent induction into the Mississippi Hall of Fame, and today's ceremony unveiling his official portrait, signals a rebirth of his fame and a reaffirmation of his enduring contributions. And he, Benjamin Leonard Covington Wailes, will indeed add a new measure of luster to this lustrous Hall of Heroes.[21]

1861 map of the University of Mississippi campus by Deborah Freeland

Endnotes

1   Benjamin L.C. Wailes, *Inaugural Address*, as the first president of the Mississippi Historical Society in 1859. There are several versions or editions of this address in the Wailes Collection in the Mississippi Department of Archives and History at Jackson, Mississippi. For a published edition, see Charlotte Capers (ed), *Journal of Mississippi History* (v 6, 1944, 161-73).

2   B.L.C. Wailes, *Address Delivered in the College Chapel Before the Agricultural, Horticultural and Botanical Society of Jefferson College on the 24th of April 1841*, The Natchez *Daily Courier*, 1841, 1.

3   Ibid, 26-27.

4   Charles Sydnor, *A Gentleman of the Old Natchez Region, Benjamin L.C. Wailes* (Durham, North Carolina; Duke University Press, 1938). See Chapter II, "Following the Frontier," for biographical information on Wailes and his family.

5   See Suanna Smith, "Washington, Mississippi: Antebellum Elysium," JMH (v 40, 1978, 143-65); Laura D. Harrell, "The Development of the Lyceum Movement in Mississippi," *JMH* (v 31 1969,187-201); Arthur H. DeRosier, "William Dunbar: A Product of the Eighteenth Century Scottish Renaissance," *JMH* (v 8,1966, 185-227); D. Clayton James, *Antebellum Natchez* (Baton Rouge, Louisiana; Louisiana State University Press, 1968).

6   A complete set of the *South-western Journal* is in the Louisiana State University Library.

7   On Wailes' contribution to Jefferson College see Edward Mayes, *History of Education in Mississippi* (Washington, D.C.; Government Printing Office, 1899), 25-38; William T. Blain, *Education in the Old Southwest: A History of Jefferson College* (Washington, Mississippi; Jefferson College Inc. and Mississippi Department of Archives and History, 1978); Sharron Lynn Dobbs, "Jefferson College: A Study of the Origins of Higher Education in Mississippi 1802-1848," (Ph.D. diss. University of Mississippi, 1987); Sydnor, *Wailes*, 204-34; "A Tribute of Respect," a resolution adopted by the Jefferson College Board of Trustees upon the death of Wailes in 1862. A copy of this resolution is in the Wailes Collection in the MDAH.

8   Sydnor, *Wailes*, 55-61.

9   Ibid, 61-91, 92.

10   Ibid, 72-75.

11   For Wailes' intellectual development, see Chapter V, "Intellectual Trends," in ibid, 120-151.

12   See Chapter VII, "Wailes as a Naturalist," in ibid, 170-203.

13   For an account of this trip, see John H. Moore, "South Mississippi in 1852," *JMH* (v 18 1955, 18-32); See also Kate Bergeron, "Benjamin Wailes: Sojourn through South Mississippi, a precious natural record," and "Wailes took to Coast — naturally," Biloxi-Gulfport *Sun-Herald*, March 3 and March 10, 1985.

14   Sydnor, Wailes, 182-203.

15   Ibid; see B.L.C. Wailes, *Report on the Agriculture and Geology of Mississippi Embracing a Sketch of the Social and Natural History of the State* (E. Barksdale, State Printer, 1854).

16   See Chapter IX, "Mississippi Historical Society," in Sydnor, *Wailes*, 234-259.

17   Ibid, 292-3.

18   Ibid, 301-2.
19   Ibid, 306.
20   Claiborne's quote is in Dunbar Rowland, *Mississippi Comprising Sketches of Counties, Towns, Institutions, and Persons Arranged in Cyclopedic Form* (Atlanta; Southern Historical Publishing Association, 1907), 889; Sydnor, Wailes, vii.
21   *Clarion-Ledger*, August 1. 1978.

The University faculty circa 1870
Professor Eugene Hilgard standing on the far right

11

PROFESSOR EUGENE HILGARD

THE FATHER OF SOIL SCIENCE

Professor Eugene Hilgard left a giant footprint in the soil. Before I researched the life and work of Professor Hilgard, I thought land was something we walked on, built houses on, and cultivated. After studying the life and work of this fascinating man, I have a much better appreciation for both Mother Earth and soil scientists.

In the 1880s, the United States Commissioner of Agriculture appointed Eugene Hilgard chairman of the Arid Lands Commission. As chairman of Arid Lands, Professor Hilgard published several scholarly papers, and some consider his work on alkali soils and arid fertility among his most significant contributions.

His biographer wrote that "Hilgard [was] the scientific conquistador… of the arid region [and] dispelled the fear of alkali soils." And, he taught farmers how to manage the soil.

California newspapers and land companies "glorified his achievements." The *San Francisco Examiner* wrote that Professor Hilgard had

made the deserts bloom and
transformed the alkali plains into fields of waving grain

Those beautiful lines in "America the Beautiful," "the amber waves of grain and the fruited plains," do we owe those lines to Hilgard? Well, maybe.

So, who was this man, and what do America and the Western world owe Eugene Hilgard? And how is his life's work linked to The University of Mississippi?

Hans Jenny titled his 1961 biography of Professor Hilgard, *E. W. Hilgard and the Birth of Modern Soil Science*. According to Jenny, Hilgard's soil studies in Mississippi, and later in California, "led to a scientific cataclysm in the earth sciences in scope and influence equal to the Darwinian theory in biology."

We will explore the life and work of Professor Eugene Hilgard, but as a historian I must add a footnote. In an article in *Footprints in the Soil* (2006), Professor Dan Brinkley of Colorado State University wrote:

The scientific investigation of soils blossomed in the U.S. with Eugene Hilgard... and in Russia under the leadership of Vasily Dokuchaev.

In another essay in *Footprints in the Soil*, Ronald Amundson wrote,

Hilgard was a towering figure in American science, education, agriculture, a farsighted pedologist who, arguably, has not yet received his due in the annals of history.

Ronald Amundson cited Hilgard's 1860 *Report on the Geology and Agriculture of the State of Mississippi* as a "landmark" in the history of soil science, and adds, "Any modern student who reads Hilgrard's [1860 Report] will be struck by its insight and modernness."

Listen to what Hilgard wrote in his 1860 Report, and bear in mind that he was only 26 years old when he made this study:

Even now the rich prairies, the garden spots of Mississippi, are giving out under the operation of [a] pernicious system.... As members of a Christian commonwealth it is our right to use, but not to abuse, the inheritance that is ours, and to hand it down to our children as a blessing not as a barren land, inert incubus, wherewith to drudge through life, as a penalty for their father's wastefulness.

Hilgard's father was an old-world aristocrat who migrated to America but returned to Europe because he could not adjust to life in America, as did two of his sisters. Hilgard also married an old-world aristocrat, and his Spanish wife never felt at home in the land of the free, and she cherished her sheltered life in academe.

Hilgard's social and political philosophy is discernable in a letter he wrote to his 13-year-old-daughter, Alice, on the eve of the 20th century:

> *In the twentieth century you will see a [common] mediocrity throughout the western world, which is the price of lifting the masses, which is their right and must be borne pleasantly.*

A hundred years later Senator Patrick Moynihan of New York would describe this process, as "the dumbing down of America."

We know a great deal about Eugene Woldemar Hilgard because he left a vast paper trail.

During his long and productive life, he published over 400 books and articles and wrote more than 20,000 letters. One of the most remarkable things about this man is that in the month he died, in January 1916, at the age of 83, he published an article in the *Proceedings of the National Academy of Science.* The article was titled "A Peculiar Clay from Near the City of Mexico."

One of the most influential men in Hilgard's life was University of Mississippi Chancellor Frederick Barnard, a preeminent scientist himself. After Hilgard had served as assistant state geologist in Mississippi from 1855-1857, Chancellor Barnard in 1858 appointed Hilgard professor of geology at the University of Mississippi.

So, where did it all begin? It began in Bavaria, Hilgard's birthplace in 1833. In 1835 his father, mother, and eight brothers and sisters migrated to Belleville, Illinois. Consider that journey for a two-year-old boy.

There was a 14-day wagon ride from his home to the Port of La Harve on the Atlantic Coast; a four-week wait to sail to America; a 62-day voyage to New Orleans, and finally a 10- to 12-day steamboat trip up the Mississippi to Belleville.

There were no schools in this frontier settlement, and during his home-schooling Hilgard read Lorenz Oken's classic, *Natural History*.

In 1848 at 15, Hilgard made a vow that he would some day become a great man.

With his brother Julius, he went first to Washington, D.C., then to Philadelphia to study chemistry, where he became a teaching assistant. There, in 1849 at age 16, he read a seminal work, Jean-Antoine Claude Chaptal's *Chemistry Applied to Agriculture*. Hilgard went to Europe with his brother Theodore, and there he met Lorenz Oken.

In 1853, at age 20, Hilgard received a *summa cum laude* Ph.D. from the University of Heidelberg where he studied under Robert Bunsen, who invented the Bunsen burner. After graduation Hilgard was ill and spent a two-year sojourn along the Mediterranean Coast. While traveling in Spain he met Jesusa Bello, his future wife.

In 1855 Hilgard returned to the United States and worked in the Smithsonian chemistry laboratory. Later that year Chancellor Barnard appointed Eugene Hilgard assistant professor of geology at the University of Mississippi, which had been founded seven years earlier in 1848.

On his way to Oxford, Hilgard went by New Harmony, Indiana, to see Dr. David Dale Owen.

Dr. Owen had recently conducted geological surveys of Kentucky and Arkansas. In their discussion, Owen advised Hilgard to highlight agriculture in his Mississippi survey that Hilgard would soon conduct. Except for a brief period in 1857, Hilgard would remain at The University of Mississippi from 1855 to 1873. His three children, Manuel, Marie Louise, and Alice Rose were born in Oxford,

In 1860 Hilgard drafted a *Geological and Agricultural Report of Mississippi*, which launched his career, although the report was not published until after the Civil War. The first sentence in the section on agriculture was a question, "What is a soil?" Hilgard spent the next 56 years of his life trying to answer that question.

After the *Report* was finished Hilgard went back to Spain to marry Jesusa. When Hilgard returned to Oxford, Mississippi and the country were on the brink of Civil War. In the fall of 1861, all the students rushed off to war, and the University closed. Chancellor Barnard went North, but Hilgard stayed South.

Mississippi was a busy place during the war. There were 300 battles and skirmishes in Mississippi, and Hilgard referred to Oxford as a strategic point on a "Belt of Desolation" that extended from Grand Junction, Tennessee, on the north to Jackson and Vicksburg on the south, and he observed the warring armies that crisscrossed and devastated that land.

When General Ulysses S. Grant and General William Tecumseh Sherman occupied Oxford in December 1862, Hilgard moved the geology survey's 3,000 specimens from the Lyceum to what is now Barnard Observatory. The Lyceum was used as a hospital.

General Grant eventually left Oxford, went to Memphis, then down the river to Vicksburg. Because Mary Todd Lincoln's brother and other relatives were Confederate gunners on the high bluffs at Vicksburg, some of the Northern press excoriated Mrs. Lincoln as a Confederate spy in the White House.

The Mississippi River became the River of Glory for General Grant, and after Grant conquered the "impregnable fortress" at Vicksburg, President Abraham Lincoln gave Grant a third star and the command of the Union army.

As the Battle of Vicksburg approached, Hilgard went to Vicksburg to install lights along the bluffs. Mrs. Hilgard refused to stay in Oxford, so she took that treacherous journey with him, by wagon west to Water Valley, then by train down to Vicksburg. Hilgard and his wife later returned to their home in Oxford. But the return trip was even more treacherous then the trip to Vicksburg. Hilgard described that trip in an article in *Civil War Times Illustrated*.

When General Nathan Bedford Forrest occupied Oxford in the summer of 1864, he tried to draft Hilgard into the Confederate army, but Hilgard protested because the governor had told him to guard the survey specimens.

General Forrest said, "damn the governor," but did not arrest Hilgard. In that summer Oxford was torched by Union troops; only one building was left standing on the Square. The University, however, was spared any extensive damage, in part because of Hilgard's intervention with the Union officers.

Few Mississippians are aware that Ole Miss was once, or at least was supposed to be a "cow college." After the Civil War, the University of Mississippi was reorganized from an "old-time classical college" to a modern, multipurpose university. That process had begun under Chancellor Barnard before the war, but was implemented under John Newton Waddel, who was appointed Chancellor in 1865. After the Civil War the University received Morrill Land Grant funds in 1871. At the request of Chancellor Waddel, Hilgard organized a School of Agriculture, but Mississippi's agricultural leadership was skeptical of "book farming," and students were reluctant to enroll. Mississippi A&M was established in 1878, and the Morrill Land Grant Funds were reallocated from Oxford to the Starkville institution.

Professor Hilgard was appointed professor of chemistry in 1870 and had offered a course in agricultural chemistry. Hilgard was very active academically from 1865 to 1873. He published 19 articles, and in 1872 Hilgard was elected to the National Academy of Science.

The most important of his publications was the 1871 report to Chancellor Waddell on the geology and agriculture of the state of Mississippi, which he had drafted before the Civil War. If Hilgard is the "Father of Soil Science," this report is its birth certificate. There were two schools of thought on agricultural education in 1870. One was the Michigan-Pennsylvania school of thought, which was based on "practical education." The other was the Sheffield School at Yale, which was based on "theoretical analysis."

At one of the first meetings of the new A&M colleges in Chicago in 1871, Hilgard rejected both extremes for the "Golden Mean." In his 1871 statement Hilgard declared that "Agriculture is the most complicated of all the arts." And, he added, "The mastery of these arts, and of the sciences applicable to them, requires an education different in kind, but as systematic and complete, as that required for the... learned professions." Then he made this remarkably modern assessment of the broader purpose of education:

Nor is it forgotten that man is something more than the artisan, and that manhood has duties and interests higher and grander than those of the workshop and the farm. Education must fit for society and citizenship, as well as for science and industry.

Hilgard insisted that "soil science" was an academic discipline, like law and medicine, to be taught in the classroom and in the laboratory. And he insisted that the purpose of the college farm was to conduct agricultural experiments.

In 1872 Hilgard's address to the Mississippi State Fair in Jackson on progressive agriculture included this remarkable statement:

If we do not use the heritage [of native Americans] more rationally, well might the Chickasaws and Choctaws question the moral right of the act by which their beautiful, park-like hunting grounds were turned over to another race, on the pleas that they did not put [those lands] to the uses for which the Creator intended them.

Then he got right to the point:

Fellow citizens... 'cotton or nothing,' has been the bane of our system of agriculture. ... The unceasing repetition of cotton cropping without rotation, return or rest, has exhausted in the course of twenty years, land that with... a rational system of culture... should have lasted a century.

Following this not-so-mild admonition, Hilgard launched into a broad discussion of how Mississippi farmers should diversify their crops and how they could restore their tired and weary soil. "The soil needs more than a winter's sleep," he told them.

One of his recommendations was the establishment of experiment stations at various locations across the state. A Mississippi agricultural journal scoffed at Hilgard's "book farming," and proclaimed, "A cotton farmer doesn't have time to plow under peas."

Hilgard Cut circa 1860

Hilgard Cut today

Soon after this speech, in August 1873, Hilgard left the University of Mississippi and accepted a position at the University of Michigan, but he stayed only one year. In 1874 Hilgard went to Berkeley as a visiting professor. He taught a course, "Origins, Properties, and Functions of Soils." He was popular at Berkeley and accepted an appointment in 1875 and remained at Berkeley for the rest of his life.

Hans Jenny wrote that Hilgard's work in Mississippi brought him national acclaim, and his career in California won him world renown.

Soon after arriving in California, Hilgard established an experiment station, which is generally considered the first in the nation. The Berkeley station was established in the spring of 1875, and a station at the University of Connecticut was opened that fall. When Hilgard moved to Berkeley, California's agriculture was dominated by the production of wheat, and he soon began urging farmers to grow more fruits and vegetables. Hilgard realized that the increased consumption of fruit would be good for the nation's health. He said, "the more fruit, the less whiskey and doctor bills."

Hilgard, however, may have been working both sides of the street. In the late 1870s he saw that California was destined to become "one of the foremost wine-producing countries in the world" and persuaded the California legislature to appropriate funds to the University of California to pursue "the arts and sciences pertaining to viticulture." Hilgard is considered the founder of California's wine industry.

When Hilgard was recommended for appointment as commissioner of agriculture, United States Senator LQC Lamar, who was Hilgard's colleague at the University of Mississippi and his old friend, advised Hilgard:

> *Let it alone! It is the most thankless station in the gift of the government — it is a post that every politician in the country thinks he could fill acceptably. ... I would think it almost rashness in you to accept the position... dearly as I would love to have you near me.*
>
> *If, however, you are anxious to attain this "crown of thorns," and questionable honor, I am ready to throw myself full length in stalwart effort to obtain it for you.*

Hilgard did not pursue the appointment, stayed in California, and became extremely popular and influential. Hilgard's career in California was incredibly busy and incredibly successful. In 1889 the United States Department of Agriculture was elevated to cabinet status, and Hilgard was nominated and approved by Congress as assistant secretary of agriculture. When he reported to the University of California regents that he would accept the appointment, they raised his salary, reduced his teaching load, and provided him with more money and assistants to run the experiment station. He declined the appointment and remained at Berkeley, where his career flourished.

In 1892 Hilgard published Bulletin No. 3, "A Report on the Relations of Soil to Climate," for the USDA Weather Bureau. This bulletin, which is frequently cited as a revolutionary document, "electrified soil scientists at home and abroad." The article was not restricted to California, or even to the United States; it encompassed the global aspects of soil formation.

Hilgard's revolutionary paper demonstrated that soil science was not just a branch of geology and that climate was a major factor, perhaps even more crucial in determining the characteristics of soils. This article elevated the study of soils to a genuine science.

In 1903 Hilgard returned to Europe for the last time to accept a Golden Degree from the University of Heidelberg, on the occasion of the fiftieth anniversary of his degree. Two years later, in 1905, after a long and distinguished career, Hilgard retired at the age of 72. In 1914 an accident caused severe damage to the old soldier, but he kept pecking away on his typewriter. He boasted that he could still type at the rate of one page a day. But he lamented to his friends, "I am beginning to feel the banquet hall is deserted." Two years later Hilgard died at the age of 83. In 1900 the life expectancy of a white male was 46 years.

Few men live long enough to hear the angels sing their praises. Hilgard was one of those fortunate enough to see his life and his work acknowledged and celebrated by his peers.

The highest accolade an academician can receive is an honorary degree from his alma mater. Hilgard not only received an honorary degree from the University of Heidelberg, his alma mater, he received honorary degrees from every university he was associated with, and from one university he was not directly associated with.

Hilgard received these honorary degrees in

1882 from the University of Mississippi

1884 from the University of Michigan

1887 from Columbia University

1903 from Heidelberg, on the 50th anniversary of his graduation

1914 from the University of California; he was surprised but pleased by this award. He thought this honor would not come until after his death.

During his life Professor Eugene Hilgard won many honors and accolades, and in death his life is celebrated by these memorials that bear his name:

A mineral

A college fraternity chapter

A World War II naval vessel

A scholarly journal of agricultural science

An academic building

A mountain

The famous railroad cut at the entrance to the campus of the University of Mississippi is fondly known as the Hilgard Cut.

John Roy Lynch

12

John Roy Lynch

An Unknown Icon

This is the story of an unknown American icon, John Roy Lynch. Who was he? He was an African American, born into slavery, who grew up as a house servant in a famous Natchez mansion. John Roy Lynch was freed by the Civil War, educated for four months in a night school taught by Northern missionaries, and rose to power and eminence on the basis of his intellect and integrity. He represented Mississippi with great distinction in the United States Congress, served in the United States army during the Cuban War, died in Chicago, and was laid to rest in Arlington Cemetery.

Lynch was also instrumental in LQC Lamar's reentry into American politics after the Civil War. Lucius Quintus Cincinnatus Lamar was a slave owner, a son of the Southern aristocracy, a distinguished professor at the University of Mississippi. He drafted the Mississippi Ordinance of Secession and entered a self-imposed exile after the Civil War. But, due in no small measure to John Roy Lynch, Lamar reentered politics, served in the United States House of Representatives, the United States Senate, as secretary of the interior, and was appointed to the United States Supreme Court.

On September 10, 1847, John Roy Lynch was born a slave on the banks of the Mississippi River across from Natchez, one of the sons of Patrick Lynch, an Irishman and the manager of Tacony Plantation near Concordia, Louisiana. His mother was Catherine, a mulatto slave and mistress of Patrick Lynch. The status of children born into slavery in the Old South was determined by the status of the mother, not the father. In 1849 Patrick Lynch bought Catherine and their children and planned to move to New Orleans where there was a large biracial community, but he died before those plans materialized.

In 1850 Catherine and her children were bought by Alfred Vidal Davis, a large, wealthy planter who owned Dunleith mansion in Natchez. Mrs. Davis was a daughter of the wealthy Surget family. Mrs. Davis was initially fond of John Roy Lynch and took him as her personal servant. He fanned her in the summer to keep her cool and fanned the dining table to keep flies away. However, Mrs. Davis eventually became upset by some of John Roy's behavior and sent him back to labor on the plantation in Louisiana.

On January 1, 1863, the Emancipation Proclamation emancipated the slaves in the Confederacy, and when Union troops occupied Natchez in the summer of 1863, the slaves were freed. Lynch came back to Natchez and lived with his mother. He worked in a photography shop on Main Street and attended a Freedmen's School for four months. His photography shop was next door to a school, and when the teachers were holding classes in the school yard, he would open the window and listen to the teachers instructing their students. An 1872 *New York Times* article on Lynch said that he had an "unquenchable thirst for knowledge."

During Presidential Reconstruction, 1865-1867, President Andrew Johnson restored civil government in Mississippi. Unfortunately, the Mississippi legislature enacted the Black Codes, which established a modified form of slavery. A Chicago newspaper declared that "the North would turn Mississippi into a frog pond before it allowed such laws to disgrace the soil in which its buried soldiers sleep." The failure of Presidential Reconstruction led to Congressional Reconstruction in 1867-1875, which established military control over Mississippi. Congressional Reconstruction established a much more severe and punitive system than the Presidential Reconstruction.

In 1867, at the age of 19, Lynch joined the Adams County Republican Club in Natchez. In 1868 the recently adopted Mississippi Constitution disfranchised most whites and ex-Confederates, and Lynch became a popular fixture in the local Republican Party. In 1869, when Lynch was only 22 years old, Military Governor General Adelbert Ames appointed Lynch justice of the peace, which was a much more significant office in 1869 than it is today.

Lynch was a highly regarded public official and bought his first piece of land. Lynch became a substantial land owner, eventually accumulating more than a thousand acres. In 1905 Lynch sold his plantation, the Grove, which was the last property he owned in Mississippi.

In 1869 the Natchez District elected Lynch to the State House of Representatives, where he was immediately recognized as a natural born leader and became a member of the ruling faction. As a member of the state legislature in the early 1870s, Lynch strongly supported the establishment of Alcorn University at Lorman as an alternative to forcing the integration of the University of Mississippi, which he saw as a hopeless cause. This was early evidence that Lynch would compromise and conciliate in the larger interest of African Americans. For his influence in getting the bill passed, he was named to the first board of trustees of Alcorn University, which was named for Governor James L. Alcorn.

On January 1, 1872, the *Jackson State Leader*, an influential Republican newspaper, praised Lynch:

> *Mr. Lynch is one of the most prominent and promising young men of his race in the State. As a member of the last House of Representatives, he won for himself a reputation for ability, integrity and industry, that was enjoyed by few, and surpassed by none. He always took a comprehensive view of questions and spoke with soundness and maturity of judgement, and depth of thought, that was remarkable.*

In 1872, at the age of 24, with the endorsement of both Adelbert Ames, the carpetbagger governor, and James L. Alcorn, the scalawag governor, John Roy Lynch was elected speaker of the house, and promised to be fair to all factions. On March 4, 1872, the *New York Times* wrote that the "coolness and sagacity" of this 24-year-old politician was "really astonishing."

Even the hardline anti-reconstruction Democratic paper, the *Clarion-Ledger*, commended Lynch for his "dignified and non-partisan leadership." The House gave Speaker Lynch a gold watch and chain and called him "an honest and fair man."

Additional evidence of the sagacity and integrity of this young former slave was his redrafting of Mississippi's six congressional districts in 1872. When the legislative redistricting committee gave up in frustration over its inability to resolve the varying conflicts, the committee asked Speaker Lynch to personally draw the state's six congressional districts. An influential Lee County politician called on the speaker in the capital while he was plotting out the districts and suggested that Lynch think about establishing five safe Republican districts and one safe Democratic district. And the visitor further suggested that he design the safe Democratic district in such a way that LQC Lamar could win that district. Lynch agreed to his suggestion. Lamar ended his self-imposed exile and was elected to the United States Congress from that safe Democratic district, and his spectacular political career was born again.

The 1872 congressional election that sent Lamar back to the United States Congress also sent John Roy Lynch to his first term in Congress, and that was his debut on the national scene. In 1872 Lynch was also a delegate from Mississippi to the Republican National Convention, and again in 1884, 1888, 1892, and 1900.

On February 3, 1875, John Lynch made what some have called his "best and most profound speech on the floor of the House of Representatives." In support of the 1875 Civil Rights Bill, he proclaimed:

> *I have never believed for a moment that social equality could be brought about even between persons of the same race. For there are hundreds of whites I know to be the social inferiors of respectable and intelligent colored people.*
>
> *No, Mr. Speaker, it is not social rights that we desire. What we ask for is protection in the enjoyment of public rights. Mr. Speaker, here am I, a member of your honorable body, representing one of the largest*

and wealthiest districts in the state of Mississippi, and possibly in the South, and yet, when I leave my home to come [by rail] to the capital of the great Republic, I am treated, not as an American citizen. Forced to occupy a [second-class, unkempt, filthy] car; and for what? Not that I am unable or unwilling to pay my way; not that I am obnoxious in my personal appearance or disrespectful in my conduct; but simply because I happen to be of a darker complexion. If this treatment was confined to persons of [the male] sex we could possibly endure it. But such is not the case. Our wives and our daughters, our sisters and our mothers, are subjected to the same insults and to the same uncivilized treatment. You may ask why we do not institute civil suits in the state courts. What a farce! Talk about instituting a civil-rights suit in the state courts where the decision of the judge is virtually rendered before he enters the courthouse, and the verdict of the jury substantially rendered before it is impaneled. The only moments of my life when I question my loyalty to my government or my devotion to the flag of my country is when I read of outrages having been committed upon innocent colored people, and the perpetrators go unwhipped of justice.

If the 1875 Civil Rights law was not passed, he concluded:

I can only say with sorrow and regret that our boasted civilization is a fraud; our republican institutions a failure; our social system a disgrace; and our religion a complete hypocrisy.

When Congress adjourned after passing the Civil Rights Act of 1875, Lynch hurried back to Mississippi to seek his reelection. In the 1876 election perhaps the most remarkable evaluation of Lynch's success as a congressman and as a human being is stated in an article in a Gulf Coast newspaper that said it would support a white candidate, providing "he was equal to Representative Lynch in intelligence, moral worth and integrity."

In the 1875 election in Mississippi, Democrats, who called themselves Redeemers, won complete control of the state legislature. When the legislature that was elected in 1875 convened, it implemented the Revolution of 1876. First, it impeached the black lieutenant governor, and then filed impeachment charges against Governor Ames. As a compromise to facilitate the transfer of power, Ames was allowed to resign.

Reconstruction was over. In 1876 the legislature established the "shoestring" district, which placed most of the black counties in one congressional district along the Mississippi River. In 1876 John Roy Lynch made an active campaign in the shoestring district but lost. He contested the election, but the U.S. House of Representatives did not even review that election.

In 1878 Lynch did not run. In 1880 he ran again and lost, but he appealed the results, and Congress ruled in his favor. In 1882 Lynch ran again and lost but did not contest that election. From 1881 to 1892 Lynch served as chairman of the Mississippi Republican Executive Committee.

After retiring from Congress in 1883, until his death in 1939, Lynch led an active life.

In 1884 Lynch was the first African American to chair a major party's national convention. He was also the first African American to present the keynote address. He was nominated for that honor by Henry Cabot Lodge, and Teddy Roosevelt seconded the nomination.

In 1885, after the election of Grover Cleveland and the installation of Democratic control of the federal government, John Roy Lynch called on his old friend and fellow Mississippian, LQC Lamar, who was then secretary of the interior. Lynch asked Lamar to protect the young African Americans he had helped get jobs in the Department of the Interior. Lynch gave him a list of names and explained that two of them had racially mixed marriages. Lamar agreed to retain all of them except the two who had racially mixed marriages. He explained what Lynch surely knew: that if it got back to Mississippi that he had hired racially mixed couples, it would be detrimental to his political career. But Lamar assured Lynch that he would retain all the others. Before the meeting was over, Lamar offered Lynch a position in the Department of the Interior, but he declined.

Lynch did remain in Washington, however, and after passing the Mississippi Bar exam in 1896, Lynch opened a law office in Washington. Although he does not explain it in his memoirs, *Reminiscences of an Active Life: The Autobiography of John Roy Lynch*, things were not going well for Lynch in 1898, and he joined the United States army during the Spanish American War. He was 51 years old and found the life of a soldier "a source of fulfillment." (Lynch's reminiscences were edited by John Hope Franklin and published in 1970.)

In 1909 Lynch explains in his memoirs that he "accidentally and providentially" met Cora Williamson. Two years later Lynch married her and retired from the army, and in 1912 he and his new bride moved to Chicago. He practiced law and bought a home on a street later named Martin Luther King, Jr. Drive. On November 2, 1939, after a long and active life, he died in Chicago. Two days later his funeral was held at St. Thomas Episcopal Church. On November 6, he was interred with full military honors at Arlington National Cemetery. The *New York Times* identified John Roy Lynch as "one of the most fluent and forceful speakers in politics in the seventies and eighties." The *Chicago Tribune* called him "the grand old man of Chicago's Negro citizenry."

But for all of his political and public service, this is not why I consider him Mississippi's most pre-eminent African American statesman. I accord him that honor because of his brief but enduring literary career. When Lynch moved to Chicago he devoted his time and effort and energy to the revision of the Dunning School, which was the prevailing historical interpretation of Reconstruction.

The Dunning School is identified with William Archibald Dunning, a renowned professor of history at Columbia University during the early years of the twentieth century. The Dunning School of Reconstruction portrayed the decade following the Civil War in the South as a period of fraud and corruption perpetrated by a marauding band of carpetbaggers, scalawags and ex-slaves who robbed the South of its remaining but meager resources. The Dunning School characterized Reconstruction as a failure that justified its violent overthrow. Prominent members of the Dunning School and the states they wrote about are Walter Fleming, Alabama (1905); Charles Ramsdell, Texas (1910); W.W. Davis, Florida (1913); J.G. de Roulhac Hamilton, North Carolina (1914); C. Mildred Thompson, Georgia (1915); Thomas S. Staple, Arkansas (1923); James Ford Rhodes, *History of the United States* [vol 6, 1906); Claude G. Bowers, *The Tragic Era, The Revolution After Lincoln* (1929); and James W. Garner, *Reconstruction in Mississippi* (1901).

John Roy Lynch's first major effort to revise the Dunning School came in 1913 when he published *The Facts of Reconstruction*. Lynch also wrote several articles in scholarly journals defending Congressional Reconstruction against such critics as James Ford Rhodes and Claude G. Bowers. In a review of Claude Bowers' book condemning Reconstruction titled, *The Tragic Era*, John Roy Lynch wrote that after carefully reading the book he thought its title should be *The Tragic Error*.

In a 1917 article in the *Journal of Negro History* Lynch expressed "the hope that a fair and impartial historian will someday write a history covering the Reconstruction period, in which an accurate account based upon actual facts of what took place at the time will be given."

Actually, an historian had already written a fair and balanced history of Reconstruction in Mississippi, and the remarkable thing is that he was a student of Professor Dunning. When James W. Garner published *Reconstruction in Mississippi* in 1901, W.E.B. DuBois considered Garner's book the fairest account of Reconstruction written by any of Dunning's students.

In 1916 this same James Garner published a review of John Roy Lynch's *The Facts of Reconstruction* in *The Mississippi Valley Historical Review*. This Dunning student wrote, "There is no evidence of bitterness or vindictiveness; and, on the whole, the [*Facts of Reconstruction*] is a fair and temperate presentation" of Reconstruction.

Two years before his death, when he was almost ninety years old, John Roy Lynch completed *Reminiscences of an Active Life, The Autobiography of John Roy Lynch*. For some reason this five-hundred-twelve-page autobiography was not published until 1970. But fortunately, a new edited version of Lynch's *The Facts of Reconstruction* was also published in 1970.

Reconstruction, especially at the state level, is one of the most complicated and convoluted periods in American history. Fortunately, William C.

Harris has written two fine books, *Presidential Reconstruction in Mississippi* (1967), and *The Day of the Carpetbagger, Republican Reconstruction in Mississippi* (1979) that illuminate this complicated period of Mississippi history.

John Roy Lynch is an intriguing and enduring figure in American history. In 2012 Matthew Lynch published *Before Obama, A Reappraisal of Black Reconstruction Era Politicians*, a two-volume study of the role that African Americans played in Reconstruction. Volume one, *Legacies Lost, The Life and Times of John R. Lynch and His Political Contemporaries*, is a must read for anyone interested in and intrigued by the life and times of John Roy Lynch. In 2015 Eerdmans Books for Young Readers published a fascinating, illustrated book, *The Amazing Age of John Roy Lynch*, written by Chris Barton and illustrated by Don Tate, which is also a must read for those interested in the life and times of John Roy Lynch.

Hopefully, an increasing knowledge and understanding of the legacy of this unknown icon will broaden and deepen Mississippi's awareness of its complicated history and its promise of a better tomorrow.

13

PROFESSOR L.Q.C. LAMAR

*It must be remembered of him that restoration of
hope renewed the spirit of a nation.*

Edward Mayes

Lucius Quintus Cincinnatus Lamar is a singular figure in American history. He was one of the few statesmen to serve in all three branches of the federal government, and his illustrious career spanned the great divide of Civil War.

Born in Georgia and educated at Emory College, Lamar was the son of a widowed mother who boarded college students to pay the tuition for her own three sons.

Lamar graduated from Emory in 1845, was admitted to the Georgia Bar in 1847, and was jilted by his first true love.

He then married Virginia Longstreet and moved to Oxford where her father, Augustus Baldwin Longstreet, was president of the University of Mississippi. That title was later changed to Chancellor. Lamar was assistant professor of mathematics from 1850 to 1852. Both his father-in-law, A.B. Longstreet, and his son-in-law, Edward Mayes, were chancellors of the university.

Lamar was one of the premier orators of his age, and his genius was evident early in his career. He was only twenty-six years old when he made his first major political speech at a great rally in Oxford during the gover-

Professor L.Q.C. Lamar

nor's race in 1851. Lamar, the young unknown assistant professor, shared the platform with Henry Stuart Foote, Mississippi's senior United States senator and an orator of national renown.

So important were such occasions in the antebellum South that the university called off classes so its students could attend the rally and hear their young professor. On the Oxford town square, Lamar delivered such a stirring speech that his exuberant students "wild with excitement and pride bore him away from the hustings upon their shoulders." One of Lamar's biographers said that speech was the flood tide that led to fame, albeit not to fortune.

Soon, though, Lamar was drawn back to Georgia. When Lamar was nine years old, his father, after returning from a Fourth of July celebration, overcome by depression, took a pistol, walked out into the family garden of their Georgia home, and killed himself. Just before he returned to Georgia, Lamar wrote to a friend, "There is one circumstance which alone is sufficient to endear me to Georgia above all other places: in her bosom rests the sacred dust of my honored father, whose blood, whose name, whose very temperament, whose everything (save his shining virtues and genius) I have inherited. Such things have greater influence on my actions than those of most men." Throughout his life Lamar battled depression, vertigo, apoplexy, and violent mood swings.

Lamar remained in Georgia only three years, then returned to Oxford, bought a plantation, which he called Solitude, cast his lot with Mississippi, and was elected to Congress in 1857.

Two months after Lamar went to Congress a fistfight broke out on the floor of the House during a heated debate over slavery. According to the *New Orleans Picayune*:

> *Quite a number of gentlemen (among them William Barksdale of Mississippi) rushed forward, some probably for the purpose of getting a better sight of 'the ring,' and others to separate the contestants. ... Potter of Wisconsin, a stout fellow with a fist like an ox, was foremost, and bombarded into the fray like a maddened tiger. Potter planted a 'sock-*

dolager' between Barksdale's eyes, which only had the effect of rousing his grit. Supposing it was Elihu Washburne who struck him, Barksdale sprang gallantly at him, and they exchanged a handsome match.... Cadwallader Washburne came to the rescue of his brother and attacked Barksdale.... Even Lamar of Mississippi and Parson Lovejoy had a little set-to in the course of the passing gust.... It was a jolly row, and no bones were broken.

The bitterness between the North and the South deepened in the late 1850s, and Lamar was disheartened by the talk of secession. He was sometimes called "Moody Lamar" by his Washington friends. In the spring of 1858 he wrote his wife, who remained in Oxford, that Capitol Hill was a beautiful and splendid scene but that he was ready to leave Washington and probably would not run for reelection. However, Lamar was re-nominated by acclamation in 1859 and reelected without opposition.

As the Southern fervor for secession intensified, Lamar became increasingly worried and warned a friend, *When the sun of the Union sets, it will go down in blood.*

In fact, Lamar was so disillusioned by the rancor of Washington politics that he wrote to University of Mississippi Chancellor Frederick Barnard, confided to him that he was abandoning politics, and asked if there were a position on the faculty that he could fill. At Chancellor Barnard's request the University's board of trustees appointed Lamar professor of metaphysics and gave him a leave of absence to complete his congressional term.

The nation was moving inexorably toward what one Northen senator called "an irrepressible conflict." But Lamar believed, or hoped, that the power of words and the force of language could calm the troubled waters and save the Union from a bloody civil war.

In December 1859 Lamar wrote to Chancellor Barnard, his friend and mentor, about his hope that someone would rise above the passions of the day and speak to this great country, not as two rival sections, but as one great nation.

Listen as he contemplates such a speech in his letter to Barnard:

The sectional war...rages with unabated violence.... But I begin to hope.... I think I can see, through all the rancor and madness of this struggle, the slow evolution of right principles. What is now the greatest need is for some one man, one true man, who, rising above the passions and prejudices of the times, will speak to both sections in a spirit at once tolerant, just, humane, and national. No one has shown himself to be that man yet. I think I know one (a friend of yours and mine) who might do it. I think he has clear perceptions of his duty, high and noble sentiment, and a heart big with pure and holy affection for the whole country; but his love of repose, shrinking from the uproar and confusion of party strife, will, I fear, cause him to be, what he has always been, wanting in the energy and courage to execute what his reason designs, his conscience approves, and his duty dictates.

Lamar was brooding over such a speech, but he was young and did not have the stature and prominence that such a speech would require, or the self-confidence to make it. After he decided that he could not or would not make that speech, Lamar decided to leave the public arena for the tranquil life of the college campus.

Perhaps Lamar's most important speech is the one he never made.

Events soon overtook Lamar, and the South, and the nation. In December 1860 South Carolina seceded from the Union, and Mississippi quickly followed in January 1861. Lamar drafted Mississippi's brief Ordinance of Secession. Mississippi's secession prompted celebrations that were more fitting for the end, rather than the beginning, of a war.

But Lamar did not celebrate the prospects of war. On the eve of war, a foreboding Lamar spoke to a festive crowd from the balcony of the Spotswood Hotel in Richmond: "We may not know," he said, "what will be the nature or result of this contest. It may be that much suffering is before us. It may be that our towns will be sacked. It may be that our fields will be desolated. It may be that... our South shall emerge from this contest exhausted, pallid, her garments dripping with blood." Lamar's somber assessment was greeted with loud cries of "No. No."

In her remarkable wartime *Diary from Dixie*, Mary Boykin Chestnut wrote that Mr. Lamar, a recent dinner guest in her Richmond home, was one of the "clear heads [who] see all the risk, the loss of land, limb, and life, home, wife, and children." She also said that Lamar no more believed in slavery then she did.

During the war Lamar served as a colonel in the 19th Mississippi Infantry Regiment, then as envoy to Russia, and finally as judge advocate in Robert E. Lee's army of Northern Virginia.

When the war was done, the South, as Lamar had feared, lay desolate and exhausted, its garments were dripping in blood. When the trumpet sounded, 78,000 young Mississippians rushed off to war. Almost half of them did not come home. Lamar lost both of his young brothers.

After the war a disconcerted Lamar returned to Oxford. He counseled the South to accept the results of the war and to safeguard the rights and liberties of the former slaves. He entered a self-imposed, seven-year political exile.

In the bitter aftermath of that bloody war Lamar blamed himself for not doing more to prevent it, for not making that speech he described to Chancellor Barnard. The self-incrimination drove Lamar to the brink of despair.

Lamar had a volcanic temper, and on one occasion in an Oxford courtroom in 1871 he physically assaulted a federal marshal.

The years between the end of the war in 1865 and his election to Congress in 1872 were years of misery for Lamar. From the front porch of his house on North Street, Lamar could see the desolate Oxford Square, burned to the ground by Union General "Whiskey" Smith, and he brooded over the future, night after night.

His son-in-law Chancellor Edward Mayes described Lamar's mental state in the early postwar years:

At this period upon almost any clement evening, if one should follow the plank walk to the white picket fence which marked the premises of Col. Lamar, there he would be found; clad in a drab study-gown, somewhat frayed and stained with ink; resting against the fence, leaning as if wounded, with his strong arms flung carelessly over it for support, and his head drooping forward; his face long, massive, and sallow; bareheaded, with his long brown hair stirred by the breeze; his deep, mysterious eyes fixed upon the yellowing western sky, or watching dreamily the waving limbs of the avenue of water oaks across the way; abstracted, recognizing the salutations of the passersby with a nod half courteous, half surly, and unconscious of all identities; a countenance solemn, somber, and enigmatical....

In those darkening twilight hours when nature gathers the wandering thoughts of men into the narrow circle of their inner selves, what mighty passions wafted upon him. ... What swirling vortices of passionate self-reproach for the tragic past, the dreary present, and the frowning future! What agonized searching of the inscrutable mysteries of the coming years!

His loving and devoted family hovered over him during those dreadful years and may have saved Lamar from the fate of his father. Mayes explains:

There were loving eyes which watched him... and loving hands... wove bonds of silk to draw him away from the perilous verge upon which he stood... more than one anxious heart interpreted those volcanic moods, and trembled lest in some weaker hour a dreadful deed, born of fury and despair, should spring like a tiger from its lair, and ruin all.

In 1872 Speaker of the Mississippi House of Representatives John Roy Lynch designed a safe Democratic district and asked Lamar to run for Congress. Forsaking his self-imposed exile, Lamar was elected to Congress. When he returned to Congress, Lamar found sectional animosity to be even more rancorous than when he left Congress in 1860.

He also found that the infamous "bloody shirt" had been added to the rancor.

Allen P. Huggins, a carpetbagger in Aberdeen, Mississippi, was assaulted and severely beaten by the Ku Klux Klan in 1871. His blood-stained shirt found its way to Washington and into the hands of Massachusetts Congressman Benjamin Butler. In a speech on the floor of the House, Butler waved that bloody shirt and declared that it was a sign of what happens to loyal men in the South.

After that dramatic display, inflammatory speeches and appeals to sectional passions by Northern politicians was called "waving the bloody shirt."

Lamar ended his political exile because he was driven by a compulsion to calm the sectional strife, to reunite the country, and to make the speech he had not, but should have made in 1860.

Two years before his famous Sumner speech he sought the counsel of a Northern friend:

> *Is it possible for a secessionist to convince [the nation] that there is common ground on which the two sections can stand and live in harmony.... He indeed would be a patriot who could awake them and say to them...'My countrymen, know one another and love one another.'*

It was a lofty and noble ambition, born in Oxford amidst the dreary ruins of war.

Lamar prepared himself and waited for the occasion.

Senator Charles Sumner of Massachusetts was perhaps America's most ardent abolitionist and the most radical reconstructionist.

After the surrender of the Confederate states in 1865, Sumner demanded that secessionists be disfranchised and declared ineligible for public office, and that the former slaves be given all the rights of citizenship, including the right to vote and to hold office.

But, by the early 1870s Senator Sumner, like Lamar, had become so disappointed with the progress of Reconstruction and Reunion that he broke with the Republican Party, called for a general amnesty for ex-Confederates, opposed the re-election of President Ulysses S. Grant, and wrote an open letter to the "colored people of America" urging them to vote with the Democrats in the 1872 presidential election.

In that letter Senator Sumner said, "Most anxiously I have looked for… reconciliation, not only between North and South, but between the two races; so that the two races and the two sections may be lifted from the ruts and grooves in which they are not fastened, and instead of irritating antagonism without end, there shall be sympathetic co-operation. The existing differences ought to be ended."

Senator Sumner died two years after writing that letter. He had been in the United States Senate for almost a quarter of a century and had, perhaps, the largest personal following of any politician in America. Of Sumner, Ralph Waldo Emerson said he never knew another man so white, as in "pure as the driven snow."

On the occasion of Sumner's passing, there were many speeches and eulogies. Lamar's invitation by the Massachusetts congressional delegation to eulogize Sumner was Lamar's second chance to make that speech he thought he should have made on the eve of war.

Listen to Lamar:

> *Mr. Speaker, I desire to add a few remarks which have occurred to me as appropriate for the occasion. Strange as the assessment may seem, impossible as it would have been ten years ago to make… Mississippi regrets the death of Charles Sumner, and sincerely unites in paying honors to his memory. Not because of the splendor of his intellect, not because of the high culture, the elegant scholarship, which reveal themselves so clearly in all his public effort… but because of his moral traits of character which gave the coloring to his singularly dramatic public career.*

As Lamar spoke these words, according to one congressman, the hush on the floor, and in the gallery, became oppressive. Pennsylvania Congressman Jackson Randall said, "Lamar just finished his Sumner speech. The House was electrified."

Lamar continued,

Charles Sumner was born with an instinctive belief that freedom is the natural right of man. ... And along with this all-controlling love of freedom he possessed a moral sensibility which would never permit him to swerve by the breadth of one hair from what he pictured as the path of duty. Thus was combined in him the characteristics which have in all ages given to religion her martyrs, and to patriotism her heroes.

To a man imbued with such a creed, to behold a human being or a race of human beings restrained of their natural right to liberty was a wrong which no logic could justify. It mattered not how humble in the scale of rational existence the subject of this restraint might be, how dark his skin... for him the great principle [was] that liberty is the birthright of humanity, and that every individual of every race is entitled to freedom. ... It mattered not that the slave might be contented with his lot; that his actual condition might be more desirable than that from which it had transplanted him, that it gave him physical comfort, mental and moral elevation, and religious culture not possessed by his race in any other condition; it mattered not that the bonds had not been placed upon his hands by the living generation; or that the social system... had been regarded by the fathers of the republic, and by the ablest statesman who had risen up after them, as too complicated to be broken up without danger to society itself; or finally, that [slavery] had been recognized and sanctioned by the [US Constitution], the organic law of the republic.

But here let me do this great man the justice which, amid the excitement of the struggle between the sections... I may have been disposed to deny him. In fiery zeal, and earnest warfare against the wrong, as he viewed it, there entered no enduring personal animosity toward [those of us] whose lot it was to be born to the system which he denounced.

It has been the kindness which in these later years he has displayed toward the impoverished and suffering people of the Southern states

that has unveiled to me the generous and tender heart which beat be-
neath the bosom of the zealot, and has forced me to yield to him the
tribute of my respect – I might even say my admiration.

By this point in the speech, many of the staid and stubborn congress-
men, North and South, were literally weeping, and one reporter saw "tears
stealing down the cheeks" of Speaker of the House James G. Blaine.

And almost every press account of the speech mentioned these next
few lines:

> *It was my misfortune, perhaps my fault, personally never to have*
> *known this eminent... statesman. The impulse was often strong upon*
> *me to go to him and offer him my hand, and my heart with it, and to*
> *express to him my thanks for his kind and considerate course toward the*
> *people with whom I am identified. If I did not yield to that impulse,*
> *it was because the thought occurred to me that other days were coming*
> *in which such a demonstration might be more opportune, and less lia-*
> *ble to misconstruction. Suddenly and without premonition, a day has*
> *come at last to which, for such a purpose, there is no tomorrow. My*
> *regret is therefore intensified by the thought that I failed to speak to him*
> *out of the fullness of my heart while there was yet time.*

By now, those assembled in the Great Hall of Congress were beginning
to realize that something historic was happening.

Lamar continued,

> *Charles Sumner, in life, believed that [the] occasion for strife and*
> *distrust between the North and the South had passed away, and...*
> *there no longer remained any cause for continued estrangement be-*
> *tween the two sections of our common country. Are there not many*
> *of us who believe the same thing? Is not that the common sentiment*
> *– or if not, ought it not to be – of the great mass of our people North*
> *and South? Bound to each other by a common constitution, destined*

to live together under a common government... shall we not now at last endeavor to grow toward each other once more in heart, as we are... linked to each other in fortunes? Shall we not, over the honored remains of this great champion of human liberty... lay aside the... misunderstanding and distrust?

The South–prostrate, exhausted, drained of her life blood... yet still honorable and true–accepts the bitter award of the bloody arbitrament... yet as if struck dumb by the magnitude of her losses, she suffers on in silence.

The North, exultant in her triumph... cherishes... a full heart of magnanimous emotions toward her disarmed antagonist; and yet, as if mastered by some mysterious spell, silencing her better impulses.

Would that the spirit of the illustrious dead whom we lament today could speak from the grave to both parties in tones that should reach every heart throughout this broad land: 'My countrymen! Know one another, and you will love one another.

When Lamar finished, there was stone silence, then thundering ovation.

"My God, what a speech, and how it will ring through the country," said New York Congressman Lyman Tremaine.

"Lamar's name has shot across the sky like a blazing meteor. From one end of the Union to the other the press teems with praises of the brilliant Mississippian," wrote the *Memphis Appeal*.

"Few speeches in American political history have had such immediate impact. Overnight it raised Lamar to the first rank in Congress and in the country, and it marked the turning point in the relations between the North and the South," wrote John F. Kennedy in *Profiles in Courage*.

After the Sumner speech Lamar became a household name throughout the country, and in 1876 Lamar was appointed to the United States Senate where he continued to charm his peers and the nation with his brilliant use of language.

In one of his most famous Senate speeches Lamar took the floor on February 15, 1877. Weeks before this speech Senator Lamar announced his intention to vote against a Senate bill to authorize the free and unlimited coinage of silver. The Mississippi legislature, which favored the silver bill, passed several resolutions instructing Lamar to vote for it. Lamar opposed the bill because it would inflate the American currency by putting cheap money into circulation.

In Lamar's day, senators were appointed by the state legislature, and if they refused to follow the legislature's instructions, they might not be reappointed.

As Lamar rose to speak, "the Chamber became as silent as the tomb."

> *Mr. President, between these instructions and my convictions there is a great gulf. I cannot pass it. Of my love to the state of Mississippi I will not speak; my life alone will tell it.*
>
> *Upon them I have always endeavored to impress the belief that truth was better than falsehood, honesty better than policy, courage better than cowardice. Today my lessons confront me. Today I must be true or false, honest or cunning, faithful or unfaithful to my people. Even in this hour of their legislative displeasure… I cannot vote as these resolutions direct. I cannot shirk the responsibility which my position imposes. My duty, as I see it, I will do; and I will vote against this bill.*

As this might be his last speech in the Senate, friends and foes alike "gathered about his desk" when he finished.

A few days later Lamar received a letter from a man whose two-day train trip "was made delightful by the generous praise I heard [for] your bold and noble act. [Your silver] speech was read aloud in the palace car that I was in, and men and women were moved as only good deeds can move the human heart."

The silver speech was not his fond farewell. Again, the people of Mississippi embraced him, and the legislature returned him to the United States Senate.

Lamar's last major Senate speech, on March 28, 1884, was an impassioned plea in support of federal aid to public education. Federal aid was necessary, Lamar explained, because Mississippi's "most eminent teachers [were] overwhelmed with work and lived on starvation wages."

In the 1880s there was an embarrassing surplus in the federal treasury, and some in Congress wanted to relieve that embarrassment by allocating the surplus funds to the nation's common schools. Lamar extolled his colleagues,

I have watched the progress of this [legislation] from the time that it was...introduced in the other House many years ago. I have watched it with deep interest and solicitude. In my opinion, it is the first step and the most important step, that this government has taken in the direction of a solution of what is called the race problem; and I believe that it will tell more powerfully and decisively upon the future destinies of the colored race in America than any measure or ordinance that has yet been adopted in reference to it—more decisively than either the thirteenth, fourteenth, or fifteenth amendments, unless it is to be considered, as I do consider it, the logical sequence and the practical continuance of those amendments.

I think this measure is fraught with almost unspeakable benefits to the entire population of the South, white and black. Apart altogether from the material aid...apart from the...bounteous donation of money, it will give an impulse to the cause of common school education in [the South] through the long coming future.

It will excite a new interest among our people; it will stimulate both state and local communities (and) encourage them in their hopes in grappling and struggling with a task before whose vast proportions they have stood appalled in the consciousness of the inadequacy of their own resources to meet it.

We have school houses; we have teachers.... All that we need is the money.

There is not a child... who would not be admitted to school should he apply. No matter what his color.

As I said at the beginning of these remarks... this bill is a decided step toward the solution of the race problem. The problem of race in a large part is the problem of illiteracy.

Unfortunately, the Blair bill that would have brought millions of dollars to the Southern school system was not passed.

During Lamar's second term in the Senate, he was appointed secretary of the interior by President Grover Cleveland.

After that appointment Lamar made only two major speeches. The first was a three-hour oration at the dedication of the John C. Calhoun monument at Charleston, South Carolina, on April 26, 1887. The other was the 1890 commencement address at Emory College.

As secretary of the interior Lamar was the custodian of America's natural resources and was among the nation's earliest conservationists. He initiated a broad range of policies that were later expanded under President Teddy Roosevelt.

In 1887, in the late afternoon of his life, three years after the death of his first wife, Lamar married Henrietta Dean Holt, his childhood sweetheart.

In the summer of that year, during a carriage ride through Atlanta, President Grover Cleveland and Henry W. Grady, the legendary editor of the *Atlanta Constitution*, were discussing the vacancy on the Supreme Court occasioned by the recent death of an associate justice.

Grady advanced the cause of L.Q.C. Lamar, saying to the President, "I believe no man from the South has ever been so perfectly equipped for public life as Lamar."

A few months after that conversation, Grover Cleveland nominated Lamar for the United States Supreme Court. Lamar's nomination sparked an intense controversy because he was a secessionist, a Confederate colonel, and he was far advanced in years. He was 63. Life expectancy for white males in 1890 was about 46 years.

In addition, Lamar's nomination came during an ugly controversy over the Rebel flag. President Cleveland had ordered the return of all captured battle flags to the states of the old Confederacy. This order outraged the Grand Army of the Republic, an organization of Union veterans. President Cleveland had paid a substitute to serve in his place during the Civil War, and Union veterans considered him a "slacker." Eventually, President Cleveland withdrew his infamous flag order.

Political cartoon published after
Lamar's appointment to the U.S. Supreme Court

Lamar's nomination to the high court was voted down in the Senate Judiciary Committee, even though one of the letters it received in support of Lamar's appointment was from James H. Pierce, the federal marshal Lamar had assaulted in an Oxford courtroom so many years earlier.

When Lamar's name was placed before the Republican-controlled Senate, two Republicans broke with their party and voted to confirm his nomination on January 10, 1888.

The two Republicans who voted for Lamar were Leland Stanford of California and William Stewart of Nevada. Senator Stewart was the son-in-law of Mississippi Governor and United States Senator Henry Stuart Foote. Lamar had debated Foote at Oxford in 1851.

Thus, Lamar became the first former Confederate and the first Democrat appointed to the United States Supreme Court following the Civil War.

After Lamar's confirmation, the *San Francisco Argos* published a cartoon symbolizing the burial of the "bloody shirt."

Lamar reached the pinnacle of American politics with his lifetime appointment to the United States Supreme Court. There are currently three hundred million Americans; only nine of them are on the Supreme Court.

In January 1893, while on a journey from Washington to the Mississippi seacoast for a period of recuperation, Lamar stopped in Georgia for a visit with friends and family. On January 23 he died at the age of sixty-eight near his boyhood home.

L.Q.C. Lamar now rests in peace, in a place of honor in St. Peter's Cemetery in Oxford, Mississippi, revered in death as he was loved in life.

In a 1938 article entitled, "The Twenty-Eight Foremost American Orators," William Brigance wrote, "I think it doubtful if any American orator exerted a more significant influence" than L.Q.C. Lamar.

And I would venture to say, that among the gifted statesmen this great nation has produced, Lamar was second, perhaps only to Lincoln, in the use of language.

Blind Jim Ivy, the model for Colonel Rebel

14

THE OLE MISS MYSTIQUE

Several years ago on a research trip in rural south Mississippi I stopped at a service station. It was a family-owned station that sold gas and groceries on credit but did not accept credit cards of any kind. As he was filling my tank the kindly old gentleman who owned the station asked me where I was from. I told him I was from Oxford, that I taught history at Ole Miss. When I handed him a card to pay for the gas, he became apologetic. He was sorry he could not accept my card and told me, lowering his voice, if I was "running a little short," I could send it to him later. I thanked him for his kindness, paid him, and turned to leave when he said, "You're from Ole Miss, hunh." Since he already knew I was, he was not asking, and knowing it called for no response I offered none. He continued in that quaint, sonorous, unreproducible, rural Mississippi accent, "Yes suh, I tell you this; I ain't no alma mater of Ole Miss, but it's sho my school."

Repressing my professorial instinct to correct his misuse of the term alma mater, I confessed that I was not an alma mater either but told him with great pride that my three children were. Then I asked him why he felt so strongly and so deeply about Ole Miss. He attempted, perhaps for the first time in his life, to translate his feelings into words, to verbalize his emotions. After a few minutes, seeing him grow uncomfortable in his verbal infelicity, I offered him the use of some colorful adjectives and a few compound nouns. Declining my offer, he finally said, "Hell, I don't know, I just love that place." Content to let it go at that, I opened the car door to leave, but his speech was not over. He kept on talking, and gradually his tone changed, and he was obviously more at ease as he began to talk about the Civil War, the Lost Cause, the federal government, about the Kennedys, race, football, pretty girls, and Miss Americas. During a convenient pause, I told him that I really had to go. But before I left I told him about the distinguished list of Rhodes Scholars Ole Miss had produced. I thought he might could use that information in some future oration.

The next day, amid the luxury of corporate headquarters in a Jackson high-rise, I had a similar conversation with a Jackson business executive who was an Ole Miss alumnus and who loved his alma mater. In the course of that conversation I asked that distinguished alumnus the same question I had asked the "good old boy" the day before. That articulate and erudite executive made a speech remarkably similar to the one I had heard the day before, with one exception. He knew about the Rhodes Scholars. After saying all the obvious things an alumnus says about his alma mater, his erudition gave way to emotion, and his practiced diction gave way to dialect, "Hell, it ain't easy to explain how I feel about Ole Miss, how much I love that place, and how much it means to me."

I once heard a man say, "I love my family and all that, but I really love Ole Miss."

The fondness Ole Miss alumni have for this place amazes me. It is more than the affection alumni have for their alma mater. It goes beyond that, much deeper. It is almost like a spell, or magic, it's metaphysical and mystical. All alumni do not have this same feeling, and it seems much stronger among older alumni than in more recent graduates. But those who are possessed of this feeling seem somehow bound by it; it becomes a commitment, a promise, an oath to be honored with a "faithful fidelity." Perhaps the best way, maybe the only way, to explain it is to say that the Ole Miss Mystique has them under its spell.

I don't think I can define the Ole Miss Mystique, but I have seen it work its way, wrap itself around, charm, disarm, and intrigue people who encounter it for the first time. I experienced this in the crowded customs office of New York's Kennedy Airport where I had gone to meet a group of German students. Acting as urbane as I could and concealing as much of my Mississippi accent as possible, I addressed the customs official who most nearly gave the impression that he knew what was going on. When I told him that I was from the University of Mississippi he asked, "Is that the same as Ole Miss?" Responding in my native dialect, I said, "Yes, Suh!" He then told me he knew all about Ole Miss because a young lady in his office had gone to school there for two years. He confessed that he had never known anyone to love a place as much as she had loved Ole Miss. Because of her and her fondness for Ole Miss, he said he would get us through customs with minimal delay.

I also saw the Ole Miss Mystique in the fascination of a young black scholar from the Midwest who attended a symposium on slavery at the University in 1976. As I drove him around the campus and through Oxford, he was intrigued by this place and its past. His interest was probably as much emotional as academic. I think I saw the Ole Miss Mystique at work among a group of Japanese journalists who had come to see where William Faulkner lived and to look at the people and places he wrote about. "Did you know him?" they asked. Unfortunately, I did not.

A mystique does not combust. It evolves long before it envelops. The Ole Miss Mystique was long aborning, and the stuff it's made of is the stuff of place and past.

Almost five years before the university was established, a town was founded by some people who believed that there is something in a name. Seeking every possible advantage, they named their town Oxford in the hope that it would be selected as the site for the new, proposed state university. In 1844, by a vote of 58 to 57, the legislature located the University of Mississippi at Oxford in the woodlands of Lafayette County rather than at Mississippi City in Harrison County. It is not likely that the Ole Miss Mystique would have evolved along the sandy shores of the Gulf Coast as it did here amid these hallowed groves.

At about the time the university was established, and the sons of Mississippi's gentry were shaping the traditions of Ole Miss, Matthew Arnold wrote these lines about Oxford University:

so steeped in sentiment as she lies,
spreading her gardens to the moonlight,
and whispering the last enchantments
of the Middle Ages

Ole Miss also whispers the last enchantments of an earlier age. Not to understand that, is not to understand the history that has shaped it, or the mystique that surrounds it.

The Ole Miss Mystique was aborning even before the university was founded. In the early 1840s a young disconsolate Methodist minister, without a charge, and worried of his future, was browsing in a bookstore in Mobile, Alabama. While flipping through the pages of a journal of the Mississippi legislature, he read that Mississippi had recently established a state university at Oxford, and an awesome premonition overcame him. In that moment, in that Alabama bookstore, he sensed that his future, his life's work, would be inextricably linked with the University of Mississippi. That young man was John Newton Waddel. In 1848 Waddel was appointed to the first faculty, and in the years of crisis following the Civil War, Waddel was appointed chancellor and perhaps saved the university.

On the occasion of the university's twenty-fifth anniversary in 1873, Chancellor Waddel addressed the graduating class. He closed his speech:

This university has my heart's affections. She was my first love. When the touch of death shall lay me in the grave, then let me sweetly sleep beneath the shadow of her fame and these classic groves.

This was one of the first references to The Grove, within which William Nichols, the university's architect, had laid out the original campus. Early in the history of Ole Miss the pristine and sylvan beauty of The Grove was superimposed upon the memories of its alumni.

In 1898, after the University of Mississippi had become known as Ole Miss, a graduating senior wrote fondly of those "hallowed groves:"

A thousand leagues of prairie
Between my heart and bliss;
How can it then be merry.
Beloved Ole Miss?
How strong so'er I be
I needs must weep at this;
Thy hallowed groves I see
No more, Ole Miss!
Let fortune smile on me,
Or O'er my failures hiss
As I am true to thee
Or false, Ole Miss.

The mystique was evolving. But first came the destruction of Civil War, and then progress with all its perils. But rather than endangering the place where Ole Miss was, both war and progress endeared it. The place became hallowed ground, and monuments were raised to the heroes of the Lost Cause. During the lumber boom after the Civil War, the virgin pines were plucked from those classic groves, but the oaks remained. They, too, are monuments, safe even from progress.

In 1928 Governor Theodore G. Bilbo wanted to move the university to Jackson. On the basis of practical economics, the proposal was sound. But Mississippians, as one writer said, were "infidels in the fold of good business." They practiced an "agnostic faith in a sort of irresponsibility" that exempted their leaders from the rigors of responsible statecraft. Decisions of consequence were not to be made on the basis of practical economics. Mississippians expected their leaders to be moved by nobler impulses. Chancellor Alfred Hume appealed to those nobler impulses in his 1928 speech urging the legislature not to move the university:

> *The University of Mississippi is rich in memories. ... Instead of*
> *moving the university away, that it might be a little easier to reach,*
> *ought not the people of Mississippi to look upon a visit here as a holy*

pilgrimage?… Gentlemen, you may move the University of Mississippi.
You may move it to Jackson or anywhere else. You may uproot it from
[this] hallowed ground… but gentlemen, don't call it Ole Miss.

Chancellor Hume also compared the barren landscape of the Jackson site, less than half of which was tree-lined, to the classic groves of Oxford. Chancellor Hume alluded to the Ole Miss oaks and rallied the poets in their defense:

Woodmen spare that tree,
Touch not a single bough,
In youth it sheltered me,
And I'll protect it now.

Sentiment and sense of place prevailed over practical economics, and the relocation was abandoned. Although some ridiculed the decision, Mississippi's disdain for progress and practical economics was seen by one writer as "a kind of stark and lonely grandeur in [a] docile world."

And so the university remained here in the sacred forest and became a lonely outpost amid the "quiet splendors of the old regime." And the Ole Miss Mystique evolved.

If Mississippians have a sense of place, they surely have a sense of history, a foreboding sense of destiny from which they derive a need for continuity. In a world of ravishing changes, Ole Miss alumni do not just stroll through The Grove; they retrace the steps of their forebears, not just over place and space, but back through time as well. Frank Everett is quite right when he says that students may graduate from the University of Mississippi, but they never leave Ole Miss because Ole Miss is more than their alma mater. It is their link, their nexus to who they were and are, and where they came from.

Who the hell are we — Ole Miss, by damn.

This is not a question and an answer; it is a confirmation. With that confirmation comes the gift of poetry and prophesy. As poets, the confirmed have license with rhyme and meter, and weights and measures and numbers. They train their gift of prophesy, not on the future, but on the past. To understand the Ole Miss Mystique one must understand what might have been, and what might have been happened a long time ago, amid "the quiet splendors of the old regime."

When the peace of those halcyon days of long ago was broken by the clanking of conflicting ideas, the statesmen of the old regime built their own university in 1848 where their sons could study the art of statecraft free from corrupting influences. The old regime was under siege.

And when that ideological siege gave way to mortal combat, their university became an early casualty. Every student at the University of Mississippi enlisted in the army of the old regime. On the afternoon of July 3, 1863, Company A, 11th Mississippi Infantry, known as the University Greys, won "imperishable glory" at Gettysburg in defense of "principles inherited from their fathers and strengthened by the teaching of their alma mater." At Gettysburg, what might have been did not happen. The University Greys scaled the rim of Cemetery Ridge in the first wave of Pickett's charge. Their advance is considered the "high watermark of the Confederacy," the farthest penetration into Union territory by any Confederate soldiers. Of the few survivors, none of the Greys returned to the university, and no reunion was ever held. The only memorial to the Greys is a stained-glass window in Ventress Hall, a beautiful but fragile reminder.

There are other Confederate memorials on campus. One is a cemetery where approximately 600 soldiers, Confederate and Union, found rest in a common grave, where *what might have been* no longer matters because *what might have been* belongs to the living.

A speaker at the 1867 commencement urged the university's graduating class to preserve "in fragrant memory that peculiar civilization which has been an ornament of the South, but which is now to pass away." He also urged them to transmit to posterity in permanent form a "record of the struggle just closed." Or else, he warned, "we have no security for the future against a thraldom far worse than that of the bayonet." Among Southerners "the pen would win what the sword has lost."

From the ruins of the old regime a New South and a New Mississippi emerged. The small farmers and laborers in the northeast hills and the piney woods finally wrested political control from the Delta and river counties. The gentry's hegemony was broken. During that bitter political struggle, the issue of class often surfaced, and it was inevitable that the university would be caught up in that struggle. The small farmers and common laborers, who were called rednecks, accused the university of pampering the sons of the gentry and neglecting the education of the sons and daughters of the working class. Eventually, Mississippi A&M College and Mississippi State College for Women were established to provide vocational training for the young white men and women of Mississippi. Recognizing in a limited way its responsibility for providing higher education for its black youth, the state also established Alcorn University.

At Mississippi A&M and MSCW students wore uniforms, and Greek societies with exclusive membership were prohibited. The practice of exclusion was a relic of aristocracy and was not in keeping with the purpose for which those institutions were founded. At the university, however, Greek societies flourished. And the Ole Miss Mystique evolved.

In 1897 Greek societies held a contest to select a name for their annual student publication. The winning entry was "Ole Miss," and the yearbook became a powerful agent in the evolution of the Ole Miss Mystique. The 1918 edition of the Ole Miss was dedicated to the young men in military service during World War I. The editor extolled the courage of those valiant soldiers who showed fidelity "to the teaching of [their] chivalric forbears [in] the cause of honor, home, and humanity." He compared their heroic deeds to those of the University Greys and pledged that they, like the Greys, would never be forgotten.

The student newspaper was also a major factor in the evolution of the Ole Miss Mystique, and when some university students were criticized for using "unparliamentary adjectives" at a sporting event, the editor scolded them:

We as students of the university represent the cream of Mississippi youth, the flower of Mississippi families. We are supposed to have been reared in homes where elegance of manners and language is atmospherical.... We must leave [profanity] for those yokels whose asininity is congenital.... We must remember that the finest families of the commonwealth are represented among Ole Miss students.

This editorial was written in 1930 and it was not a parody.

By the 1930s the Ole Miss Mystique was evolving apace, and one of the most intriguing aspects of that mystique was the origin of Colonel Rebel. Since the introduction of football as an intercollegiate sport in 1893, the Ole Miss team had been called the Red and Blue. Those colors were selected by Professor Alexander Bondurant, a Latin scholar and the team's first coach. This lackluster, though colorful, designation did not capture the fancy of those who were coming increasingly under the spell of the Ole Miss Mystique. The student newspaper conducted a contest in 1929 to select a name for the university's athletic teams that would "symbolize the spirit, traditions, and ideals of the University of Mississippi." The 800 entries included Young Massers, Magnolians, Confederates, Invincibles, and Mississippi Mudders. The winning entry was Mississippi Flood. Democrats and Rebels tied for second, and Ole Marsters came in third. However, the name Flood did not catch on and was rarely used in the 1930s.

On May 2, 1936, the student newspaper announced another contest. From the 600 entries a committee selected forty names, which were eventually reduced to five. The five final names were sent to a group of sports writers who were asked to rank them according to their preference. Eventually, the name Rebels was selected, and in 1937 an image of Colonel Rebel that bore striking resemblance to Blind Jim Ivy appeared on the cover of the Ole Miss yearbook. In 2010 Journalism Professor Charlie Mitchell cited an unpublished article by Frank Everett that affirmed that Blind Jim Ivy was the model for Colonel Rebel. Frank Everett of Vicksburg received a BA in 1932 and a law degree in 1934, and was a devoted alumnus. Mitchell quoted Everett as saying that Colonel Rebel was "ageless and raceless [and] belongs to no era... his eye is set steady to the future. He is history and hope."

Blind Jim Ivy was the legendary and beloved vendor on the campus who was named honorary dean of the freshman class. When he died on October 20, 1955, Ole Miss students and alumni endowed a scholarship in his honor. The Blind Jim Scholarships would enable "Mississippi Negro youngsters to attend Negro institutions of higher learning." Because of the complexities of race, the young African Americans who would benefit from the affection Ole Miss students had for Blind Jim could not attend the school he loved and had been a part of for so long.

All the stuff that mystiques are made of were present by the 1940s: a place, with its hallowed ground; a past, with its memories of imperishable glory; and symbols that enticed loyalty and devotion. Some great triumph, a string of victories won under those symbols, and the Ole Miss Mystique would envelop.

Then came the glory days when the Ole Miss Rebels won several football conference championships, started a string of bowl games, was named the team of the decade for the 1950s, and won a national championship in 1960.

In those Glory Days it was on the gridiron that the Ole Miss Rebels won their "imperishable glory." Football is a grand and colorful spectacle. The great crowds, the banners, the symbols, the bands, and the music spark our martial instincts. When I first came to Ole Miss in 1970 and saw Archie Manning and the Rebels take the field, and heard the stirring strains of Dixie, and saw all those Rebel flags, I thought of the University Greys's famous charge at Gettysburg.

In the 1981 edition of the *Ole Miss* is a double-page spread of Vaught-Hemingway Stadium filled to capacity. The green field glistened under the autumn sun; it was a grand spectacle. A small insert pictured Coach Steve Sloan looking tense but confident, his arms around his blue-helmeted quarterback. The caption read:

The Glorious Cause was gallantly surrendered in 1865, but true Southern spirits rise today on a new battlefield. Rebel warriors again battle to overcome the enemy amid the excitement and pageantry that is uniquely Southern. Their struggle is our struggle, together we strive for glory under the same banner. Win or lose we have taken our stand in Dixie.

As I looked at that picture and the caption, I thought of something Faulkner wrote in 1948:

It's all now you see. Yesterday won't be over until tomorrow and to-morrow began ten thousand years ago. For every Southern boy fourteen years old... it's still not yet two o'clock on that July afternoon in 1863, the brigades are ...waiting for Longstreet to give the word and it's all in the balance, it hasn't happened yet... it not only hasn't begun yet there is still time for it not to begin... yet it's going to begin, we all know that, we have come too far with too much at stake and that moment doesn't even need a fourteen-year-old boy to think this time. Maybe this time with all this much to lose and all this much to gain... the golden dome of Washington itself to crown with... unbelievable victory the desperate gamble.

Professor C. Vann Woodward, one of the South's premier historians, has written about memory and the "burden of Southern history." Ole Miss bears the burden of its history, and it was at Gettysburg on that July after-noon in 1863 that the Ole Miss Mystique was born.

And it was here at Ole Miss in the 1960s that Mississippi experienced some of its greatest triumphs, its brightest moments, and its darkest hours. In 1962 Ole Miss, this lonely outpost, became a national battleground. Change like a terrible swift sword came to Mississippi, and not even Ole Miss was beyond its reach.

But Ole Miss endured, and in the intervening years the university has prevailed, not in spite of, but because of those changes. A shining example of those changes was the enrollment of Coolidge Ball in 1970. Coolidge Ball was Ole Miss's first African American athlete. He scored more than a thousand points during his basketball career at Ole Miss and was inducted into the Ole Miss Sports Hall of Fame in 1991, named an SEC Basketball Legend in 2005, and inducted into the Mississippi Sports Hall of Fame in 2008.

The admission of black students to Ole Miss enlarged it, enhanced it, enriched it, and enlightened it. Who would have imagined on that dark night in 1962 that the grandson of Mohandas Ghandi would come to the University of Mississippi in 1987 to study race relations in America? Who would have believed that one of Ole Miss's recent Rhodes scholars would be Damon Moore, an African American? Who would have believed that "Gentle Ben" Williams would be an All American and Colonel Rebel, or that Chucky Mullins would become a Favorite Son of Ole Miss, and have one of the main entrances to the campus named in his honor, or that Debbie McCain would be elected most beautiful in 1996, and Courtney Pearson would be elected homecoming queen in 2012 and that Asya Branch would be named most beautiful in 2018? Who could have imagined in the aftermath of the Meredith crisis that in its centennial season the Ole Miss football team would start a black quarterback, or that when the team takes its ceremonial walk through The Grove, more than half of the players would be African Americans?

Another African American student with an enduring legacy was John Hawkins, Ole Miss's first African American cheerleader. Although he did not make a big issue of it personally, he declined to wave the Rebel flag during the 1982 football season. Ole Miss students and alumni would eventually agree to not wave the Rebel flag, would take Colonel Rebel off the field, and not play Dixie at football games.

The University of Mississippi is no longer a small state university nestled in the hallowed groves of north Mississippi and has in recent years achieved international distinction of some renown. There are ten colleges and schools at the Oxford campus that offer approximately two hundred academic programs. More than twenty percent of its students are minorities, and its student body has included students from all fifty states and eighty nations.

Coolidge Ball

The flags of those nations are proudly displayed in the Student Union. The chairman of the Arch Dalrymple III history department is a Harvard-educated scholar of Japanese history who teaches courses in Japanese, Korean, and Chinese history. The university's office of global engagement, which includes the office of international programs, "is a multidisciplinary network of people and programs that continuously strive to bring the world to Mississippi and take Mississippi to the world in ways that engender the development of global citizenship, scholarship, and human development."

One of the most important and prestigious positions at the University of Mississippi is the office of general counsel, which is currently held by Erica McKinley, an African American who holds a BA from Tougaloo College and is a 1998 *summa cum laude* graduate of the Ole Miss Law School. In announcing her appointment in June 2018, Chancellor Vitter stated, "Ms. McKinley is a highly-respected attorney with exceptional legal experience in corporate, government, and private practice. We are thrilled to welcome Erica back to Ole Miss."

There are those who still hear the whispers of an earlier age and are enchanted with its past, but the University of Mississippi, under Chancellor Jeffrey Vitter, and its faculty, staff, and student body tarries not with yesterday. Ole Miss can't wait until tomorrow.

15

OLE MISS

THE ORIGIN AND MEANING OF THE TERM

In the waning years of the nineteenth century the fundamental character and function of the University of Mississippi was transformed. It became coeducational, and two new forces in American higher education appeared with enormous impact. Those two forces were the alumni movement and intercollegiate athletics, and they intersected and interacted with each other. "The alumni movement," Frederick Rudolph wrote in his classic study of the American collegiate system, "had its own rationale, its own purposes, its own life, and [was remote] from the purposes of the professors."

University of Chicago President Robert Maynard Hutchins mused that college is "one of life's climactic experiences, and it grows rosier in memory as it recedes in time." He concluded, "In some as yet undefined way renewed contact with intercollegiate athletics revives [our] youth as no other experience could."

The American college campus became a self-contained community with its own traditions and value system. There were so many non-intellectual and extracurricular activities at the University of Mississippi in the 1890s that the YMCA began publishing a handbook for new students.

Student publications were among the most influential agents in creating college traditions and were instrumental in forming an institution's identity. In 1896 the Greek societies at The University of Mississippi an-

James Meredith at Harvard

nounced that they would begin publishing an annual, or yearbook, and invited students and alumni to submit suggestions for its title. Elma Meek suggested the name *Ole Miss*, which the board of editors adopted, and they published the first issue of the *Ole Miss* in 1897.

An article in the October 10, 1936, issue of *The Mississippian*, under the heading, *Name 'Ole Miss' Given Years Ago—Miss Elma Meek Author*, stated that "The identity of Miss Meek as the originator of the name, 'Ole Miss,' finds definite confirmation by Mrs. Maud Morrow Brown, member of the original committee and who is now the wife of Dr. Calvin Brown, professor of modern languages and literature at the university." Maud Brown also wrote several books about Oxford and the University of Mississippi.

The term "Ole Miss" was a term of respect and endearment for the mistress of the plantation used by slaves in antebellum Mississippi, and by former slaves who survived well into the 1930s. Elma Meek had heard former slaves use the term. Most students at the University of Mississippi in the 1890s were from well-to-do families that employed African Americans, and they were familiar with the term. In the 1930s there were approximately 20,000 former slaves still living in Mississippi, and many of them continued to use the phrase "Ole Miss" in reference to the mistress of the household. Of those 20,000 former slaves 450 were interviewed in the 1930s by researchers employed by the WPA. Those interviews were subsequently transcribed and published in the multi-volume collection, *The American Slave: A Composite Autobiography*. The researchers who transcribed those interviews were meticulous in their effort to capture and reproduce the dialect of the former slaves. One of those former Mississippi slaves whose interview was published was Barney Alford of Pike County, who spoke in glowing terms of the *Ole Missus* of his plantation.

By suggesting the term Ole Miss, Alma Meek did not intend to reminisce or regale slavery. She wanted to preserve the high regard accorded Southern women. That regard for Southern women was explained in 1900 by Dunbar Rowland, the director of the Mississippi Department of Archives and History:

It is impossible to picture in words the wife Mother of a Mississippi plantation home, she was the grandest, noblest and best type of woman that ever brought joy and happiness to the world [and they] are rapidly passing away. Their memories, deeds, and virtues must be preserved by their sons and daughters. They must be preserved on the living pages of history, in story, poetry, song, in sculptured marble.

Let me reiterate that Elma Meek's intention was not to recall or reminisce slavery, but to link her alma mater to those grand women of the antebellum South. The term Ole Miss was so popular with students and alumni that it immediately became interchangeable with the University of Mississippi. In the first edition of the *Ole Miss* published in 1897 the alumni offered this poetic tribute to their alma mater:

> To the Beloved Mother of this Fair
> > Daughter and namesake
> > Ole Miss, thy name is dear
> > Ole Miss, we cannot fear
> > > To Praise thee.
> > Ole Miss, our hearts are thine
> > Ole Miss, we ever pine
> > > When from thee.
> > Ole Miss, our lady fair,
> > Ole Miss, beyond compare
> > > We love thee.   Alumni

In the next issue editor Durrell Miller also lauded his alma mater:

> Ole Miss
> A thousand leagues of prairie
> Between my heart and bliss;
> How can it then be merry.

Beloved Ole Miss?
How strong so'er I be
I needs must weep at this;
Thy hallowed groves I see
No more, Ole Miss!

In that issue there was also a section titled "Rooter's Brigade" that includes rousing cheers for the athletic teams that used Ole Miss and the University of Mississippi interchangeably:

Don't you see those boys? Don't you see those boys?
They are playing for the glory of Mississippi!
Don't you see those boys? Don't you see those boys?
They are playing for the glory of "Ole Miss"
Who dat say Mississippi can't play ball?
Whoever said so lied, and dat ain't all—
We ain't skeered of any ole team;
'Cause we ain't as weak as we seem.
Who dat say Ole Miss can't play ball?

The editors of the 1900 edition of *Ole Miss* articulated the university's subliminal link to the Old South and the Civil War by dedicating the yearbook to the unknown soldiers in the Civil War Cemetery on campus:

To… these unknown sons of our Southland's lost hope… and with sympathy and sorrow for their mothers who know not where their beloved boys sleep.

The section devoted to athletics also includes a cheer for the baseball team that identified the University of Mississippi as Ole Miss:

And when "Ole Miss" gets after Tulane
What is the mischief she will do.

In the 1905 *Ole Miss* one short line about the football game between the University of Mississippi and the University of Nashville in the athletics section indicates just how transposable the terms Ole Miss and the University of Mississippi had become by 1905:

> *Well, to make this short, when the whistle blew for the last of the second half, Ole Miss was 12 and Nashville 5.*

The senior poem in the 1908 *Ole Miss* indicates that the term "Ole Miss" was not only interchangeable with the University of Mississippi, but it was also an expression of the deep affection alumni had for their alma mater:

> *When we look back on our school days, just about four years ago,*
> *Then we think of all the good times and the days that are no mo',*
> *On June the third comes our departure from the place we love so*
> *   well,*
> *Whose ground we trod for four years each hour, at the ringing of*
> *   the bell.*
> *And now, "Ole Miss," good bye to you, the class of nineteen eight*
> *   must go.*
> *We'll love the good times spent with you, and all the days that are*
> *   no mo'.*

The 1909 *Ole Miss* features a steaming locomotive on its cover identified as Ole Miss with the date 1909. The cover also includes a discombobulated duck that seems to be fleeing the oncoming train, and a frantic figure of Father Time, with his scythe, who also seems to be running for safety. In Chancellor Andrew Kincannon's inaugural address on September 19, 1907, he asked the alumni and students to join him in transforming Ole Miss into "The Greater University of Mississippi." His ambition for the transformation of the university was embraced by students and alumni, and the phrase "Greater University of Mississippi" became a powerful slogan during Chancellor Kincannon's administration. The 1907 student newspaper included that phrase on its masthead. In February 1908 the campus magazine conceded that the Greater University of Mississippi was a dream at that time but predicted it would be "a reality in the future."

The editorial staff of the 1909 *Ole Miss* also embraced the concept of a Greater University of Mississippi and predicted even greater things to come:

> *Throughout the Commonwealth the Alumni of Ole Miss are dominating and molding public policy. ... We know it is our University's golden hour. The stage is cleared for the Greater University, and with confidence we await its entry.*

It may be that the steaming locomotive labeled Ole Miss is symbolic of The Greater University of Mississippi that is roaring toward its "golden hour."

In the 1910 yearbook there is a toast that bespeaks of the emerging mystique of Ole Miss.

> *To thee Ole Miss, with hearts of love,*
> *To thee whose traditions are dearer to us*
> *Than personal fame or renown,*
> *To thee, Alma Mater, our dear Ole Miss,*
> *We propose our humble toast.*

By the time the Alma Mater was adopted in 1925, the term Ole Miss was used in reference to the university almost as often, maybe even more, than its legal and formal designation. In fact, the alma mater does not include the term "University of Mississippi." The first stanza reads,

> *Way down south in Mississippi, there's a spot that ever calls,*
> *Where among the hills enfolded stands old Alma Mater's halls,*
> *Where the trees lift high their branches to the whispering Southern breeze*

There Ole Miss is calling, calling to our hearts' fond memories.

Students and alumni, especially the editorial staff of *The Mississippian*, were possessive and protective of the term Ole Miss. In the November 11, 1929, issue of the student newspaper, under the caption "Mississippi is not Ole Miss," a somewhat irate student editor declared:

> *The name 'Ole Miss' is the private property of the University of Mississippi. It is undisputedly a University product, intended solely for reference to the University. Nowhere else is there a name so beautiful and appropriate.*

But in the creeping passage of time, facts are sometimes lost, forgotten, or muddled. In the November 1932 issue of the *Ole Miss Alumni News* is an article titled "Origin of Ole Miss." The editor explained, erroneously, that the term "Ole" was for the period before and during the Confederacy, and "Miss" was an abbreviation of Mississippi.

The misinformation about the origin and meaning of the term Ole Miss in that 1932 article may have prompted the October 10, 1936, article in *The Mississippian* mentioned previously. But there are a few sentences in that 1936 article that bear repeating:

> *The identity of Miss Meek as the originator of the name 'Ole Miss' finds definite confirmation by Mrs. Maud Morrow Brown. ... 'I was a member of the committee appointed to suggest names suitable for the annual. ... Miss Elma Meek had suggested Ole Miss.'*

This 1936 article was followed three years later by a May 13, 1939, front-page article in *The Mississippian* reiterating the origin and meaning of the term Ole Miss.

Following World War II, when the university's enrollment increased dramatically, and student life was getting back to a more normal routine, it was only natural that the name Ole Miss would become the focus of interest and inquiry. On October 29, 1947, the Department of Public Relations issued a formal statement explaining the origin and meaning of the term Ole Miss. That document was basically an expanded and updated version of the article that appeared in the October 10, 1936, issue of *The Mississippian*.

In 1948, during the University of Mississippi's Centennial Celebration, the board of editors of the *Ole Miss* dedicated that issue to Miss Elma Meek:

> *Through her origin of the name Ole Miss, Miss Elma Meek has won a merited place in the hearts of all who have been in any way connected with the University of Mississippi, and it is in sincere appreciation of Miss Meek's contribution that we issue this volume of The Ole Miss.*

By 1948 the terms Ole Miss and University of Mississippi had become so synonymous that the first line in the historical sketch of the university in the centennial issue of the *Ole Miss* reads:

> *It was on a bright, brisk, Monday morning in November, in the year 1848, that the University of Mississippi, now affectionately known as Ole Miss, came into existence.*

In the years since the admission of James Howard Meredith in 1962 the origin and meaning of the term Ole Miss has been lost in the misty memories of yesterday. The term Ole Miss no longer refers to "what used to be." Ole Miss is about "what is, what ought to be, and what can be."

In 2013, on the fiftieth anniversary of his graduation from Ole Miss, Harvard University presented James Howard Meredith the prestigious *Medal for Education Impact*. Mr. Meredith is pictured in newspapers across the country accepting that award and wearing a red shirt bearing the name of his alma mater, Ole Miss. James Meredith's legacy to Ole Miss, to Mississippi, and to America symbolizes a major event in the history of the United States of America.

Since James Meredith's admission in 1962, African American students have enrolled at The University of Mississippi in increasing numbers and have been front and center in student affairs and athletics, and have held virtually every elective office on campus. Since the admission of African American students, Ole Miss has discontinued playing "Dixie" and waving the Confederate flag. In 2003 the University discontinued Colonel Rebel as the official mascot, and eventually replaced him with The Black Bear, which was never really popular with either students or alumni. And then something very special happened.

Late in the fourth quarter of the Ole Miss-Florida football game in Gainesville on September 27, 2008, with Ole Miss ahead by one point, Florida Quarterback Tim Tebow was leading No. 4 Florida on what would have been a winning drive. But on fourth down Tebow was brought down for a loss, which ended the Florida drive and preserved one of the grandest wins in the history of Ole Miss football. After that sack Ole Miss linebacker, Antonio D. "Tony" Fein, flashed, perhaps for the first time in an Ole Miss football game, the Landshark sign. And the rest is history.

Tony Fein was an African American, a United States army veteran who had won a Purple Heart in Iraq and had received the Pat Tillman Award, which honors athletes for their military service. After his honorable discharge, Fein played football for two years at Scottsdale Community College in Arizona before coming to Ole Miss in 2007. After Fein displayed the Landshark salute in the Florida game, the gesture was immediately popular among Ole Miss players and fans. Ole Miss athletes in other sports and fans of all sports adopted the tradition of flashing the Landshark salute.

Tragically, Tony Fein died in 2009 because of an accidental drug overdose, but he will long be remembered for his devotion to his country and his legacy at Ole Miss.

The growing popularity of the Landshark salute prompted the Ole Miss student body to conduct a September 29, 2017, referendum on the formal adoption of the Landshark as the university's official mascot. In that referendum eighty-one percent of the students who voted supported the adoption of the Landshark as the university's mascot.

Two weeks after that vote, Chancellor Jeffrey Vitter announced the he and Athletics Director Ross Bjork, in consultation with various other uni-

Tony Fein

versity constituencies, approved and supported the adoption of the Land-shark as the Ole Miss mascot. The adoption of the Landshark as the mascot did not, however, mean the discontinuation of the term Rebels. Chancellor Vitter said that "we are—and always will be the Ole Miss Rebels."

While walking through The Grove not long ago, I asked an African American student who was wearing a red sweatshirt with Ole Miss on the front, what Ole Miss meant. He looked at me kind of funny, and said, "The university!" I did not have to ask him what university.

16

THE DIGNIFIED LYCEUM

REDEDICATION CEREMONY, APRIL 27, 2001

If there is one single edifice or structure or scene that conjures up the whole history of the University of Mississippi, if there is one image that symbolizes the glorious past of this great institution and its troubled history, it is this building we celebrate today, known simply and fondly as the Lyceum.

When I wrote the sesquicentennial history of the university there was never any question about what would be on the cover. The only question was which picture of the Lyceum would decorate the book jacket.

Governor Albert Gallatin Brown, who signed the law establishing the state university, admonished the board of trustees to consult economy rather than ornament in the construction of the university's original buildings. Nevertheless, George Frederick Holmes, the university's first chancellor, who had seen the architectural splendors of the Old Dominion, Georgia, and South Carolina, called the Lyceum "one of the most elegant structures in the South."

The origin of its name is shrouded in the mists of history. According to Professor Franklin Moak, from whose treasures of Ole Miss history I have pilfered many golden nuggets, the building's name was derived from an Oxford/Lafayette County literary society, called the Lyceum, which held its meetings in the university's principal building.

The Lyceum

The Lyceum was designed and built by William Nichols, one of antebellum America's most renowned public architects. His state capitols, county courthouses, and college campuses decorated the Southern landscape from North Carolina to Louisiana.

Long before its walls were raised, or its roof was set in place, or its doors were hinged, the Lyceum was dedicated on July 14, 1846, almost a year and a half before its completion. I believe that early dedication was a deliberate act to save the university.

Just three months before the Lyceum was dedicated, a bill to revoke the university's charter and establish several colleges around the state was defeated in the Mississippi House of Representatives by the slim margin of three votes. It is highly probable that the board of trustees held the cornerstone ceremony at the earliest possible opportunity to forestall the effort to disestablish the University of Mississippi.

The dedication ceremony was conducted with great pomp and circumstance, with military fanfare, and, of course, a parade. That auspicious occasion also required many orations, the main one delivered by a twenty-eight-year-old Holly Springs attorney William Forbes Stearns, who later became the first dean of the University Law School.

The founding of the University of Mississippi had been delayed for so many years, and there was still so much opposition to it, that its future was by no means secure. Stearns was frank with his listeners: "The experiment is now about to be tried in earnest, whether or not an institution of learning can be established in [Mississippi] upon a permanent foundation. There is no good reason why an institution may not here be founded, which shall rank [among] the first in any portion of our [great republic]." Stearns concluded his oration in a flourish of high optimism: "Let this institution succeed, and no man can estimate how many poets, orators, [and] statesmen… may here be formed," nor can any man measure "the influence that will be exerted for good, through its agency, upon the generations who are to succeed us."

When John Millington, the professor of natural sciences, arrived on campus in mid-October 1848, three weeks before the university opened its first session, he found the construction crews putting the finishing touches on the university's six original buildings.

The campus was in a setting of great natural beauty, with the buildings arranged in a semicircle at the crest of a slight eminence. The six original buildings, of which only the Lyceum remains, included two dormitories, two faculty houses, and a steward's hall.

The Lyceum, where classes were held and learning flourished, loomed above the eminence and towered above the other buildings, greeting students and visitors to the nation's newest temple of learning.

In 1856 following his appointment as the university's third chancellor, Frederick Barnard devoted his every effort to the single goal of placing the University of Mississippi in the front ranks of the nation's institutions of higher learning, and the Lyceum figured prominently in his ambitions for the university.

Chancellor Barnard emphasized the natural sciences over moral philosophy and metaphysics and began accumulating the latest scientific apparatus. To house this new equipment he built a 36-foot addition to the Lyceum, which included a chemistry laboratory and a lecture hall. He designed the laboratory and lecture hall himself, proudly sketching it out in a letter to Eugene Hilgard. After the completion of this addition, *DeBow's Review*, a Southern business journal published in New Orleans, described the university's laboratories and scientific apparatus as "the most perfect in… arrangement and appointments now existing in the Union."

Barnard's ambition for the university and for himself was unfortunately interrupted by the Civil War. In the early months of 1862 the Confederates established a hospital on the university campus, and the Lyceum sheltered wounded Southern soldiers. After General Ulysses S. Grant occupied Oxford in December 1862, the Lyceum was used as a federal hospital. In a cemetery behind the Tad Smith Coliseum, the boys who died in the Lyceum, blue and grey alike, were buried in a common cemetery, a silent reminder of the unspeakable tragedy of that war.

In the decades following America's Civil War many Ole Miss traditions were formed. Among them were football, Rhodes Scholars, student publications, and the storied beauty of the Ole Miss campus. In 1894 the campus magazine wrote of this tradition:

> *Imagine yourself this beautiful October day, a visitor who is approaching, for the first time, the campus of the University of Mississippi.... You approach from the town of Oxford, and as you approach through University Street you see the... spire and roof of the Library.... You cross the railroad bridge and find yourself beneath the spreading arms of these matchless [oaks] and passing over grounds that exhibit... nature's [finest] handiworks.... Here and there, in artistic order, a dignified old building of venerable style reaches up into the lofty trees as if to dispute a question of height with the sturdy hickories.... There at the end of the main walk stands the grand old Lyceum with its...columns and classical outline. How serenely and grandly does it look down upon you and how suggestive its towering grandeur.*

Writing in the campus newspaper in the spring of 1902, a student called the campus "the prettiest place I ever saw." Spring is "busting out," he wrote, and the "magnificent oaks are beginning to cast an inviting shade [on] those hot spring days." Students could not "resist the temptation [of] passing a ball," playing "leap frog," and "lounging upon the green sward."

How could change and modernity dare intrude upon such an idyllic scene? But it did. First came the bicycles. Many of the same complaints we now make about automobiles were made then about bicycles. In 1904 the communication revolution reached the university with the installation of telephones in the Lyceum.

A more unsettling manifestation of change and modernization was the construction of wings on the Lyceum in 1903. In a section called "Pertinent Questions," the *University Magazine* said that it did not wish to be disrespectful of Chancellor Robert Fulton but did feel compelled to express its disappointment that the classic lines of the Lyceum were compromised by the attachment of the two annexes. After the new gymnastics room and the swimming pool, which were located in the south wing, opened in February 1904, the *University Magazine* made no further complaints about stylistic compromises. However, the journal did complain that the gymnasium and the swimming pool were too small and urged the university to build a new and larger sports facility.

By far the most dramatic change in the Lyceum's external appearance occurred in the 1920s. After voting not to consolidate the four existing white state institutions of higher learning during the 1920 legislative session, the legislature voted for what I believe was the university's first million-dollar state appropriation. The 1920 appropriation launched a construction program that eventually transformed the overall appearance of the campus. The allocation was used for a chemistry-pharmacy building, four boys' dormitories and one girls' dormitory. The new science hall, now known as the Old Chemistry Building, was a beautiful structure of neoclassical design. The fifty-thousand-square-foot building, which housed the chemistry department and the pharmacy school, was occupied in the spring of 1923.

With the opening of the new science building, the chemistry laboratory in the Lyceum was converted into four classrooms. Several other major structural changes were made within the Lyceum, and its external appearance was also dramatically altered in 1923 with the addition of columns at the west entrance to replicate the appearance of the east entrance that had been the main entrance. Four years later, in 1927, a handsome clock and bell system were added to the eastern face of the Lyceum.

Over the next several years, with the construction of new classroom buildings, the Lyceum gradually became less an academic and more an administration building.

By the end of the 1920s it had become an Ole Miss tradition for the freshman class to assemble on the Lyceum steps on Thursday night during the first week of the fall semester to receive a special welcome and words of wisdom from their unofficial dean, Blind Jim Ivy. Blind Jim was a one-man vending operation who was given special dispensation to sell his wares in the Lyceum corridors.

The relationship between Ole Miss students and James Ivy broke none of the codices of white supremacy, and their affection for him was genuine. But all of that changed in 1962 during what Ellen Douglas has called "a long night." On Monday, October 1, 1962, the morning after that long night, James Meredith registered in the Lyceum as the university's first African American student, and the Lyceum was pictured on the front page of newspapers around the world. Seldom has a school building been seen by so many in such distant places.

James Meredith's registration as a student at Ole Miss changed Mississippi, and indeed America, and our lives, forever. And we are all better because of that change, not in spite of it.

More than a hundred and fifty years ago the Lyceum was built by slave labor. Today, in a spacious second-floor office an African American, Thomas Wallace, presides over one of the university"s largest and most important divisions, which is but one measure of the change that has swirled through its corridors since the laying of its cornerstone.

If a building can have dignity, and I think it can, then this one, the Lyceum, is a dignified building. Now restored in all its glory it shall stand for the ages as a symbol of continuity, a memorial, a monument to what has been, what is, and what can be.

Dedication of the Arch Dalrymple III Department of History

17

A Tribute to
Arch Dalrymple III

On the Occasion of Naming the History
Department in His Honor
April 27, 2012

It was my good fortune to know Mr. Dalrymple. He was a man of great dignity and decorum, and he lived a full life for 85 years. He was a man of significant means, and a giving and sharing man. The Dalrymple Family Foundation has made the town of Amory and the world a better place. He devoted much of his time and energy to public education. He was a member of the Amory School District Board of Trustees and a founding member and president of the Mississippi School Boards Association. To read a biographical sketch of Arch Dalrymple is to marvel at the breadth of his varied interests and the sweep of his pursuits. Just one sentence from a recent newspaper account of his life will illustrate: "Mr. Dalrymple's business interests included farming, timber, real estate, oil and gas, heavy equipment, construction machinery, and for many years he served on the board of directors of Trustmark National Bank."

In addition to his varied business interests and his devotion to public education, he was also active in the Mississippi Historical Society and was its president in 1976. Mr. Dalrymple served on the board of trustees of the

Mississippi Department of Archives and History with his Ole Miss classmate William Winter for more than thirty years. The distinguished director emeritus of the Department of Archives, Mr. Elbert Hilliard, who served with Mr. Dalrymple for many of those years, is here today, and I would like to thank him for joining us as we honor Mr. Dalrymple.

Arch Dalrymple III was in the best and truest sense of the term a Southern Gentleman. His roots ran deep; he was a member of the Society of the Cincinnati. He loved history, but he was not bound by the past. He was a man of his time, and a man ahead of his time.

In 1943, at the age of nineteen, Mr. Dalrymple interruped his collegiate career to enter the United States military service. Discharged in 1945 as a second lieutenant, he returned to the University of Mississippi, where he majored in history and graduated in 1947. He studied under Professor James Wesley Silver, a circumstance that would reach long into the life and legacy of Arch Dalrymple. One of his classmates was another young veteran and history major named William Winter. They knew well the impact James Silver had on their lives as students, but little did they know nor could they have anticipated what a major role they would later play in Professor Silver's life and in the course of Mississippi history.

After their graduation William Winter became a prominent attorney, chairman of the board of trustees of the Department of Archives and History, and governor of Mississippi. And, as Arch Dalrymple was becoming increasingly prosperous and prestigious, they maintained an enduring friendship with Professor Silver and with each other.

On one occasion, I think it was in 1949, the three of them took a trip through north Mississippi to identify historic sites where the Department of Archives would place historical markers. In the rural environs of Lee County, out from Tupelo, they were trying to locate the site of the famous Battle of Ackia, where the Chickasaw Indians defeated French troops under Bienville in 1736. That historic battle virtually ended French dominion over the geographic area that later became Mississippi. The Daughters of the American Revolution had placed a small stone marker at the site many years earlier, but they could not find it. They stopped at a country store out in the middle of nowhere, and Mr. Dalrymple asked the lady at the cash register if she knew where the great Indian battle between the French and the Chickasaws had taken place. She said she did not. But she would ask her husband, who was in the back of the store, if he could tell these gentlemen where that famous Indian battle had taken place, and if it was some place around there. Governor Winter, who told me this story many years later, said the kindly old gentleman came up to the front, with a funny look on his face, and said, "I've lived here all my life, and there ain't never been no Indian battle nowhere 'round here." They thanked him, left the store, walked down the gravel road a little way, and there it was, the DAR stone marker identifying the site of the Battle of Ackia. That encounter prompted Arch Dalrymple to initiate a statewide historical markers program.

In the late 1950s a much more significant experience linked Arch Dalrymple, Governor Winter, Professor Silver, and The University of Mississippi. In several speeches, one of which was titled, "The Lunatic Fringe and the Moderates—A Hundred Years Ago and Now," Professor Silver criticized the state's political leadership for resisting the impending racial and social changes and accused them of making the same mistakes their forebears had made on the eve of the Civil War.

An angry outcry from the press and politicians prompted the introduction of bills in the legislature and resolutions on the College Board to dismiss that "communist agitator up there at Ole Miss." While William Winter helped calm the waters among the politicians, Arch Dalrymple worked the college board. There are two letters in Professor Silver's papers in the J.D. Williams Library from Arch Dalrymple to his former, and now infamous, history professor.

Mr. Dalrymple explained in those letters that he had persuaded Professor Silver's detractors on the college board not to push for his dismissal.

Professor Silver survived another day, in part because of Arch Dalrymple's support, and wrote another book, *Mississippi, The Closed Society*. Professor Silver's classic study, which he first published in 1963, prompted a reexamination of Mississippi history by academics and by the public at large. Professor Silver's book was a prologue to what some historians now call The New Mississippi.

And Arch Dalrymple was present at its creation.

And so today, we dedicate The Arch Dalrymple III Department of History, at The University of Mississippi. I think Mr. Dalrymple would be so pleased that his memorial is not of bricks and stones, but of students and faculty, of research, teaching and learning, because he understood that it is what happens inside these hallowed halls that endures and makes a difference. And I am certain that he would be pleased that the Dalrymple Department of History includes the William Winter Chair of History, and that a memorial to his beloved Professor Jim Silver is nearby.

On behalf of the students and faculty at The University of Mississippi, and for future generations, may I express to the Dalrymple Family our deep and abiding gratitude.

18

THE BILBO PURGE, 1928-1932

Chapter 5 in
A Troubled History: The Governance of Higher Education in Mississippi

> *But I was looking fifty years ahead for Mississippi.*
> Governor Theodore G. Bilbo

In the fall of 1927, Michael O'Shea published his Study of Higher Education in Mississippi, which had been commissioned by Mississippi Governor Henry Whitfield. At that time Mississippi was in the midst of a heated gubernatorial campaign between Theodore Bilbo and Dennis Murphree. The state's institutions of higher learning, as usual, were in the thick of the fray, and as the campaign progressed Bilbo became increasingly troubled by the political involvement of college officials.

President J.C. Fant of Mississippi State College for Women had given a glowing introduction of Dennis Murphree at a special student assembly that left little doubt about his personal preference for governor, and MSCW alumni made no effort to conceal their support for Murphree. Var-

Theodore Bilbo

ious alumni groups bought newspaper advertisements and wrote letters on his behalf. Two members of the college board and the wife of a former board member who had ties to MSCW were members of Murphree's state campaign committee. The opposition to Bilbo among MSCW supporters stemmed in large measure from his support of the Sheldon-Zeller bill in 1920, which would have consolidated the three white colleges into one university located at Jackson. There was also open opposition to Bilbo among the staff and alumni at Mississippi A&M College and State Teachers College at Hattiesburg. Bilbo was made aware of that political involvement by his own partisans at those institutions.[1]

It was the opposition of Ole Miss officials, however, that most troubled Bilbo, a seasoned veteran of six campaigns. Robert Farley, a young law professor, wrote letters to friends and alumni urging them to work for Bilbo's defeat. "A vote for Bilbo is a vote against Chancellor Hume," Farley explained. Farley's conjecture was based on rumors that Bilbo, if elected, would fire Chancellor Alfred Hume and reinstate his old friend Joseph Neely Powers, who had been fired four years earlier by Governor Whitfield. The fact that Powers was campaigning for Bilbo and had endorsed his populist promise of free textbooks lent credence to Farley's accusation. When Bilbo learned of Farley's letters, he asked Chancellor Hume to reprimand Farley and instruct him to quit the campaign against him. Chancellor Hume refused to do so, telling Bilbo that Farley's private political opinions did not come under his jurisdiction, and he would not intervene.[2]

There were several other university officials who campaigned against Bilbo including William Hemingway, the former mayor of Jackson and a professor of law who in his law classes openly ridiculed Bilbo and his redneck politics. Thomas Turner and other Bilbo partisans kept records on university personnel who campaigned against him and passed that information on to the governor. Turner later served on the board of trustees of State Institutions of Higher Learning, from 1964 to 1976.[3]

Bilbo was embittered by the politics of Ole Miss officials, and their opposition to his populist platform was proof, in his mind at least, that the university was still catering to Mississippi's old aristocracy. Like his predecessor, Henry Whitfield, and some other Southern governors, Huey Long of Louisiana in particular, Bilbo looked to the state university as a catalyst in the solution of the state's social and economic problems. As Governor Whitfield and Michael O'Shea had found, Ole Miss was still under the sway of the "Genteel Tradition" and the notion that a university should train the mind and build character. The success of Bilbo's populist platform of economic development would in some important aspects depend upon a progressive, problem-solving state university. Bilbo was convinced that Ole Miss as it existed in 1927, an isolated liberal arts college in poor repair in a "sylvan exile," could contribute little to Mississippi's "progress and future glory." He now had the findings of the O'Shea Study as he began to formulate his plan to restructure Mississippi's system of higher education during the political canvas of 1927.[4]

As the reorganization plan was being formulated, bits and pieces of it leaked to the press. One version of the plan called for sweeping changes in the system's leadership, and rumors ran amok about who would be dismissed. Another feature of Bilbo's plan that became the subject of increasing speculation was the relocation of the university to Jackson. The possibility of moving Ole Miss to Jackson first surfaced in the days just before the Civil War, resurfaced around 1900, and again soon after the establishment of the central board of trustees in 1910, and again in 1920. The central board of trustees governed the university, Mississippi A&M, and MSCW. Some legislative leaders had considered the relocation of the university to be such a likely possibility that they were reluctant to build up the Oxford campus. In 1927 "the university was slowly dying of neglect, and drastic measures were necessary if the institution was to be revitalized."[5]

As the question of moving the university to Jackson became increasingly the subject of public discussion, the tone of that discussion became increasingly emotional and sentimental. In December 1927 Chancellor Alfred Hume issued a public statement opposing the relocation of the university. Many Mississippians of that era had been baptized in "the blood of the lost cause," and Chancellor Hume played upon those precious memories with great skill and success:

The University of Mississippi is rich in memories and memorials and a noble history. … The memorial window in the old library erected in loving memory of the University Grays, the Confederate monument nearby, and the Confederate soldiers' cemetery a little farther removed are as sacred as any ancient shrine, altar, or temple. Instead of moving the university away that it might be a little easier to reach, ought not the people of Mississippi to look upon a visit here as a holy pilgrimage?[6]

Governor Bilbo was inaugurated on January 17, 1928. His inaugural address was well crafted, and even editor Fred Sullens of the *Jackson Daily News*, one of Bilbo's bitterest critics, gave grudging due. Sullens wrote that Bilbo's inaugural was one of "the ablest messages… in the memory of this writer." Other papers, even some that had opposed his election, praised his inaugural address, though many expressed reservations about the cost of his agenda, which was estimated at one hundred million dollars.[7]

The high cost of Bilbo's legislative program triggered a conditioned response from a powerful coalition known as the "low-pressure" faction of the Democratic Party. The low-pressure faction was composed of fiscal conservatives who were dedicated to the proposition of low taxes and economy in government. Bilbo represented the populist, or redneck, faction, which outnumbered the low-pressure group but enjoyed little legislative success because it was out maneuvered by the crafty conservatives who controlled both houses of the legislature. The low-pressure faction was stunned by the visionary and costly proposals in Governor Bilbo's inaugural address, and they, with help from the Great Depression, ultimately defeated his legislative program.

Bilbo's inaugural address embraced a wide range of reforms and other programs that he considered essential to Mississippi's social and economic development. He reiterated his campaign proposal for free textbooks, a modern mental hospital, two charity hospitals, a separate correctional facility for young inmates, and a massive highway program. But it was his proposal to reorganize and restructure the governance of higher education that created a firestorm.

After citing some of the O'Shea Study's recommendations, Governor Bilbo proposed sweeping changes in the governance of higher education. One of his priorities was the establishment of an eight-member central governing board, one from each of the eight congressional districts, who would serve eight-year staggered terms with one member going off the board each year "so that no governor could appoint the majority of said board." The governor also recommended a five-member "largely advisory" board for each of the six institutions of higher learning, who would serve four-year terms. To coordinate the governance of higher education, Governor Bilbo recommended the establishment of a "director of higher education [who would be] placed in charge of all institutions of college rank."

To these recommendations Bilbo proposed the establishment of what he called "The Greater University of Mississippi" at Jackson:

> *If I were called upon to name the one thing that would do more to develop Mississippi and bring to her the highest degree of progress and future glory than anything else, I would not hesitate in saying that [moving] the University of Mississippi to the capital city of Jackson and the building and equipment of a twelve- or fifteen-million-dollar institution would be that thing.*[8]

The day after Bilbo was inaugurated, Senator Linton Glover North introduced a resolution to relocate the University of Mississippi to Jackson. Senator North was a native of Vicksburg, a graduate of Mississippi A&M College and, according to the *Jackson Daily News*, was "an upstanding, progressive young man" who was motivated by "the sole hope of building a bigger and better university." The *Daily News* reminded its readers that Senator Julius Zeller had recommended the establishment of one consolidated university in Jackson eight years earlier. "But the legislature," said the *Daily News*, "lacked the largeness of vision to see it."[9]

Jackson business leaders heartily endorsed the relocation of the state university, but they had some reservation about the twelve- to fifteen-million-dollar cost of the new institution. Governor Bilbo's response to their concern is an indication of just how committed he was to the establishment of a great university:

> *I fully understand that the proposal suggested in my inaugural address is a big one, but I was looking fifty years ahead for Mississippi... the start could be made in a smaller way, but the plans must be made for the distant future.*[10]

While the populist governor and the Jackson plutocrats were forming what some may have considered an unholy alliance, Chancellor Hume was plotting to keep Ole Miss at Oxford. His strategy, based not on reason but sentiment, appealed to sense of place and evoked the memory of the Lost Cause. Chancellor Hume expressed that sentiment in an address to the legislature:

> *Gentlemen, you may move the university of Mississippi. ... You may uproot it from the hallowed ground on which it has stood for eighty years. You may take it from these surroundings that have become dear to the thousands who have gone from its doors. But, gentlemen, don't call it Ole Miss.*[11]

The legislature was persuaded by the Chancellor's rhetoric and voted 109 to 9 to leave Ole Miss at Oxford. Two weeks later Governor Bilbo addressed a joint session and conceded that the university would not be relocated. He then entreated the lawmakers to build a Greater University at Oxford and asked for a special appropriation of five million dollars for new buildings. He also urged the legislature to build hard-surfaced roads from various points in the state to Oxford to make Ole Miss more accessible.[12]

Bilbo's entreaties went unheeded, and the legislature appropriated only $1,500,000. The governor was irked by that paltry appropriation, but he was more upset with the board of trustees and Chancellor Hume for not asking for more. In 1927 Chancellor Hume had asked for $165,000 for capital improvements and, in spite of the dire needs of the university, he requested only $265,000 in 1928.[13]

As concerned as Governor Bilbo was about the university's physical condition, he was even more concerned about its academic programs that had come under heavy criticism in the past few years. In 1927 the Ole Miss law school lost its accreditation, and the university's medical school was placed on probation. Two years later the Southern Association of Colleges and Schools found that the university's general academic program did not meet several of its standards. The Southern Association singled out the faculty for special criticism and noted that a "large proportion" of the faculty had taken their degrees at the university. SACS did not rescind the university's accreditation but recommended that Chancellor Hume eliminate those deficiencies as soon as possible.[14]

That $1,500,000 appropriation that Bilbo secured in 1928 enabled Chancellor Hume to remedy some of the most glaring deficiencies and infused the university with new vigor. Chancellor Hume reported that a "transformation is being wrought." Hoping to capitalize on the expansive spirit of that transformation, a department chairman went to Chancellor Hume with a request to buy "the back issues of an important professional journal" at a cost of $125. According to procedures then in place all library purchases were personally approved by the Chancellor. In spite of the fact that part of the special appropriation was slated for library improvements, Chancellor Hume denied the professor's request. Chancellor Hume told the department chairman that he "found it difficult to persuade the students to read the textbook, much less outside reading assignments [and] saw no reason why $125 should be spent on old periodicals."[15]

When Chancellor Hume announced that the university would use some of the 1928 appropriation for the purchase of new steel library shelves, the *Mississippian* proclaimed, "Let's first get a library." W.A. Lomax, the student editor, ridiculed the library's holdings in philosophy, science and mathematics, most of which, he said, had either been "donated [or] bought at auctions." If a book "even hints at disturbing the established political, social, or religious questions of the day, it is not on the university library shelves" and that, Lomax asserted, should "not be the case in a great university, the alleged home of free thought."[16]

It was obvious to Governor Bilbo that Ole Miss was not a great university in 1928; it was not even a good university, and he was convinced that under Chancellor Hume it would not become one. Known fondly as "Little Allie," Chancellor Hume was perhaps the most popular and beloved chancellor in the institution's history. In 1930 he was sixty-four years old and had been at the university forty years. Hume was a devout Presbyterian, and when he assumed the office of chancellor in 1924 he announced the singular goal of his administration.

> *My greatest aspiration for the present administration is... not that we excel in scholarship and athletics. ... I am hoping that it may be truthfully said that it was characterized by the exalting of character, by putting the emphasis on things moral, by stressing religious and spiritual values.*[17]

Chancellor Hume's administrative policies were an extension of his personal faith, and he cloaked the university in a religious atmosphere. Students were not allowed to smoke, drink, dance, wear shorts on campus, or play tennis on Sunday and were required to attend daily chapel services. Ole Miss was often called, in jest, "Hume's Presbyterian University." Michael O'Shea's pointed criticism that Mississippi institutions of higher learning planned their "courses so as to develop character" was probably directed at the university.[18]

According to Hardy Poindexter Graham, Chancellor Hume also embraced "the university's traditional role" as the institution devoted primarily to the needs of the upper classes of Mississippi society. But Governor Bilbo was determined that the University of Mississippi would not remain a liberal arts academy or a provincial university hidden away in the hills of northeast Mississippi. He would transform the university if he could not relocate it.[19]

In June 1928 Bilbo announced his intention to replace Chancellor Hume if he could persuade the board of trustees to do so. The board rejected Governor Bilbo's recommendation, and Hume was reelected. Governor Bilbo was successful, however, in persuading the board that governed the

State Teachers College at Hattiesburg to dismiss Joseph Anderson Cook, the school's first and only president. President Cook had come under heavy fire from former students, alumni, and public school teachers who believed that his administrative philosophy was antiquated. He routinely locked the gates to the campus at twilight, and movement on and off the campus after dark was restricted. Many professional and business leaders in Mississippi's rapidly growing coastal region envisioned a much broader role and scope for the State Teachers College, and they were doubtful that Cook, who was then sixty-five years old, had either the vision or the vigor to develop its enormous potential. Governor Bilbo agreed with that assessment and recommended that the board replace him with a younger, more progressive administrator. The board initially refused to dismiss President Cook, but when Robert E. Lee Sutherland resigned from the board, his replacement voted not to renew President Cook's contract. Claude Bennett, the superintendent of Biloxi city schools, replaced President Cook in October 1928.[20]

Governor Bilbo in 1929 renewed his effort to remove Chancellor Hume, and he was more convinced than ever that Hume was "temperamentally unfit" to be chancellor of a modern, comprehensive state university. The incident that strengthened his resolve was Hume's dismissal of the editors of the college yearbook. Chancellor Hume decreed that some of the yearbook's poetry and puns were "libelous slurs at girlhood and womanhood," and he impounded the annual, expelled the editors, and established a board of control to censor future student publications.[21]

The expulsion was given extensive press coverage, and Hume came under heavy criticism for the arbitrary manner in which he handled the entire affair and was under intense pressure to reinstate the students. Eventually, Chancellor Hume did reinstate one of them but denied that he had done so under pressure from the board or anyone else. Chancellor Hume explained that his reinstatement of the student was an "act of free grace" and that he had meted out "mercy not justice" because the student had come to him as a "penitent child or sinner." Hume proclaimed that he would never compromise a principle because, in an obvious reference to Bilbo's characterization of him, he was "temperamentally unfit" for that sort of thing.[22]

In his 1929 report to the board of trustees, Chancellor Hume explained the expulsion of the two students and addressed the larger issue of freedom of thought at a university. In most cases, he conceded, faculty members should be given the right to express their opinions. "[But] occasionally freaks are found," he said, "who prove exceptions to the rule." Academic freedom may sometimes be academic nonsense, the Chancellor added, and offered two illustrations for which a college president or a board of trustees would be at liberty to dismiss a faculty member or otherwise restrict his right of expression. The first example was a professor who teaches that the world is flat and square. The other hypothetical case was a professor of history who might teach that secession was treason and that Robert E. Lee was a traitor. Hume said if an Ole Miss professor made such a claim, his chair of history should become "instantly vacant." And if the professor should claim that his academic freedom had been abridged, "The emphatic answer, coming quick and hot," would be, according to Chancellor Hume, "Sir, ... you may not trample under foot what we regard as sacred as long as you hold a position in our institution."[23]

As *ex officio* chairman of the board of trustees, Governor Bilbo received Chancellor Hume's report, but he was not swayed by it, and shortly before the 1929 summer board meeting he announced that he would again recommend that Chancellor Hume be replaced. The board again rejected Bilbo's recommendation and reelected Hume for another year. After this second setback, Fred Sullens, in an editorial entitled "Forget It, Theodore," advised Bilbo to give it up. Sullens warned him that Hume's removal would provoke "bitter resentment among hundreds of 'Ole Miss' graduates, many of them prominent in public life."

"It would mean," Sullens said, "that these men will... throw every possible obstacle in the path of your administration."[24]

But Governor Bilbo would not abandon his goal of restructuring the governance of higher education or his effort to remove Chancellor Hume. In his third annual message to the legislature on January 6, 1930, Bilbo repeated his recommendations for a central board of trustees and a commissioner of Higher Education. He also requested a one-million-dollar bond issue for capital construction at Ole Miss.

To those requests Bilbo added a rather startling addendum. Bilbo announced that he would recommend sweeping personnel changes, including faculty as well as presidents, at all of the state's institutions of higher learning. He had only two years left of his four-year term, and at that point he had achieved virtually none of his major goals.[25]

Governor Bilbo was determined to improve Mississippi's institutions of higher learning, and if necessary he would start at the top and work down. The Jackson Daily News reported the governor's annual message under the caption, "Bilbo promises Clean Sweep," and quoted the governor as saying that younger men were needed to lead the state's institutions of higher learning.[26]

Over the next few months the subject of age and length of service figured prominently in any discussion of the impending shakeup at the state institutions of higher learning. It was frequently noted by the press that President Buz M. Walker of Mississippi A&M was approaching seventy years of age and that he had been associated with the college in one capacity or another for nearly fifty years. Robert E. Lee Sutherland, a former member of the board of trustees who was under consideration for president of MSCW, refused to tell reporters his age. "If it is necessary to say anything about my age," he told them, "you might say that I would pass for 48, perhaps younger." Sutherland was fifty-two at the time of his appointment as president of MSCW.[27]

Age and energy were not the only considerations in Bilbo's determination to bring new leadership to the state institutions of higher education, especially in Chancellor Hume's case. Bilbo had stated publicly several times that Chancellor Hume's educational philosophy was outmoded and that he did not have the vision to transform Ole Miss into the Greater University of Mississippi that he believed was essential for the state's economic and social development. Not only did he favor the removal of Hume, Governor Bilbo also wanted to increase the chancellor's salary from $4,800 to $25,000, a whopping five-hundred-percent increase, which would enable the board of trustees to recruit an educator of national prominence.[28]

The board had rebuffed Bilbo in 1928 and 1929. In 1930, however, when he decided to extend his purge to the faculty, he would operate from a much stronger advantage. Because of several additional appointments, Bilbo controlled a majority of the central board of trustees that governed the university, Mississippi A&M, MSCW, and Alcorn A&M. He did not control the board that governed Delta State Teachers College, and his effort to replace President William Kethley was unsuccessful. He had already replaced the president of State Teachers College in Hattiesburg. Bilbo made no effort to replace Alcorn President Levi Rowen or reorganize the faculty.[29]

For several weeks before the June 1930 meeting of the central board of trustees, some MSCW alumni had lobbied for the appointment of Dean Nellie Keirn as president. She had been acting president since the death of President Fant in 1929. Dean Keirn "did not desire the presidency on a permanent basis" and advised the board that she preferred to remain as dean of the college. The alumni effort on behalf of Dean Keirn was linked to the broader effort to secure the appointment of a woman president. Even though MSCW was the first state-supported women's college in the country, it had never had a woman president. It was not until 1989, and after it had become coeducational, that Clyda Rent became MSCW's first woman president.[30]

The two candidates most seriously considered for the MSCW presidency were Claude Bennett, president of State Teachers College, and R.E.L. Sutherland, the former president of Hinds Junior College and a former member of the central college board. After Bennett announced that he intended to stay at State Teachers College, the board of trustees elected Sutherland president of MSCW in 1930.[31]

Speculation over who would be appointed president of Mississippi A&M obscured the circumstances under which President Buz M. Walker was vacating that position. Walker was known as a Bilbo partisan and had helped raise funds for Bilbo's 1927 campaign. Because of Walker's alliance with Bilbo, the *Clarion-Ledger* assumed that Walker's position was safe and predicted that he would be reappointed. The assumption that President

Walker would be reappointed because he was a Bilbo supporter is a telling point, and his subsequent removal is evidence that Bilbo's determination to reform higher education was not an effort to punish his enemies or a political maneuver to reward his friends.[32]

President Walker had been the subject of widening criticism for several months before the June board meeting, and he was personally blamed by some alumni for the lack of growth at Mississippi A&M. Anticipating the worst, President Walker secured a position in North Carolina and announced his intention to leave Mississippi A&M at the end of his current contract in June. However, on the day of the board meeting a group of A&M alumni met with the board and informed them that they had persuaded President Walker to reconsider, that he had done so, and that he wished to remain as president. That eleventh-hour maneuver was not successful because Bilbo and the board of trustees had already decided not to reelect President Walker.[33]

There had been some speculation that Alfred Butts, a popular professor of education at the Agricultural College, might be elected president of either Mississippi A&M or Ole Miss. That possibility prompted some backroom maneuvering by Ole Miss alumni. They wanted to get Butts elected to the A&M position because they did not believe Bilbo had enough votes to dismiss Chancellor Hume and reinstate Joseph Powers. Their strategy was simple. Getting the A&M presidency for Butts would save Chancellor Hume. The Ole Miss faction was frustrated, however, because Butts was so complacent about either position that he was eventually eliminated from both. His elimination guaranteed that Hugh Critz would get the A&M presidency.[34]

Critz's appointment at A&M sealed the fate of Chancellor Hume. At the June board meeting A.B. Schauber, a member of the board of trustees when Chancellor Powers was fired in 1924, nominated the former chancellor. Paul Bowdre, a Bilbo appointee, nominated Alfred Hume. Powers was elected by a vote of 6 to 4.[35]

It is probable that the shake-up of the college presidents would have provoked no more than the customary gust of outrage, which would have soon faded. However, at the June meeting, and a later meeting on July 5, the board of trustees reorganized the faculty and staff at MSCW, Mississippi A&M, and the university. At Mississippi State College for Women ten faculty members out of a total of fifty-three were dismissed, and at least four staff members were not retained.[36]

At Mississippi A&M, in addition to President Walker, the director of extension, and the director of experiment stations were also replaced. The athletic director was relieved of his duties but retained as "professor unassigned, outside of athletics, at the same salary." It is difficult to determine how many support personnel were fired or reassigned; there were slightly more than one hundred changes. That figure includes some home demonstration agents, county agents, experiment station workers, and clerical personnel and does not include faculty members. The best estimate of the number of faculty who were relieved or reassigned is twenty, certainly no more than twenty-five, out of a total of ninety-one. Exact figures are difficult to determine.[37]

The purge at the University of Mississippi has been researched by Hardy Poindexter Graham, who found that it involved a relatively small number of professors and staff. The board minutes also contain much more information about the changes at Ole Miss than it does about the changes at A&M and MSCW. On the same day that Joseph Powers was elected chancellor, Julius Zeller was elected vice chancellor. Zeller was a state senator at the time of his appointment, and he listed farming as his occupation in the biographical section of the senate journal. The appointment of Senator Zeller is often cited as evidence that Governor Bilbo put hacks in high places because they were his friends and that he took no accounting of their qualifications. Senator Zeller is the worst possible example. He had several college degrees, two from the University of Chicago, and a doctor of civil law from Illinois Wesleyan University. He had also served as president of the University of Puget Sound. In 1930 the *Jackson Daily News* wrote that "there is not an abler member in either branch of the lawmaking body than Senator Zeller. He is both a scholar and a statesman." For several years Zeller had been anti-Bilbo, but after failing to relocate the university, they joined in a common cause to enlarge and upgrade Ole Miss.[38]

Two weeks after Zeller's appointment, Chancellor Powers presented his faculty nominations to the board of trustees. The board declined to re-elect eighteen faculty members. The minutes of that meeting list the age and credentials of those eighteen faculty members, and in most cases include the credentials of their replacements. In every case they were replaced by a professor with bona fide academic credentials equal to or superior to the individual being replaced. In most cases the credentials of the new faculty members were superior. A good example is the dean of the graduate school. The graduate dean, who had been at the university for thirty-seven years, did not have a Ph.D. Governor Bilbo insisted that the dean of the graduate school be replaced by a younger man with a doctorate. The new graduate dean was Nathaniel Bond, who held a Ph.D. from Tulane University.[39]

Most of the Ole Miss professors who were dismissed were in their late sixties or early seventies. Governor Bilbo recommended that faculty members in their mid-sixties who were not retained be given emeritus status with some compensation. But the legislature did not appropriate the necessary funds. Only a few of the faculty who were dismissed held graduate degrees, and several of them had only a bachelor's degree, which they had taken at the University of Mississippi. The unusually "large proportion" of faculty holding degrees from the University of Mississippi had been noted by the Southern Association of Colleges in 1929 and had brought an admonition to upgrade the university's faculty. Although most departments were affected by the purge, Bilbo and the board did not disturb the history department, which was chaired by Professor Charles Sydnor, who held a Ph.D. and later enjoyed a distinguished career at Duke University.[40]

At least thirteen clerical and staff personnel were also replaced in addition to eighteen faculty members. One of those was the director of buildings and grounds. When he was informed of his dismissal he fired off a letter to Governor Bilbo demanding an explanation: "Everyone in Lafayette County knows that I have championed your cause from your entry into Mississippi politics until the present time. So come clean. ... I want to know why." Several days later Governor Bilbo replied: "The chief cause of complaint seems to be that you were lazy or in other words, not as alert on the job as you might have been."[41]

One of the first and fiercest condemnations of the purge came from Bilbo's old nemesis, Fred Sullens, who predicted that political intrusion into higher education would continue "until some clever brain devises a plan to remove our colleges wholly beyond the realm of political influence." He took no notice that Governor Bilbo had recently recommended such a plan to the state legislature.[42]

John Hudson, a free-lance writer, described the purge in a 1930 article, "The Spoils System Enters College," in *The New Republic*. Hudson reported that Bilbo had fired 50 professors at Ole Miss, 129 at other colleges and that 233 more were in jeopardy. Hudson's estimate of faculty members who were fired or in jeopardy totaled 412, when, in fact, there were only about 300 faculty members in the entire college system. According to Hardy Poindexter Graham, Hudson's article was an "extreme example of distortion and falsification."[43]

The best estimate of the Bilbo purge includes three college presidents, eighteen faculty members at the university, ten at MSCW, and approximately twenty or twenty-five at Mississippi A&M. The number of staff and support personnel who were fired was no more than one hundred twenty-five. The reaction to the purge was swift, severe, and subject to the most partisan interpretation. Lucie Robertson Bridgforth, in her 1984 history of the University of Mississippi School of Medicine, was among the earliest historians to offer a fair and balanced assessment of the Bilbo purge. "In retrospect," she wrote, "there is little doubt that the university benefitted from the Bilbo changes in terms of personnel. There is also little doubt that Bilbo's intentions were honorable, for he clearly was determined to build a great university which would serve the state and all its people, not just the privileged sons of the upper classes." Bridgforth also explains the complicated situation involving Joseph Crider, the dean of the medical school, who was fired but rehired, and then resigned. Historian Chester Morgan, in his biography of Governor Bilbo, also provides a more accurate appraisal of the Bilbo purge and an explanation of how it has lingered as an historical inaccuracy for more than eighty years. "While some of the changes were patently political," Morgan explains, "there is ample evidence that the overall design was a sincere effort to improve higher education. ... Although the extent of the dismissals, which included several Bilbo supporters, was greatly exaggerated, and that most of the replacements bore impeccable academic credentials, the almost universal enmity in the Mississippi press turned the whole affair into just another Bilbo scandal."[44]

Criticism from the opposition press was hardly more than a nuisance. But the loss of accreditation by educational associations was a repudiation of Bilbo's determination to modernize Mississippi's institutions of higher learning. The most serious damage to state institutions was the loss of accreditation by the Southern Association of Colleges and Schools. The Ole Miss law school was also expelled from the American Association of Law Schools, and the medical school was placed on probation. But one medical association wrote to Chancellor Powers that "great good will no doubt come out of the whole mess. ... Maybe the new dean can and will do what is needed... to build up the school." Two professional associations that conducted on-site investigations did not censure the university. The American Pharmaceutical Association commended the new dean and allowed the school of pharmacy to retain its "A" rating. President Emeritus W.O. Thompson of The Ohio State University and the chairman of the American Association of State Universities' committee that investigated the Bilbo purge, stated that John Hudson's New Republic article included many exaggerations and distortions. On the basis of Thompson's report, the Association of State Universities declined to censure the University of Mississippi and expressed its disagreement with the accrediting agencies that had done so.[45]

Some members of the board of trustees believed that the Southern Association's action was punitive and not entirely free of political taint. Whatever may have been the motive that caused SACS to suspend Mississippi's institutions of higher learning, Fred Sullens did not like it. Sullens wrote that the suspension was "cruel, wanton, brutal, unnecessary, and devoid of any semblance of constructive thought." Many Mississippians shared Sullens's anger at both the Southern Association and Governor Bilbo. And some saw it as an opportunity to "devise a plan to remove our colleges wholly beyond the realm of political influence," and they would cite the Bilbo purge as proof that some dramatic reforms were necessary.[46]

Theodore Bilbo might have been "Governor Inglorious" as Wigfall Green called him, or "a slick little bastard" as William Alexander Percy described him. But for all the bad he did, he did some good, and he tried to do right, so the evidence suggests, in restructuring Mississippi's system of higher education. That is not to say that Bilbo was not guilty of wreaking revenge upon some of his enemies in higher education. It is to say that Bilbo tried to do what needed to be done. The Brookings Institution conducted a study of higher education in Mississippi a year after the Bilbo purge and repeated with only slight modifications most of Bilbo's recommendations. As the Brookings study was being conducted, Mississippi was in the process of choosing a successor to Governor Bilbo, and its institutions of higher learning were again a prominent issue in the campaign.[47]

Endnotes

1   *Jackson Daily News*, May 27, 1927; *Clarion-Ledger*, August 19, 1927. For general information and analysis of the Bilbo Purge at Mississippi institutions of higher learning, see Allen Cabaniss, *The University of Mississippi* (1971); David G. Sansing, *Making Haste Slowly: The Troubled History of Higher Education in Mississippi* (1990); *The University of Mississippi, A Sesquicentennial History* (1999), and *A Troubled History: The Governance of Higher Education in Mississippi* (2016); John K. Bettersworth, *The Peoples University, The Centennial History of Mississippi State* (1980); Michael Ballard, *Maroon and White: Mississippi State University, 1878-2003* (2008); Chester M. Morgan, *Redneck Liberal: Theodore G, Bilbo and the New Deal* (1985) and *Dearly Bought, Deeply Treasured: The University of Southern Mississippi, 1912-1987* (1987); Bridget Smith Pieschel and Stephen Pieschel, *Loyal Daughters: One Hundred Years at Mississippi University for Women* ((1984); Lelia Rhodes, *Jackson State University: The First 100 Years* (1978); Josephine McCann Posey, P*ushing Forward: A History of Alcorn University in its Second Century* (2017); Lucie Robertson Bridgforth, *Medical Education in Mississippi: A History of the School of Medicine* (1984); Jack Gunn and Gladys Castle, *A Pictorial History of Delta State University* (1980).

2   Interview with Robert Farley May 15, 1979, at Oxford; Hardy Poindexter Graham, "Bilbo and the University of Mississippi, 1928-1932," (M.A. thesis, University of Mississippi, 1965), 14.

3   Thomas Turner Interview Oral History Collection, University of Southern Mississippi, Hattiesburg, Mississippi.

4   See T. Harry Williams, *Huey Long* (1969), Chapter 18, "I've Got a University," 491-526; for a study on the social and economic role of the American state university see Norman Foerster, *The American State University, Its Relation to Democracy* (1937).

5   Graham, "Bilbo," 5, 12; on Bilbo's determination to restructure higher education and move the University of Mississippi to Jackson, see Larry T. Balsamo, "Theodore G. Bilbo and Mississippi Politics, 1877-1932" (PhD diss., University of Missouri, 1967) and Sansing, *University of Mississippi*, Chapter 9, "Bilbo and the Greater University," 215-247.

6   Cabaniss, University of Mississippi, 142; see also Charles Reagan Wilson, *Baptized in Blood: The Religion of the Lost Cause, 1865-1920* (1980).

7   Balsamo, "Bilbo," 163, 166; *Clarion-Ledger*, January 18, 1928.

8   McArthur, *Inaugural Addresses, 1890-1980*, 134-187; on the Greater University of Mississippi see 146-147 and on restructuring higher education see 152-153.

9   *Jackson Daily News*, January 19, 1928; see also Wigfall Green, *The Man Bilbo*, (1963) and Chester M. Morgan, *Redneck Liberal*, 10; *Clarion-Ledger*, January 19, 20, 1928.

10   *Clarion-Ledger*, January 19, 20, 1928.

11   Cabaniss, *University of Mississippi*, 141-142; for a text of this and other speeches by Chancellor Hume, see Myra Hume Jones, "Tenets and Attitudes of an Old-Time Teacher," (M.A. thesis, University of Mississippi, 1949); for additional arguments against moving the university, see Friends of the University, *Some Facts Against Removal of the University of Mississippi* (n.d.).

12   *Oxford Eagle*, February 23, 1928, March 8, 1928; *Jackson Daily News*, February 15, 1928, March 7, 1928, September 18, 1928.

13   *Mississippian*, January 13, 1928.

14   Graham, "Bilbo," 3.

15   See Richard Aubrey McLemore, "Higher Education in the Twentieth Century," McLemore [ed.], *History of Mississippi* (Chapter 39, vol 2, 415-445); Graham, "Bilbo," 37-38.

16   *Mississippian,* April 6, 1928.

17   Cabaniss, *University of Mississippi,* 135. 141-143; Graham, "Bilbo," 32, 36.

18   Graham, "Bilbo," 32-33. 36-37.

19   William D. McCain interview at Hattiesburg, Mississippi on January 30, 1979; Graham, "Bilbo," 32-33; Francis Egger Watson, "Dr. Alfred Hume: His Leadership as Vice Chancellor, Acting Chancellor, and Chancellor of the University of Mississippi (1905-1945)," (PhD diss., University of Mississippi, 1987), 71-73.

20   Balsamo, "Bilbo," 210; *Hattiesburg American,* June 20, July 1, 1928; New Orleans *Times Picayune,* May 31, 1928; *Jackson Daily News,* June 12, 1930; *Commercial Appeal,* June 2, 1930; *Jackson Daily News,* March 6, 1940; Willard F. Bond, *I Had a Friend* (1958), 80-81; Alma Hickman, *Southern As I Saw It: Personal Remembrances of an Era, 1912 to 1954* (1966), 73, 84; Morgan, *Dearly Bought, Deeply Treasured,* 45-52.

21   *Mississippian,* April, 27, September 28, 1929; Board of Trustees, *Biennial Report 1927-1929,* 14-21.

22   Graham, "Bilbo," 13-15; *Mississippian,* September 28, 1929; Sansing, *University of Mississippi,* 226-233.

23   University of Mississippi Board of Trustees, *Biennial Report 1927-1929,* 14, 17.

24   *Jackson Daily News,* June 20, 1929.

25   *Senate Journal 1930,* 8-9.

26   *Jackson Daily News,* January 7, 1930; *Clarion-Ledger,* June 14, 1930.

27   Bettersworth, People's College, 280; Balsamo, "Bilbo," 208; *Clarion-Ledger,* June 11, 14, July 6, 1930; *Jackson Daily News,* June 12, 1930; *Clarion-Ledger,* July 6, 1930; *Jackson Daily News,* June 15, 1930; *Commercial Appeal,* August 5, 1930.

28   Graham, "Bilbo," 15.

29   Bond, *I Had a Friend,* 141; *Clarion-Ledger,* June 12, 1930; Gunn and Castle, *A Pictorial History of Delta State,* 27.

30   *Jackson Daily News,* June 11,15, 1930; *Clarion-Ledger,* June 12, 15, 1930; Pieschel and Pieschel, *Loyal Daughters,* 88-90.

31   *Jackson Daily News,* June 11, 1930; *Board of Trustees Minutes,* June 13, 1930.

32   *Clarion-Ledger,* June 5, 11, 1930; *Board of Trustees Minutes,* June 13, 1930.

33   *Clarion-Ledger,* June 5, 11, 1930.

34   Ibid; *Jackson Daily News,* June 12, 1930.

35   *Board of Trustees Minutes,* June 13, 1930; *Clarion-Ledger,* June 14, 1930.

36   *Board of Trustees Minutes,* June 13, July 5, 1930; *Clarion-Ledger,* June 28, July 6, 1930; *Jackson Daily News* June 16, 1930; Pieschel and Pieschel, *Loyal Daughters,* 90-91.

37   *Board of Trustees Minutes,* June 13, July 5, 1930, *Clarion-Ledger,* June 12, 28, July 3, 6, 1930; Ballard, *Maroon and White,* 44-46.

38   *Board of Trustees Minutes,* June 13, 1930; Graham, "Bilbo," 40; *Jackson Daily News,* June 13, 1930; for a biographical sketch of Senator Zeller, see *Official and Statistical Register of the State of Mississippi, 1920-1924,* 135-140.

39   For a comparison of the credentials of the faculty dismissed and those who replaced them, see Graham, "Bilbo," 44-64.

40   Ibid.

41   These letters were in a folder marked "Higher Education" in the Theodore G.

Bilbo Papers, William D. McCain Library, University of Southern Mississippi, Hattiesburg, Mississippi.

42   *Jackson Daily News*, June 15, 1930

43   John Hudson, "The Spoils System Enters College," *The New Republic* LXIV, (September 17, 1930), 123-124; see also Clarence Cason, "The Mississippi Imbroglio," *Virginia Quarterly Review* (April, 1931), 229-240; *Mississippi Educational Advance* (October 1930), 9 and also (November 1930), 41; Bettersworth, *People's College*, 208, relied on Hudson's figures and included this statement, "Before the 'terror' ended 112 members of the faculty at A&M had been dismissed and the positions of 233 others were in jeopardy;" Allen Cabaniss, *University of Mississippi*, was more careful in describing the purge, but he did not challenge Hudson's figures.

44   Bridgforth, *Medical Education in Mississippi*, 74; for a more recent history of the Medical School, see Janis Quinn, *Promises Kept, The University of Mississippi Medical School* (2005); and for an interesting reminiscence of the medical school, see Robert D. Currier and Maurine Twiss, *Pressure From All Sides, The University of Mississippi Medical Center in the 60s* (2006); Morgan, *Redneck Liberal*, 45-46; see also Sansing, *University of Mississippi*, Chapter 9 "Bilbo and the Greater University, 1927-1935," 215-246.

45   Graham, "Bilbo," 78-79, 80-85, 91-94, 95-98, 98-99; see *Proceedings of the Thirty-fifth Annual Meeting of the Association of Colleges and Secondary Schools of the Southern States, Atlanta Georgia December 4-5*, 1930, 35-36.

46   *Jackson Daily News*, December 7, 1930

47   Green, Bilbo, 72; William Alexander Percy, *Lanterns on the Levee, Recollections of a Planter's Son* (1941), 148.

19

THE MEREDITH CRISIS, 1962-1963

Chapter 8 in
A Troubled History: The Governance of Higher Education in Mississippi

> *I returned to my home state to replace the old*
> *unsuitable customs with more desirable ones.*
>
> James Meredith

The admission of James Howard Meredith to the University of Mississippi was a crucial event in the Civil Rights Movement and a turning point in the history of Mississippi. In the summer of 1962 Chancellor John D. Williams asked the alumni to help him protect freedom of speech at Ole Miss; in the fall he would be as asking them to help him save the university.[1]

Meredith's application triggered a mechanism that had been in place since 1954. A copy of his application and other correspondence was sent to the executive secretary of the board of trustees, and six copies were sent to the state attorney general. The number of copies sent to the attorney general was later reduced because university officials were concerned that some

James Meredith at graduation

copies might fall into the wrong hands.[2]

Mississippi's white power structure, in consort with the board of trustees, employed a strategy of delay in the hope of dissuading Meredith from his bid to break the color barrier in Mississippi. Their strategy was based in part on their experience with Charles Dubra, Medgar Evers, and Clennon King, but mainly on their hope that Meredith might just go away if they did not let him in. Dubra, Evers, and King had attempted to integrate the University of Mississippi but did not pursue the matter through the court system. Before he filed his application, Meredith wrote the NAACP Legal Defense Fund requesting legal assistance in the event a costly court case would be necessary to gain admission. After receiving Meredith's application, the registrar informed him that the deadline for applications had expired and advised him not to appear for registration.[3]

After that initial rejection Meredith informed the justice department of his application to the University of Mississippi. His letter recalled the anguish that he and "his people" had experienced in a Closed Society:

> *Whenever I attempt to reason logically about this matter, it grieves me keenly to realize that a... citizen of a free democratic nation has to clamor with such procedures... to gain just a small amount of his civil and human rights.*[4]

James Meredith was seeking the rights that Hodding Carter, in a 1948 commencement address, had told Alcorn University graduates were "the least that they deserve."

Until Meredith received the letter of rejection, he had maintained a low profile, and university authorities and state officials maintained strict secrecy. But after his official rejection James Meredith filed a class-action law suit on May 31, 1961, in the federal district court. His NAACP attorney, Mrs. Constance Baker Motley, had wanted to appeal directly to the college board. Meredith preferred a suit because he believed the courts would decide the issue swiftly and painlessly.

In a court hearing Federal District Judge Sidney Mize ruled that university officials "gave no consideration whatsoever to the race or the color of the plaintiff." Judge Mize further ruled that the admission policies adopted by the board of trustees, even those enacted after Meredith filed his application, were not designed "in any attempt direct or indirect, to discriminate against anyone solely on the grounds of race and color." Judge Mize concluded: "The testimony shows, and I find as a fact, that there was no discrimination against any student... solely because of his race or color."[5]

Meredith appealed Judge Mize's ruling to the Fifth Circuit Court of Appeals in New Orleans. Circuit Judge John Minor Wisdom was baffled by the hearing in the district court that he said had been "tried below and argued in the eerie atmosphere of never-never land." The court of appeals ordered a trial on Meredith's request for a permanent injunction.[6]

After a sometimes bizarre trial, Judge Sidney Mize ruled on February 5, 1962, that Meredith was not denied admission because of his race.[7]

Meredith appealed Judge Mize's ruling, and on June 25, the fifth circuit reversed the district court and directed Judge Mize to order Meredith's admission. "In every other state but Mississippi that would have solved the matter," according to Ole Miss Professor Russell Barrett. "Instead," he wrote, "it soon became clear that he had reached but one more detour of the many that remained."[8]

As incredulous as Judge Mize's initial ruling was, the board of trustees adopted a policy that was even more incredulous. The trustees divested the university of its authority over "the application of James Howard Meredith" and vested that authority "exclusively unto this Board of Trustees of Institutions of Higher Learning." A week later, on September 10, 1962, United States Supreme Court Justice Hugo Black ordered the admission of James Meredith, and on September 13 Judge Mize directed the University of Mississippi to admit Meredith.[9]

On the evening of Judge Mize's order to admit Meredith, Governor Ross Barnett addressed the people of Mississippi on a statewide television network. He said that Mississippi had only one of two choices:

We must either submit to the unlawful dictates of the federal gov-

ernment or stand like men and tell them NEVER!

Governor Barnett pledged to go to jail if necessary and called upon all other public officials to make a similar commitment, and he promised that no school would be integrated as long as he was governor. Under a 1954 amendment to the Mississippi Constitution, Governor Barnett had the authority to close any or all of the state's public schools to prevent integration, and his oblique reference to that authority startled many Ole Miss alumni, who feared that Barnett's counselors might actually persuade him to close Ole Miss. Within a few days after Barnett's speech, Ole Miss alumni organized a secret committee with the singular purpose of keeping the university open, even if it meant admitting Meredith.[10]

The day after Governor Barnett's televised address, the board of trustees held a called meeting in Jackson. The discombobulation of the board began at that three-hour "stormy" session on Friday, September 14. During the weekend, while board members were anxiously awaiting an explanation of his strategy to prevent Meredith's admission, Governor Barnett began a series of telephone conversations with President John Kennedy, Attorney General Robert Kennedy, and other officials at the justice department.[11]

Bill Minor's memoir, *Eyes on Mississippi, A Fifty-Year Chronicle of Change*, which includes his articles that were published in the New Orleans *Times Picayune* from September 16, 1962, to May 19, 1963, provides a fascinating contemporary account of the Meredith crisis.

On Monday, September 17, board members returned to Jackson for a closed meeting with Governor Barnett, who discussed the options in their legal battle with James Meredith. Governor Barnett mentioned two possibilities that shocked the board members. First, he raised the possibility of closing the university. Then, he asked the board if they would be willing to accept contempt citations and go to jail. After Governor Barnett left the meeting, the trustees held a lively discussion.[12]

After that stormy meeting a reporter asked several trustees if the university would be closed. The board president explained that the trustees did not have the authority to do so, but the governor did. The intimation that the university might be closed, subtle though it was, sounded an alarm. The Ole

Miss alumni realized that the university was in jeopardy and that some, even in high places, would sacrifice the University of Mississippi in the cause of white supremacy and segregation. Although board members had agreed not to make any public statements, Verner Holmes thought that "was a great mistake" and decided that "somebody from the board should say something." As Holmes was leaving the September 17 meeting a reporter asked him if he was willing to go to jail. Holmes, an Ole Miss alumnus and vice president of the board, declared: "I am not willing to go to jail [and] I will not vote to close the university."[13]

As tension and speculation mounted, and as the date of Meredith's registration neared, a Hinds County justice of the peace issued an injunction setting aside the United States Supreme Court order to admit James Meredith to the University of Mississippi.

Editor Ira Harkey wrote, *In a madhouse's din, Mississippi waits. God help Mississippi.* Ira Harkey was the Pulitzer Prize-winning editor of the *Pascagoula Chronicle* and one of the few editors who opposed Governor Barnett's policy of defiance.[14]

While Mississippi was waiting for some final dispensation, the board of trustees met in a midnight secret session to give Governor Barnett one last chance to convince them that he had a legal way "to keep him out." Verner Holmes remembered that five-hour meeting at the medical center "as the worst experience of the whole thing." After hours of a rambling discussion, a frustrated trustee shouted to the governor: "We've got to know what is the legal way to keep him out; that's all we want to know." The governor's exasperated reply shocked his supporters and confirmed the worst suspicions of his detractors: "The only way I know to keep him out is just don't let him in." When it became apparent that Governor Barnett actually had no plan, no way of keeping Meredith out of Ole Miss, tempers began to flare, and angry words and threats were exchanged.

During that frantic session the board found an alternative to compliance or contempt. On September 4, the board had assumed the authority to act on the application of James Meredith to shield Chancellor Williams and other university officials. If the board had the power to divest the University of Mississippi of its authority to register James Meredith, the board had the power, they reasoned, to confer that authority upon the governor of Mississippi. At that midnight meeting at the medical center, the board designated Governor Barnett registrar of the University of Mississippi. That stratagem had been considered among Barnett's advisers and was brought before the board when a trustee blurted out to Governor Barnett in frustration, "We'll let you do it. We'll let you reject him." That desperate strategy was soon implemented.[15]

On Thursday afternoon, September 20, 1962, James Meredith and a small escort of federal officials arrived on the Ole Miss campus and were led through a noisy but not unruly crowd of students to a small auditorium where Governor Barnett and Registrar Robert Ellis were seated at a table. Following an exchange of friendly greetings, according to folklore, Governor Barnett asked, "Which of you gentlemen is Mr. Meredith?" Meredith identified himself, and Governor Barnett then read a Declaration of Interposition, which he said allowed him to interpose himself as governor between an unlawful dictate of the federal government and the execution of that dictate in the sovereign state of Mississippi. Then, on the basis of the authority vested in him by the board of trustees as registrar of the University of Mississippi, Governor Barnett denied James Meredith admission to the University of Mississippi. Following another brief but polite exchange, Meredith and his escort left the campus and returned to Memphis.[16]

Because James Meredith had now been officially denied admission, a three-judge federal panel in Hattiesburg issued a contempt citation against the board of trustees and ordered the board to appear in New Orleans on September 24 to show cause why they should not be held in contempt. University officials were also ordered to appear with the board in New Orleans.[17]

The news that the board had been cited for contempt raised the anxiety level among Governor Barnett's counselors. Some of them had already advised the governor to vacate the existing board and appoint a more stalwart group. On Saturday, the day after the board had been ordered to New Orleans, Governor Barnett huddled with his advisors at the governor's mansion for a strategy session. "It was the day of the Mississippi State-LSU game," is how one board member remembered the day of that meeting. The meeting was attended by fifteen or twenty of Barnett's advisors, including the executive secretary of the Citizens' Council. There was no focus to the meeting, and a wide ranging, free-wheeling review of circumstances and possible options were discussed. The only agreement among the various constituencies represented at the meeting was that compliance or capitulation were "unthinkable."[18]

On Sunday afternoon, the day after that strategy session in the Governor's Mansion, a different kind of meeting was held in Jackson. William Mounger, president of Lamar Life Insurance Company; Baxter Wilson, an executive in the Mississippi Power and Light Company; Tom Hederman, publisher of *Jackson Daily News-The Clarion-Ledger*; and Calvin Wells, chief counsel for Lamar Life, met in Wilson's office to discuss the general state of affairs. They were convinced that Mississippi's business leadership should do something, and they agreed to talk with their colleagues and get back together as soon as possible.[19]

In federal court in New Orleans on Monday morning September 24, Board President Thomas Tubb informed the court that the board of trustees would register Meredith at two o'clock the next day in Jackson. The board was polled in the courtroom, and each member present voted yes. The one absent member was polled by telephone, and he also agreed.[20]

Realizing that the board's decision would excite the public, William Mounger and Calvin Wells directed the management of WLBT and WJDX, which were owned by Lamar Life, to "tone down" their editorials. At a meeting at the medical center Monday night, Mounger, Wilson, and Wells were joined by Ed Brunini, Bob Herrin, Joe Latham, and one or two other Jackson businessmen. They all agreed that the college board had no other choice. But they were concerned about the repercussions and agreed to call other businessmen across the state and invite them to a private meeting in Jackson to discuss the crisis, which they feared could lead to massive violence. They also agreed to meet again the next night.[21]

On Monday night, September 24, Attorney General Robert Kennedy called Governor Barnett to arrange for Meredith's registration the next day.

Governor Barnett was so upset by the board's decision that he could not carry on a coherent conversation with Kennedy and frequently interrupted their talk to confer with his advisors. The governor finally ended the conversation: "I am in a big hurry here now. I appreciate your calling. I will let you know tomorrow whether or not I can advise you of our proceeding and," Attorney General Kennedy interrupted, "And work out his protection?" Barnett answered, "I will let you know what our proceedings will be."[22]

The next morning, as board members were returning to Jackson from their New Orleans court appearance, a large crowd gathered at the Woolfolk building, and Governor Barnett and his emissaries occupied the board office. When President Tubb learned that the board office had been commandeered, he instructed Executive Secretary Jobe to tell the board members to meet him in the restaurant at the Sun-N-Sand, a motel across the street from the Woolfolk building. Back on Mississippi soil, under threat of imprisonment, meeting in a motel coffee shop, and with two members absent, the board of trustees reaffirmed its unanimous vote to admit James Meredith to the University of Mississippi.[23]

When Executive Secretary Jobe got to his office he found Governor Barnett sitting at his desk, talking on the telephone to Robert Kennedy, who had just informed the governor that Meredith was on his way to the Woolfolk building to register. When Chief United States Marshal James McShane and James Meredith arrived at the Woolfolk building they were led through a milling crowd of two thousand to the boardroom. A Barnett aide rapped sharply on the closed door; the governor appeared and again asked, this time for the television cameras, "Which of you gentlemen is Mr. Meredith?" After Meredith identified himself, the governor again read a proclamation denying him admission to the university and added that he did so politely. The federal officials, mocking the governor, agreed to leave politely. As they walked down the corridor, Governor Barnett called out, in a practiced afterword, "You'll come see me at the Mansion." He turned back into the crowded boardroom amid cheers and Rebel yells.[24]

James Howard Meredith is a remarkable man. He marches to the beat of a different drummer; he recognized history when he saw it, and he made history. As Meredith and his federal escort were leaving the Woolfolk build-ing, their car stopped at a traffic light, and he saw history happening on a street corner, as he recalled in his memoirs:

> *Just as the light was about to change, Marshal McShane asked me if those were some of my friends, indicating a group of six or seven Ne-groes standing on the corner. I waved at them as we pulled away... they were all common folk, my people, maids still in uniform and common laborers, but... the pride they displayed [was] overwhelming. This is what I was fighting for, and I had my reward in the brief seconds that I saw my unknown friends on that corner.[25]*

Early the next morning in search of some final resolution, Assistant Attorney General Burke Marshall called Tom Watkins, one of Governor Barnett's most trusted advisors. Watkins suggested that on the next effort to escort Meredith onto the campus to be registered, federal officials should "gently" push the governor aside, but they should use "the mildest kind of force." Watkins explained that this would make the governor's point and give him an out because the federal government would have forcibly brought about desegregation. That pantomime was put to a quick test.

When Meredith and his escort arrived at the campus on Wednesday morning, September 26, they were blocked by Lieutenant Governor Paul Johnson and several highway patrolmen. When John Doar of the justice department and Marshal McShane attempted to "gently" push their way through, Lieutenant Governor Johnson jostled with McShane and Doar. After a few minutes McShane doubled up his fist, shook it in the face of Lieutenant Governor Johnson and said, or perhaps he was asking, "You un-derstand that we have got to break through." Apparently, Johnson did not understand or was not let in on the deal or, more likely, he did not want to be remembered as the "one who stepped aside." When all the fist-shaking and shoving were over, Doar, McShane, and Meredith left Oxford and re-turned to Memphis.

And the telephones started ringing. When Burke Marshall called Tom

Watkins and asked him what went wrong, Watkins told him that he "had not used enough force." How much force is enough force, Marshall asked? Watkins suggested that the next escort should include "twenty-five marshals with side arms." Marshall agreed to bring Meredith back to the campus the next day, Thursday, September 27, with an escort of twenty-five armed marshals "if it were clearly understood that the resistance to this amount of force would be token." Watkins said he would talk to the governor and get back with him.[26]

Over the next several hours a bizarre haggle ensued. It was first agreed that the lead marshal would draw his gun, but Governor Barnett later decided that was not enough show of force. It was then agreed that the lead marshal would draw his gun, and that the other marshals would slap their holsters as if ready to draw. That was acceptable, at first, but Governor Barnett began to have second thoughts, and he told the attorney general:

> *General, I was under the impression that they were all going to draw their guns. This could be very embarrassing. We got a big crowd here, and if one pulls his gun and we all turn, it would be very embarrassing. Isn't it possible to have them all pull their guns?*[27]

As this haggling continued, Robert Kennedy pressed the governor for a guarantee that he would keep the peace and protect Meredith and the marshals. When Barnett wavered, Kennedy called the whole deal off and directed McShane and Doar not to take Meredith to the campus Thursday afternoon.[28]

After this impasse developed, President Kennedy decided to call Governor Barnett on Saturday morning to join the search for a peaceful resolution of the Meredith crisis. The affable young president from Massachusetts and the wily old governor from Mississippi had a pleasant talk. President Kennedy advised the governor that he would use all the resources of his office to carry out the court order. The governor explained to the president that his aide, Tom Watkins, was at that very moment trying to work out a plan to resolve the situation.[29]

Within less than an hour the President and the governor were back on the telephone. The President called Barnett back to discuss a proposal Tom Watkins had just made to the attorney general. President Kennedy put Robert Kennedy on the line to explain the plan. Watkins had suggested a "hidden ball trick." The plan was for federal authorities to announce that Meredith would go to the campus on Monday, October 1. On the basis of that information, Governor Barnett and Lieutenant Governor Johnson would both be at Oxford to block his admission. In the meantime, Meredith would actually go to Jackson where he would be registered in the board office. Governor Barnett could claim that the Kennedys had misled him. President Kennedy even agreed to let Barnett scold him in the sternest language if that would serve his political interest. With Meredith registered, Barnett would declare the battle was lost and would allow Meredith to attend the University of Mississippi. Governor Barnett was enthusiastic about the proposal as a solution to the impasse.[30]

While President Kennedy and Governor Barnett were working out the details of the "hidden ball trick," about one hundred businessmen and women were meeting secretly in Jackson on Saturday morning. They had come to that clandestine meeting in response to telegrams and calls from Mounger, Brunini, and the small group of Jackson businessmen who had met several times over the last week or ten days. They represented the power structure in Mississippi, but they had waited too long to influence the course of history and prevent a violent confrontation between federal and state authorities.[31]

Throughout Saturday afternoon and into the early evening, Governor Barnett tried to persuade his counselors to accept the agreement he had made with the President. By game time Barnett had lost his own resolve to honor it. At the Ole Miss-Kentucky football game that night in Jackson, Governor Barnett was called to speak at half time. As the governor was speaking, the world's largest Rebel flag was unfurled to the stirring strains of "Dixie." The stands were awash in a sea of Rebel flags. On that haunting night those flags were more than a symbol of college spirit; they were a political statement.

Known fondly as Ole Ross, Governor Barnett was one of Mississippi's last great stump speakers. In his raspy, throaty voice, his right fist clinched, rising and falling, circling in rhythm with the words, Ole Ross proclaimed from the fifty-yard line:

> *I love Mississippi...*
> *I love her people...*
> *I love her customs...*[32]

Governor Barnett's half-time speech was thrilling to many but puzzling to some. After the game, former Governor J.P. Coleman talked briefly with former Governor Hugh White as they were leaving the stadium. Governor White said, "J.P., do you know what's going on about this Meredith business?" Coleman replied that he did not know what the situation was at that point. Governor White surprised Coleman by saying, "I don't understand Ross making that speech because I know that he has already agreed to admit Meredith."[33]

After the game Governor Barnett called the justice department. His call was forwarded to Attorney General Kennedy, who had gone home. Governor Barnett told Robert Kennedy that he wanted to call off the deal. Kennedy was startled by that unexpected turn of events and accused the governor of breaking his word to the President. The two men ended the conversation amicably with Barnett agreeing to keep working on the situation. Governor Barnett also promised to call Kennedy early Sunday morning to let him know if the situation changed through the night. President Kennedy was called at the White House and told that the deal was off. He reluctantly signed the documents federalizing the Mississippi National Guard, and authorized Secretary of the Army Cyrus Vance to send troops to Oxford and the university if it became necessary.[34]

On Sunday morning, September 30, 1962, Governor Barnett called Attorney General Kennedy. That disjointed conversation dragged on for thirty minutes, and Governor Barnett made one last desperate effort to postpone the whole affair. Failing at postponement, Governor Barnett proposed another mock confrontation between federal and state authorities. His suggestion was fraught with calamitous potential. Robert Kennedy rejected it and threatened to reveal the secret tapes that had been made of their conversations.

Governor Barnett was startled to learn that his conversations with federal authorities had been taped and that President Kennedy might reveal those negotiations on national television unless a solution was found to the Meredith crisis. Bobby Kennedy realized that he had finally gotten through to the governor, and he took advantage of Barnett's fear of exposure. Tom Watkins and Burke Marshall then worked out a plan to bring Meredith to the campus later that afternoon. Unfortunately, and unbelievably, university officials were not notified that Meredith and a federal escort were on the way to the campus.[35]

Through the late afternoon and early Sunday evening, a milling crowd of students gathered in front of the Lyceum, which had been cordoned off by federal marshals. Meredith had moved into his dormitory room in Baxter Hall and would register in the Lyceum the next morning. The crowd was gradually augmented by "outsiders," and by nightfall the crowd was much larger and more restive. At 7:30 p.m. Governor Barnett announced on a statewide radio and television network that Meredith was on the campus. He explained that he had been forced to yield to the "armed forces and oppressive power" of the United States and that he had conceded to Meredith's admission to prevent violence and bloodshed.[36]

At approximately eight o'clock, just moments before President Kennedy went on national television to announce that Meredith was safely on the campus and would register the next morning, the crowd surged toward the marshals, and the order to fire the tear gas was given. As the marshals fired the gas into the surging mob, several people, including some highway patrolmen, were hit by the canisters and suffered fractures and broken bones. The pep rally atmosphere was gone, and most of the college kids, who had just come to see what was happening, went with it. Only the real resisters, the true believers, remained to fight what Willie Morris has called the "Echos of a Civil War's Last Battle." Two men were killed on that tragic night. Hugh Clegg, Chancellor Williams' executive assistant, blamed the "trigger happy" federal marshals who "jumped the gun" for causing the riot.[37]

Early on Monday morning, October 1, 1962, James Meredith went to the Lyceum, registered for classes and paid his fees. He then hurried off to an eight o'clock history class. Before James Meredith enrolled at Ole Miss, no other public school in Mississippi, not a grammar school, high school, or college, had been integrated. Public parks, playgrounds, libraries, beaches, theaters, doctor's offices, lunch counters, cafes, water fountains, hospitals, hotels, motels, cemeteries, everything in Mississippi was segregated. James Meredith graduated from the University of Mississippi in August 1963.

The color barrier was broken, and a crack appeared in the Closed Society.

Endnotes

1   For a chronology of the legal steps leading to Meredith's admission, see Russell Barrett, *Integration at Ole Miss* (1965), Appendix A, 247-251; for Meredith's discussion of his admission, see his book *Three Years in Mississippi*, (1966) and James Meredith, with James Doyle, *A Mission From God, A Memoir and Challenge for America* (2012); see also Walter Lord, *The Past That Would Not Die* (1966); James W. Silver, *Mississippi: The Closed Society* (1966); Nadine Cohodas, *The Band Played Dixie, Race and the Liberal Conscience at Ole Miss* (1997); William Doyle, *An American Insurrection, James Meredith and the Battle of Oxford, Mississippi 1962* (2003); Henry T. Gallagher, *James Meredith and the Ole Miss Riot: A Soldier's Story* (2012); Meredith Coleman McGee, *James Meredith: Warrior and the America That Created Him* (2013); Allyson Hobbs, *A Chosen Exile: A History of Racial Passing in American Life* (2014); for the definitive study of James Meredith and Ole Miss see Charles Eagles, *The Price of Defiance, James Meredith and the Integration of Ole Miss* (2009).

2   Hugh Clegg, "Someone Jumped the Gun," Unpublished Manuscript, Special Collections John D. Williams Library, University of Mississippi; for a recent biography of Hugh Clegg see Ronald F. Borne, *Troutmouth, The Two Careers of Hugh Clegg* (2015).

3   Meredith, *Three Years in Mississippi*, 58.

4   Ibid., 59.

5   Ibid., 105ff; *Meredith vs. Fair, Transcript of Record*, II, 217, 220.

6   *Meredith vs. Fair*, II, 228, 232, 238-239, 241-243.

7   See *Transcript of Record*, III, for the testimony and the court's ruling; see also Jack Bass, *Unlikely Heroes*, (1981), Chapter 9, "Crisis in Mississippi," 172-201.

8   See *Transcript of Record*, V, 734, 737-739; Bass, *Unlikely Heroes*, 180-181; Barrett, *Integration at Ole Miss*, 82.

9   *Minutes*, September 4, 1962; Barrett, *Integration at Ole Miss*, 249.

10   For a complete text of Governor Barnett's speech, see the *Clarion-Ledger*, September 14, 1963; interview with Charles Fair, Chairman of the Board of Trustees, September 18, 1978, Louisville, Mississippi; *Jackson Daily News-The Clarion-Ledger*, September 16, 1962; see also Clegg, "Jumped the Gun" for the names of an alumni steering committee that he said "saved" the university; see also David G. Sansing, "Standing Guard, 150 Years of The University of Mississippi Alumni Association," *Ole Miss Alumni Review* (Fall 2002), 36-50.

11   *Minutes*, September 14, 1962.

12   For the positions of various board members, see transcripts of interviews in the Holmes Collection; also Verner Smith Holmes-Euclid R. Jobe Interviews; a copy of the Transcripts of the Barnett-Kennedy telephone conversations is in the Holmes Collection.

13   *Jackson Daily News*, September 18, 19, 1962; *Washington Post*, September 20, 1962.

14   *Pascagoula Chronicle*, September 19, 1962; see also Ira Harkey, *Dedicated to the proposition... Editorials from The Chronicle, Pascagoula, Mississippi* (1963) and *The Smell of Burning Crosses* (1967); Carl Wiesenburg, *The Oxford Disaster... The Price of Defiance* (1962); Weisenburg, a member of the state legislature from Jackson County, and Joe Wroton of Greenville, were the only two state legislators who publicly opposed Barnett's policy of defiance.

15   See Interviews with Tubb, Fair, Evans, Riddell, Stone and Holmes-Jobe in the Holmes Collection.

16   Barrett, *Integration at Ole Miss*, 107-108.

17   *Jackson Daily News*, September 21, 1962, New Orleans *Times Picayune*, September 22, 1962; Barrett, *Integration at Ole Miss*,109; Lord, *The Past That Would Not Die*, 157.

18   Interview with S.R. Evans, a member of the board of trustees, on October 13, 1978.

19   Interview with William H. Mounger on September 21 and 28, 1978 at Jackson, Mississippi.

20   Interview with Thomas J. Tubb on September 18, 1978 at West Point, Mississippi.

21   Mounger Interview.

22   Transcripts of the Barnett-Kennedy Tapes, September 24, 1962; Verner S. Holmes and Euclid R. Jobe Interviews.

23   Tubb Interview.

24   Tubb interview; *Jackson Daily News*, September 26, 1962; *Times Picayune*, September 26, 1962; see also Robert Canzoneri, *"I Do so Politely:" A Voice from the South* (1965).

25   Meredith, *Three Years in Mississippi*, 196.

26   Transcripts of the Barnett-Kennedy Tapes, September 26, 1962; *Daily Mississippian*, September 27, 1962; Meredith, *Three Years in Mississippi*, 202-203; Transcripts of the Barnett-Kennedy Tapes, September 27, 1962.

27   Transcripts of the Barnett-Kennedy Tapes, September 26 and 27, 1962.

28   Ibid.

29   This conversation is not included in the Transcripts of the Barnett-Kennedy Tapes, but excerpts from this conversation, from which the above quotation is taken, may be found in Hugh Clegg, "Jumped the Gun," 179-181.

30   Ibid.

31   Mounger Interview; copies of those telegrams are in the Holmes Collection.

32   *Jackson Daily News-The Clarion-Ledger*, September 30, 1962; interview with Gerald Blessey, July 22, 1975, by Hank Holmes, in Mississippi Department of Archives and History, Jackson, Mississippi.

33   Holmes-Coleman Interview.

34   George B. Leonard, T. George Harris, and Christopher S. Wren, "How A Secret Deal Prevented a Massacre at Ole Miss," *Look* (December 31, 1982), 22 ff.

35   Transcripts of the Barnett-Kennedy Tapes, September 30, 1962.

36   Barrett, *Integration at Ole Miss*, 146.

37   Willie Morris, "At Ole Miss: Echoes of a Civil War's Last Battle," *Time* (October 4, 1982), 8-11; Eagles, *The Price of Defiance*, Chapter 18, "The Riot," 340-370.

Top: Federal troops around the
Oxford courthouse

Right: *The Personal Memoirs of
Ulysses S. Grant*

20

Oxford, the Town That Saved America, Twice

Perhaps no town and college in America have been more closely identified with each other than Oxford and Ole Miss, and there are few collegiate environs where the town and gown relationship has been more congenial, mutual, and enduring. Oxford is a town with two histories, one in fact and one in fiction. It can be found on any standard map of Mississippi. It is also a site in the "postage stamp" world of William Faulkner.

Within three years after Oxford's founding in 1837, a guide to Mississippi towns and cities described Oxford as one of the most pleasant towns in all that region. Its 400 good citizens had constructed a brick courthouse, organized two churches, built two hotels, and opened six mercantile establishments, one of which was Neilson's Department Store, which is still in operation. Soon after its founding, Oxford would include the largest assembly of doctors and lawyers of any town its size in the region.

Also located in this tiny frontier town deep in the southern forest were two preparatory academies. As the founders of Faulkner's fictional Yoknapatawpha County were laying off the square of Jefferson, the county seat, one of them said, "And we're going to build a school too soon as we get around to it. But today we're going to build the courthouse." Oxford's founders, in fact and in fiction, linked statecraft with schooling and liberty with learning.

Thomas Dudley Isom, one of the founders of Oxford, was only nineteen years old when he came to work in his uncle's trading post in the Chickasaw

Territory. Isom had not come to trade with the Chickasaws; they were being resettled in Indian Territory west of the Mississippi River. He would trade with the white settlers, who would soon appear by the thousands to clear the land, grow cotton, establish towns and villages, and found a university.

One of the new counties created from the Chickasaw Cession was Lafayette County, named for the Marquis de Lafayette, the young French general who fought along side his hero, George Washington, in the American Revolution. General Lafayette, like Isom, was only 19 years old when he landed on America's golden shores. When the Lafayette County Board of Police was considering a name for the county seat, Thomas Isom suggested Oxford, hoping that name would give the town an advantage in persuading the legislature to locate the state university there.

Five years after the founding of Oxford, the state legislature considered forty-eight prospective sites for the state university. Cud-de-hunk, Mount Pleasant, Redbone, Bare-foot, Brandywine, Sweet Water, and Good Springs were all eliminated in the early balloting. On the final ballot the seven finalists were Louisville, Kosciusko, Mississippi City, Brandon, Oxford, Middleton, and Monroe Missionary Station.

Each site, except Middleton, lobbied for its selection. A flourishing village with a small liberal arts college and two preparatory academies, Middleton proudly called itself the "Athens of Mississippi" and, ironically, it was originally named Oxford. Realizing that their small liberal arts college would be displaced by a public university, the supporters of the local college lobbied against its selection. The citizens of Middleton fulfilled the ancient prophecy "where there is no vision, the people perish."

When the Mississippi Central Railroad was built in the 1850s, it bypassed Middleton. Had the state university been located there, the railroad would certainly have been routed through Middleton. Time and the railroad bypassed Middleton, and the Athens of Mississippi, like so many other promising villages in the Southern forest, gradually "marched back into the wilderness."

Unlike the village elders of Middleton, Oxford's founding fathers were visionaries who lobbied diligently, and successfully, for its selection. On

January 21, 1841, the lawmakers selected Oxford over Mississippi City by a margin of one vote, fifty-eight to fifty-seven.

Oxford was "romantically situated" on a ridge between the Tallahatchie and the Yockony Patawfy rivers, and established on a parcel of land that once belonged to Hoka, Princess of the Chickasaw Nation. This elevation, slight as it was, gave Oxford an advantage over the other sites, because higher elevations were believed to be freer of fevers and other contagious diseases. Oxford offered several other advantages in addition to its healthy elevation. It was "situated on the great stage road, leading from Jackson… to Memphis."

It was also linked by a stage road to Columbus, where several other major stage lines intersected. As remote as the university was, students could reach it from almost any region of the state by stagecoach. The stagecoach from Jackson to Oxford, with nighttime layovers, took three to four days.

Since its founding, Oxford has remained a small town with a special charm. Oxford natives and visitors alike, then and now, speak of its charm and beauty and its graceful hospitality. The citizens of Oxford, according to an early student publication, were "noted for their kindness and hospitality, especially to students." The student publication also noted that Oxford merchants were "generally busy counting students' money."

Three months after the University of Mississippi was chartered on February 24, 1844, the Oxford Observer described the village where the university would be located:

> Our village at this time presents a beautiful and most lively aspect. The splendid four-horse mail coach… comes dashing through every day, save Monday. Our beautiful shade trees, so nicely arranged, are in full vigor. Our academies and schools are flourishing.

A year after the university graduated its first class in 1851, a visitor who identified herself as "The Cumberland Girl" recorded her impression of Oxford: "This modern Oxford we find to be a neat, cheerful, social, homelike place; just as beautiful as a sonnet, as bright as Eden ever was." Her explanation for Oxford's charm was simple: "Good kind hearts and happy faces, the holiday robes of most villages... are worn here as an everyday dress."

The editor of the *Ripley Advertiser* predicted that the university would flourish in the "beautiful village of Oxford" and would become as famous as its "transatlantic namesake."

When the university was swept up in the sectional crisis in the decade before the Civil War, there was talk of moving it to Jackson where it could be under the watchful eye of the legislature. According to the *Pontotoc Examiner*, "The university's problem was its Yankee chancellor, Frederick Barnard, and its Northern-born professors."

J.D. Stevenson, editor of the *Oxford Mercury*, was extremely critical of the university and endorsed its relocation. The *Oxford Intelligencer*, which was established in the summer of 1860 as an alternative to the *Oxford Mercury*, condemned any talk of moving or closing the university. The *Intelligencer* estimated that the University of Mississippi brought at least a hundred thousand dollars in business to Oxford every year and had transformed it from "an insignificant county seat... to a thriving, prosperous town."

To the youthful editor, there was more to the relationship between Oxford and the university than just money. In the summer of 1860, the editor complained about how dull Oxford was when all the students were gone. "When the university is in session the town presents an aspect of cheerfulness and activity," he wrote, "but now that the students have departed to their several homes, the stillness is scarcely broken." But in early September 1860, the editor could hardly contain his glee: "Persons who have only known Oxford in the vacation would hardly recognize it as the same town, now that the university [is] in full operation. The stores are crowded; the merchants are in good humor [and] the streets... resound with the... hearty laughter of... students."

But in the early fall of 1860, the editor was distraught by the appearance of the university's classic groves. "There are hundreds of persons—former and present students of the university," he wrote, "who will be sorry to learn that, of all the magnificent trees that once adorned the campus, and with which so many dear associations are connected, naught now remains save a few tall, unsightly stumps." The editor conceded that the trees had been "topped" and that "they will eventually be improved by the mutilation." But he feared "the promised improvement will not occur in our lifetime."

The thirteenth session of the university opened in September 1860 in a time of great political excitement. The election of Abraham Lincoln was quickly followed by the secession of several Southern states and the establishment of the Confederate States of America. On May 1, 1861, the University Greys, a military company composed of university students, left the happy environs of Oxford for the fields of battle. The Greys were regaled for their heroism on the front line, and on July 3, 1863, won "imperishable glory" in the Battle of Gettysburg. After the Greys left Oxford in 1861, the university would remain closed until after the war.

In my classes at Ole Miss I would often draw a wide, sweeping curve on the chalk board and say to my students, "That is what history looks like; that is how history moves." Rarely ever does history take a right turn or move at a 90-degree angle. To most people history is something that happened to someone else, a long time ago, and far away.

But the great English historian, Arnold J. Toynbee, wrote, "Had I been born in the American South... I would have known that history had happened to me and to my people."

History did happen to the South, not once but twice, and history took a right turn in 1861. Southerners went off to war in 1861 and came home in 1865 to a different world.

Between the inauguration of John F. Kennedy in 1961 and the passage of the Voting Rights Act in 1965, our world changed again, and history took another right turn.

The Civil War was a defining moment in American history. So, too, was the Civil Rights Movement.

The University of Mississippi was founded in the midst of America's bitter sectional strife over slavery and states' rights. A state university was the necessary alternative to sending the sons of the gentry to the North for their schooling. Said one state official, "Those opposed to us in principle cannot be entrusted with the education of our sons."

"Send your sons to other states," said another, and "you estrange them from their native land, [and] our institutions are endangered."

As the University Greys were beginning their long and perilous march toward Gettysburg, General Ulysses S. Grant and William Tecumseh Sherman were assembling a hundred-thousand-man army on a broad tableland on the west bank of the Tennessee River, near a small Methodist church called Shiloh.

In the aftermath of bloody Shiloh, in the spring of 1862, Grant and Sherman launched the Vicksburg Campaign, an overland assault on the last Confederate stronghold on the Mississippi River. And the road to Vicksburg led through Oxford, which General Grant occupied in early December 1862. With the arrival of the Union army the university campus became a military post. In the Lyceum's classrooms and lecture halls, populated by young scholars and learned professors only months before, federal soldiers wounded at Shiloh sought rest and healing.

One hundred years later, on the night of the Meredith riot in September 1962, young soldiers in the Army of the Lost Cause, wounded in what some have called an echo of the last battle of the Civil War, were treated in the spacious halls of this grand old building hallowed by time and history.

In preparation for the Vicksburg campaign, Grant stockpiled his supplies for several months at Holly Springs, a sleepy little town 26 miles north of Oxford. To provision a large army marching through hostile territory, those supplies, and a direct line to them, were absolutely essential, according to prevailing military theory.

Grant's march against Vicksburg was delayed as his army got bogged down in the wetlands between the Tallahatchie River, just north of Oxford, and the Yoknapatawpha, Faulkner's fabled river, just south of Oxford. This delay in Grant's movement made his supply depot at Holly Springs vulnerable to Confederate attack.

In a daring nighttime raid on December 20, 1862, a Confederate cavalry regiment swooped into Holly Springs and destroyed the Union supply depot and almost captured Julia grant, General Grant's wife. Mrs. Grant, with her four-year-old son, Jesse, and her personal slave, Jule, were on their way to spend Christmas with the general in Oxford.

There was just enough warning of the raid to get Mrs. Grant out of Holly Springs in the late afternoon of December 19. Years later Jesse remembered that hasty evacuation from Holly Springs and recalled the image of his mother sitting in a chair in an otherwise empty boxcar during their nighttime ride to Oxford.

After the loss of his supply base, General Grant was forced to change his plans for an overland attack of Vicksburg. He ordered his army to march from Oxford to Memphis where he reestablished his supply line and then moved down the Mississippi for an amphibious assault of Vicksburg. As Grant was preparing to leave Oxford, he sent out troops and wagons fifteen miles in every direction to confiscate all the food and forage and supplies they could find. Grant told Adam Badeau, a member of his staff, and the first writer to chronicle Grant's Civil War campaigns, that he was astonished by the success of those foraging expeditions. Grant learned, here at Oxford, that his army could live off the land. That realization would inform his Vicksburg strategy and influence all of his future campaigns. In his memoirs Adam Badeau recalled:

> *General Grant told me, when discussing [the Vicksburg Campaign] that had he known then, what he soon afterwards learned—the possibility of subsisting an army of thirty thousand men without supplies, other than those drawn from an enemy's country—he could, at that time, have pushed on to the rear of Vicksburg and probably have succeeded in capturing the place. But no experience of former wars, nor of the war of the rebellion, warranted him in supposing that he could feed his army exclusively from the country. ... But the country was abundantly stocked... and the lesson was taught which Grant afterwards applied in the rear of Vicksburg, and which Sherman, having seen the application, practiced on a still larger scale, in his marches through Georgia and the Carolinas.*

Top: Federal troops
around the Lyceum

Right: *Mission from God*

A
Mission
from God

A Memoir and Challenge
for America

James Meredith
with William Doyle

After several unsuccessful and costly assaults against Vicksburg in the winter and spring of 1863, General Grant secluded himself, and without consulting his corps commanders, designed a bold, daring and dangerous plan.

Grant would cross the river, march his men down the Louisiana side of the Mississippi, cross over into Mississippi at Bruinsburg, cut himself off from his supply line, and attack Vicksburg from the high ground south of the city. General Sherman was startled that Grant would sever his supply line and warned his commanding officer that the plan could not succeed. Sherman even complained to higher authorities. But General Grant was undeterred by Sherman's reluctance because he had learned at Oxford that his army could live off the land. In his memoirs Grant recalled:

> *I was amazed at the quantity of supplies the country afforded.... Our loss of supplies was great at Holly Springs, but it was more than compensated by those taken from the country and by the lesson we learned.*

Weeks later, from the high ground of Haines Bluff, at the beginning of the siege of Vicksburg on May 18, 1863, Grant recalled that Sherman "turned to me, saying that up to this minute he had felt no positive assurance of success. This, however, was the end of one of the greatest campaigns in history, and I ought to make a report of it at once."

General Sherman learned during the nineteen-day march from Bruinsburg to Vicksburg what Grant had learned at Oxford. And for the remainder of the war, Grant says in his memoirs, General Sherman lived off the land "while marching through four states of the Confederacy with an army more than twice as large as mine at this time."

After General Grant's victory at Vicksburg, President Lincoln brought Grant to Washington, gave him another star, and command of the Army of the Potomac. It was Lincoln's fervent hope that Grant, who alone among his generals, Lincoln said, understood the arithmetic of war, could bring an end to the death and destruction unbridled by this, the first of the new modern wars.

In the next year and a half Grant swept across Virginia, living off the land, in relentless pursuit of General Robert E. Lee. Ultimately Grant would prevail, and in April 1865 Lee surrendered the remnants of his Army of Northern Virginia. As the Confederate banner was furled, a young Rebel soldier said, "Damn me, if I ever love another country."

In the century between the surrender of the revered Virginian, Robert E. Lee, and the election of Mississippi's "Unreconstructed Governor," Ross Barnett, America had been transformed from a rural, agricultural country to an urban, industrial nation, from a weak and divided country to a powerful, but still divided nation. Much of the South was poor, rural, and agricultural; it had not shared in the bounty of industry and enterprise.

And, as Charles Reagan Wilson has written, the South was "baptized in the blood of the Lost Cause." And Ole Miss was the last bastion of the Lost Cause and whispered the last enhancements of an earlier age

On March 28, 1961, dressed in a Confederate uniform, in front of Mississippi's antebellum Governor's Mansion, Governor Barnett reviewed 6,000 Confederate-clad marchers in a re-enactment of a Civil War parade of troops.

That parade was one of the opening events in the state's Civil War Centennial Celebration and drew thousands of cheering spectators. In the midst of the most serious challenge to the state's racial and social customs since the 1860s, Mississippians paused to recall the glories of former times and to remember the Lost Cause.

Only the day before and just a block away, there had been another parade of sorts. But in the language of the sixties it was called a demonstration. A group of Jackson State University students were protesting the arrest of several Tougaloo College students for attempting to use the Jackson public library. Jackson State University was Mississippi's largest black institution of higher learning, and Tougaloo was a black college founded in the aftermath of the Civil War.

Among the students then enrolled at Jackson State was James Howard Meredith. Two months after Governor Barnett "reviewed the troops," Meredith filed a suit in federal court seeking admission to the University of Mississippi. His initial application had been declined.

When James Meredith applied for admission to Ole Miss, Mississippi was by law and custom a Closed Society. No school, college, church, café, park, water fountain, or waiting room was integrated. In a brilliant and dispassionate chronicle of his quest to break the barriers of race in Mississippi, Meredith wrote,

> *I returned to my home state to accomplish my divine mission... I had developed a master plan to replace what I... considered the Negro's worst enemy, the doctrines and principles of white supremacy.... I intend to build a better system and to replace the old unsuitable customs with more desirable ones.*

Gaining admission to Ole Miss and breaking the color barrier there were only part, important as they were, of Meredith's ultimate goal. He wanted to change the system. He was trying to get into Ole Miss, but what he really wanted was to open up the Closed Society, which had shut him and other blacks out for so long.

After his application was denied, Meredith filed a federal suit on May 31, 1961. One hundred years earlier, the University Greys had withdrawn from the university and boarded a train bound for glory and Gettysburg.

On September 10, 1962, after much legal wrangling and several appeals, the United States Supreme Court ordered the university to admit James Meredith. Three days later Governor Barnett promised to go to jail and threatened to close the yniversity before he would allow Meredith to enroll at Ole Miss. Governor Barnett also issued a Proclamation of Interposition, interposing himself between the Meredith order, which he dismissed as an unlawful dictate of the federal government, and the implementation of that unlawful dictate in the sovereign state of Mississippi.

Soon after the United States Supreme Court issued that order to admit Meredith, a Hinds County Justice of the Peace issued an injunction setting aside the U.S. Supreme Court Order.

I am not making this up!

During the weeks following his proclamation, Governor Barnett personally barred Meredith's enrollment on two occasions. On one occasion Lieutenant Governor Paul Johnson, flanked by state police, blocked the entrance to the campus and personally rejected Meredith's admission.

After several mock confrontations between state and federal officials, Governor Barnett and Attorney General Robert Kennedy agreed that Meredith would be brought to the campus on Sunday afternoon, September 30, under heavy guard and would register Monday morning, October 1, 1962. According to the agreement, Governor Barnett would remain in Jackson, and he could then say that the Kennedys had tricked him by taking Meredith to Oxford to register. As with most of the negotiations between Barnett and the Kennedys, university officials were not made aware of this plan until about two hours before Meredith arrived on campus.

On Sunday afternoon, as these plans were being set in motion, and as rumors that Meredith would be brought to the campus circulated, large numbers of both students and non-students were converging on the Ole Miss campus. Meredith arrived at about 5:30 Sunday afternoon and moved into his dormitory room. A few of the federal marshals remained at his dormitory, while a much larger contingent surrounded the Lyceum where Meredith would register the next morning. The appearance of the marshals surrounding the Lyceum angered the crowd in The Circle.

The Meredith crisis was perhaps the crucial event in the American Civil Rights Movement. It was an unprecedented judicial confrontation over states' rights and federal authority, and the most serious constitutional crisis since South Carolina seceded from the Union in 1860.

The Meredith crisis measured the limits to which state officials would be willing to go in defiance of the United States Supreme Court, and it demonstrated the extent to which federal authorities were determined to enforce the orders of the High Court.

The deployment of federal troops in Oxford in 1962 obliterated any notion that a state or a mob would be allowed to defy a federal mandate. And no other state attempted to do so.

After the Meredith crisis there were no more questions, no speculation, or debate about the relationship between states' rights and federal authority. Federal law and federal courts take precedence over state law and state courts.

And it was forever decided, on that night in Oxford, that a justice of the peace court could not set aside a Supreme Court order.

During the Meredith crisis, President Kennedy sent thirty thousand federal troops to Oxford, about the same number General Grant had during his occupation of Oxford a century earlier.

In 1862, at Oxford, General Grant devised a strategy that enabled him to win the Civil War. In 1962 the Union army returned to Oxford to put down what may have been an "echo of the last battle of the Civil War."

The Civil War was not over after the surrender of Vicksburg, but what General Grant learned here at Oxford, and General Sherman implemented in later campaigns, may have determined the outcome of the war.

The Civil Rights Movement was not over after James Meredith's admission to Ole Miss, but the ultimate outcome of the movement was decided here at Oxford on that Monday night in 1962.

Is it then too much to say that Oxford may have saved America—twice?

Billy Sylvester Guyton Hall

21

PROFESSOR BILLY SYLVESTER GUYTON, 1883-1971

HIS LIFE AND LEGACY

In 1908 when Billy Sylvester Guyton was in the happy days of his youth, long before his life had run its course and his legacy had been formed, his college peers said of him: "He lives to build, not to boast." Today, nearly a half century after his death, we gather in this special place to celebrate his life, a lifetime of building. It is perhaps not too much to say that the University of Mississippi Medical Center is the House that Guyton Built. If he did not build it, he surely saved it.

This is not to take away the high regards due to Dr. Leathers, Dr. Mull, Dr. Anderson, Dr. Cully, Chancellor Butts, Dr. Pankratz, Chancellor Williams, Dr. Holmes, Dr. Arthur Guyton, Dr. Hardy, Dr. Nelson, Dr. Conerly, and many others; it is not to dim the luster of their shining deeds to make this great institution what it is today. It is only to say that if it had not been for Billy Guyton's devotion to the two-year medical school at Oxford and his commitment to keep it open and accredited, the history of medicine in Mississippi, especially academic medicine, could have and probably would have followed a different course. If the two-year program had collapsed and closed, the University of Mississippi Medical Center, with its schools of medicine, nursing, dentistry, and other health professions, along with its magnificent teaching hospital, might still be aborning, or at best still in its infancy. Now, celebrating the fortieth anniversary of its founding and having secured its standing among the nation's most respected medical institutions, the Mississippi Medical Center is an enduring monument to Dr. Guyton, and to all of the others who labored against such great odds just to keep it going.

Let me say how pleased I am to have the honor of presenting the second annual Dean Billy Guyton lecture on the history of medicine, especially since it is being held in conjunction with the university's sesquicentennial celebration and the dedication of the Billy Guyton Archives and History Reading Room of the Rowland Medical Library. I also want to express my appreciation to Ada Seltzer, director of the Rowland Library, and to Virginia Segrest for their assistance in locating sources on the history of medicine in Mississippi. Allow me to express my thanks also to Barbara Austin and Janice Quinn, and especially to Dr. Robert Lewis. Dr. Arthur C. Guyton and Ruth Guyton, and Dr. Julius Cruse, who were also very helpful to me by providing valuable information and insight into the life and work of Dean Billy Guyton.

Billy Sylvester Guyton was the scion of a pioneer Mississippi family that migrated to Tippah County from the Union District of South Carolina in the early 1850s. His father, John Franklin Guyton, was a cotton farmer, and his mother, Mary Letitia Thornton, was a school teacher. Born on January 11, 1884, one of nine children, Billy chopped cotton as a small boy on his father's farm, learned to read and cipher in a one-room school, finished Blue Mountain Military Academy in 1901, and enrolled in Mississippi College at Clinton. His college days were intermittent. He would go to school for a while, then drop out for a while to work in a New Albany bank so he could help pay the tuition and other costs for a younger brother who also attended Mississippi College.

Established as Hampstead Academy in 1826, Mississippi College was a flourishing institution of higher learning at the beginning of the twentieth century. Although it was a Baptist institution, it was not a "nursery for ministers." Among its strongest departments was the School of Natural Sciences in which Billy Guyton earned a BS degree in 1908. Among his professors was John William Provine, who held the chair of chemistry. Professor Provine joined the faculty in 1893 after receiving his doctor of philosophy degree from the University of Gottingen. Dr. Provine taught several generations of pre-med students, and it was in his classroom that Billy Guyton was first introduced to the marvels and mysteries of modern medicine.

Although a dedicated student academically, he was a Phi Beta Kappa at the University of Virginia, Billy also participated in social activities, athletics, and literary societies. He was business manager of the college yearbook, treasurer of the athletic association, president of the Baptist Young People's Union, captain of the tennis team, and critic of the Philomathean Literary Society. Although the minutes of the Philomathean Society do not indicate precisely what the duties of the critic were, they do offer early evidence of how seriously Billy Guyton took even a small responsibility. Somehow, at that early age he understood that if you were responsible in little things, later, you would be responsible in bigger things. The November 1907 minutes of the Philomathean Literary Society include this statement:

> One of the most pleasing features of the meeting was the report of the critic. For the first time in many months the duties of the critic were performed as they should be, and it is greatly hoped that the example Mr. Guyton has set will be followed by all others elected to this office.

Across the next seven decades thousands of young men and women would strive to meet the standards set by Billy Sylvester Guyton. He would lead by deed as well as by words.

Following his graduation from Mississippi College in 1908, Billy served two years as principal of Dexter High School in Walthall County in order to accumulate the necessary funds to enroll at the two-year medical school at Ole Miss. When he matriculated at the university in 1910, the medical department was just seven years old. A medical school had been envisioned as early as 1870 by Chancellor John Waddell when he reorganized the university's academic departments and schools. At that time the board of trustees expressed its intent to organize a medical college "on the plan of the University of Virginia" as soon as funds became available.

After the plan suffered several false starts in the late nineteenth century, Chancellor Robert Fulton finally established a two-year program in 1903. Sixteen students were enrolled in the first class. The medical department was immediately admitted to the Southern Association and to the American Association of Medical Colleges. The first medical certificate was awarded in 1904.

During its first four years the medical department occupied two upstairs rooms in the Lyceum. Dissecting procedures were conducted in a small frame building about fifty yards north of the Lyceum. The construction of this facility brought strong protests from the librarian and several other faculty members who complained of the noxious odors emanating from the shack. So persuaded were they by the power of suggestion that they were only slightly mollified when they were told that there had been no dissecting up to that time because the legislature had made no provisions authorizing the medical department to procure cadavers.

The difficulty of securing dissecting material was alleviated by the legislature in 1906, and the problem of severely cramped quarters was resolved by the construction of a science building in 1907. One other problem, however, continued to plague the fledgling institution. Oxford was a small town without adequate hospital facilities to supplement the classroom instruction.

In a premature and perhaps naive attempt to rectify that problem, Dean Walter Leathers, Chancellor Andrew Kincannon and the board of trustees entered into an arrangement with the city of Vicksburg in 1909 to use the state charity hospital for a second two years of medical school. That arrangement, which was plagued from the beginning by a lack of teaching facilities, a competent faculty, and adequate funds, lasted only two years and produced only four graduates.

Undoubtedly, some of the impetus to upgrade the two-year course to a four-year degree program was derived from the growing popularity of the Mississippi Medical College, a four-year proprietary medical school at Meridian. Although it was chartered in 1882 as Kirk's Clinical Institute of Medicine and Surgery, the school did not open until many years later. On April 27, 1906, a group of local physicians met at Kendall's Drug Store in Meridian and organized the Mississippi Medical College, formulated a curriculum, appointed a faculty, and announced the date for the opening of the fall term. Six months later the state's second medical college opened with sixty-three students enrolled.

Mississippi Medical College was a product of a "wave of degradation and exploitation of medical education [that] swept the United States" in the late nineteenth and early twentieth century. This institution was Mississippi's only contribution to that generation of proprietary schools, but there were 18 in Tennessee, 27 in Indiana, 39 in Illinois, and 42 in Missouri. In fact, there were more medical schools in America at that time than there were in the rest of the world.

In 1909, in the midst of this flurry of fledgling institutions, Abraham Flexner conducted a Carnegie Foundation-sponsored, on-site inspection of the 131 existing medical schools in the United States. During his tour Flexner visited the medical college at Vicksburg and anticipated its quick demise. He also visited and dismissed the Mississippi Medical College at Meridian as a diploma mill. The only virtue he found there was its fostering of medical education for women. Flexner also inspected the two-year medical department at Oxford.

Flexner's influential study, which was published in 1910, was one of several steps taken by the medical profession to elevate the standards and establish a greater degree of uniformity in the nation's medical schools. Two powerful accrediting agencies, the American Medical Association Council on Medical Education and the American Association of Medical Colleges, emerged from those early efforts. Dean Guyton would become intimately acquainted with both of those agencies during his tenure as dean of the Ole Miss Medical School. But those days and those troubles were far, far away when Billy Guyton first crossed the bridge above Hilgard's Cut when he came to Oxford in the fall of 1910 as a first-year medical student.

The remarkable promise of this young man from Ingomar —his family had since moved to Union County—became increasingly evident during his two years at Ole Miss. He was a member of the Ole Miss Athletic Association; the YMCA; Phi Sigma, the university's oldest literary society; and he held a seat on the university's prestigious Honor Council. In addition he was selected by his professors as student assistant in histology and elected president of the senior class by his peers.

After receiving a second bachelor of science degree and a master of science degree in 1910 and 1911, Billy Guyton enrolled at the University of Virginia at Charlottesville. Following his graduation in 1913, the newly minted M.D. interned at Martha Jefferson Sanatorium in Charlottesville (1912-1913).

During the Christmas season of 1913 Billy came home to marry a childhood acquaintance, Mary Katherine Smallwood. Kate, who was born in New Albany on February 8, 1886, was as remarkable in her own way as was her distinguished husband. She graduated from Mississippi Industrial Institute and College, now known as Mississippi University for Women, with a degree in music and science. She took further study at Scarritt College in Kansas City. In September 1908, at the tender age of twenty-two, Kate fulfilled a pledge to go to the mission fields of China. Her local newspaper announced her departure:

> *Miss Kate Smallwood, who will leave here tomorrow for China, is the youngest missionary ever sent out by the Woman's Board of the Southern Methodist Church. She will teach in a mission school for girls either in Soochow or Shanghai.*

During her five-year sojourn, Katherine Smallwood from New Albany, Mississippi taught science and mathematics to young girls in Soochow, China. Like her husband, Kate Guyton was not an ordinary person.

The first year of their marriage was spent in Orange, New Jersey, were Billy spent a second-year internship at the Orange Memorial Hospital. In 1914 the young couple came home to Ingomar where Billy opened a private practice. But the quiet life of a country doctor was not to be his destiny. In 1915 the University of Mississippi school of medicine offered him a professorship, which he accepted. Billy Guyton was the first graduate of the two-year medical course to enter academic medicine, but he would not be the last.

A study of graduates of the Ole Miss two-year program, conducted by William Fisher and directed by Dr. Julius Cruse, found a "surprisingly large" number of graduates, especially for a state-supported institution, who went into academic medicine. Fisher concluded that the high percentage of graduates going into academic medicine was due to the inspiration of the faculty and noted that most medical students who choose an academic career do so during their first two years when they are concentrating on theoretical rather than clinical medicine. During Professor Guyton's first year at Ole Miss, 12.5 percent of the graduates went into academic medicine. During the school's fifty-two-year existence over 126 graduates of the two-year course went into academic medicine. Dr. Cruse informs me that recent findings, which were not included in Fisher's original study, have actually increased the number of Ole Miss graduates who have chosen academic careers over private practice.

During his early years at Ole Miss Dr. Guyton decided to specialize in ophthalmology, which required additional post-graduate work. In 1919 he enrolled at the University of Colorado where he spent the next several summers studying for an advanced degree. Mrs. Guyton and the small children accompanied their father to Colorado. Because of Colorado's salubrious climate, and because the university offered Dr. Guyton a teaching position, the Guytons decided to remain out West. As Billy and Kate were about to purchase a home and begin a new life, John Franklin Guyton interceded and persuaded his son to come back home to Mississippi. After his return Dr. Guyton combined a highly successful private practice in Oxford with his continuing interest in academic medicine as an adjunct professor in the university's medical department.

During the 1920s and early 1930s Ole Miss was Mississippi's "neglected child of higher education." The neglect of the state university was due in equal parts to legislative penury and the increasing probability that the university would be relocated to Jackson. The continuing and mounting support for consolidation of the various white institutions of higher learning and the construction of a "Greater University of Mississippi" at Jackson culminated in January 1928 when Theodore G. Bilbo was inaugurated for his second term. In his inaugural address Governor Bilbo announced a costly and controversial proposal:

> *If I were called upon to name the one thing that would do more to develop Mississippi and bring to her the highest degree of progress and future glory than anything else, I would not hesitate in saying that the moving of the University of Mississippi to the capital city of Jackson and the building... of a twelve- or fifteen-million-dollar institution would be that thing.*

In an emotional response to Bilbo's proposal to move the university to Jackson, Chancellor Alfred Hume invoked the memories of the "Lost Cause" with great rhetorical skill, and success:

> *The University of Mississippi is rich in memories and memorials and a noble history. ... The memorial window in the old library erected in loving memory of the University Greys, the Confederate monument nearby, and the Confederate soldiers' cemetery a little farther removed are as sacred as any ancient shrine, alter, or temple. Instead of moving the university away that it might be a little easier to reach, ought not the people of Mississippi to look upon a visit here as a holy pilgrimage?*

In 1930, after failing on two previous occasions, Governor Bilbo renewed his effort to remove Chancellor Hume because he was more convinced than ever that Hume was "temperamentally unfit" to be chancellor of a modern comprehensive state university. The incident that strengthened his resolve to remove Hume was the chancellor's action concerning the college yearbook. Chancellor Hume considered some of its content "libelous slurs at girlhood and womanhood." He impounded the annual, expelled the two editors, and established a board of control to censor future student publications.

When Governor Bilbo gained a controlling majority on the board of trustees in 1930 he decided to reform higher education in Mississippi, not from the bottom up, but from the top down. The board of trustees, at Bilbo's direction, did not renew Chancellor Hume's contract. Instead, the board reinstated Chancellor Joseph Neely Powers, who had been fired four years earlier. The medical chool, like all other departments at the university, was subject to the "Bilbo Purge." The aging professor of pharmacology, Dr. Peter W. Rowland, who had been born two months before the firing on Fort Sumter, was dismissed along with Dean Joseph Crider, who had become dean in 1924 when Dr. Leathers resigned.

The American Association of Medical Colleges and the American Medical Association promptly notified Chancellor Powers that such obvious political intervention would not be tolerated and that the medical school faced the possibility of expulsion if the dismissals were allowed. Consequently, Chancellor Powers reinstated Dean Crider and Professor Rowland. However, two days before the opening of the fall semester Dean Crider resigned. Dr. John Cully, the university physician and a loyal supporter of the medical school, declined the appointment. Dr. Phillip Mull, a former professor of anatomy, was then offered and accepted the appointment.

Chancellor Powers's acquiescence to the accrediting agencies' demands saved the medical school's "A" rating, at least temporarily. Both agencies advised Chancellor Powers that they would keep the institution under close scrutiny for the foreseeable future and that significant improvement must be made if the medical school were to retain its membership in both associations. After the Southern Association of Colleges and Schools suspended the university, both medical accrediting agencies placed Ole Miss in a special category that required continual updates on the improvements being made.

One of the most loyal and constant friends of the University Medical School was Dr. W.H. Anderson, editor and publisher of the *Mississippi Doctor*, a medical journal published at Booneville by the Northeast Mississippi Medical Society. Dr. Anderson, a 1916 graduate of the two-year medical course, made the pages of the *Mississippi Doctor* available to Dean Mull in his efforts to gain financial and moral support for the medical school. In the December 1931 issue Dean Mull listed eight areas that the Association of Medical Schools had cited as deficient. Number one on the list of needs was "A medical library in the medical building with an all-time librarian in charge."

A state that could not pay its university faculty could hardly buy books for a medical library. The January 9, 1932, issue of the university student newspaper, *The Mississippian*, included this editorial:

HATS OFF TO OLE MISS PROFESSORS
At midnight tonight it has been exactly ten months and nine days since the professors at Ole Miss have received a salary check.

Shortly after this editorial was printed the Mississippi Senate Committee on Colleges and Universities recommended closing the university medical department because Mississippi could not afford to meet the accrediting standards. But the accrediting agencies were accommodating to Mississippi, the poorest state in the Union. They realized that the state could not afford the capital outlays necessary to meet the standards required of fully accredited medical schools. Consequently, they placed the university on a state of conditional probation that allowed the institution to retain its accreditation on a year-to-year basis.

In 1935, after five years in what was described as "a particularly trying post," Dean Mull resigned. Two months after his resignation representatives of the AMA and the Association of Medical Colleges visited the medical school. The purpose of that visit was not part of the evaluation process for accreditation. The two associations were conducting another national survey of medical schools much like the Flexner Study of 1910. This latest survey, sponsored in part by the Federation of State Medical Boards, was an effort to ascertain if medical schools were incorporating into their curriculum the revolutionary changes that were taking place in medical science.

The university's two-year medical course received a negative evaluation. The inspectors questioned the feasibility of even continuing the program. In the spring of 1935 the medical school's future was as gloomy and grim as it had been during the darkest days of the Great Depression. Dean Mull told the chancellor, "We have about come to the end of our period of grace." *The Mississippian* reported that the medical school was "on the verge of being discontinued." So uncertain was its future, the medical school did not enroll a class in the fall of 1935.

As the gloom of night was descending upon this small and struggling medical school, the university's newly appointed chancellor, Alfred Benjamin Butts, addressed a special convocation of faculty and students in Fulton Chapel on April 4, 1935. His speech was an affirmation of the university's future, and it provoked "an outburst" of applause. "I am interested and greatly appreciative of the history of the University of Mississippi," Chancellor Butts said, "but I am frank to say that I am more interested in its present and its future than I am in its past. This, then, will be my policy: to keep ever in mind that the university is, above all, an intellectual enterprise."

One of Chancellor Butts's first and most notable achievements was to persuade a reluctant Billy Guyton to accept the "particularly trying post" of dean of the medical school in 1935. In accepting the post Dr. Guyton became the first graduate of the two-year course to enter academic medicine and the only alumnus of the institution to serve as its dean.

Initially, Dr. Guyton agreed to serve only one year as acting dean. But a lesson he had taught to so many others he could not forsake himself. In a reminiscence of his "two-year hitch at Ole Miss," Dr. W.H. Anderson wrote fondly of his year as the laboratory assistant to Professor Billy Guyton. "By his kindness," Anderson remembered, "he taught us never to fail our work." After a year as acting dean, Dr. Guyton agreed to serve until he finished the job.

The medical school crisis consumed much of the time and energy of Dean Guyton and Chancellor Butts. No longer just a matter of accreditation, the crisis was a matter of survival. The AMA was already on record as opposing the continuation of two-year programs, and the Association of Medical Colleges had to be convinced on a school-by-school basis that two-year programs were still viable. At a critical meeting in Chicago in February 1936 Dean Guyton won the university a timely reprieve. He persuaded a special joint committee of the Association of Medical Colleges and the AMA to validate the credits earned by the class of 1934 and the upcoming class of 1936. That action would allow the students to transfer their work from Ole Miss to four-year institutions.

With the problem of transfer credits resolved, at least temporarily, Dean Guyton turned his attention to the problem of money. The grim prospects of the medical school induced Dean Guyton; Chancellor Butts; Calvin Wells, chairman of the board of trustees; and Governor Hugh White to beseech the legislature to find the funds necessary to save and sustain the medical school. Their appeal was heard. The legislature made a substantial appropriation, and a freshman class was enrolled in the fall of 1936. The rejuvenation of the medical school over the next two years was quite spectacular. The medical school was removed from probationary status, and its "A" rating was reinstated without conditions by the Association of Medical Colleges in November 1937 and by the AMA in February 1938. It may not be fair to say that Dean Guyton alone saved the two-year medical school. But it is safe to assume that if the school had failed and closed, Dean Guyton would have gotten most of the blame.

When the medical school was restored to full standing in 1938, its staff numbered 33, four times as many as there had been in 1930. The enlarged staff enabled Dean Guyton to expand the curriculum, and the new facilities allowed him to supplement the antiquated lecture system with laboratory and clinical instruction. Dean Guyton not only directed the recovery of a declining program, he presided over the medical school's most significant expansion since its founding. The campus development program that was begun with Governor Bilbo's urging and assistance in 1929 was abandoned during the Depression. One of the buildings included in that ambitious program was a student hospital and medical building. Constructed in the early 1930s at a cost of $125,000, the building that was eventually named for Dean Guyton in 1961 sat idle and empty for several years. After Guyton

Hall was finally completed, furnished, and occupied in 1937, it was featured in a special issue of the *Phi Chi Quarterly*.

One of the criticisms of the Ole Miss Medical School in its early years was the lack of a medical library and, later, the inadequacies of the makeshift library that did exist. When Guyton Hall was refurbished in 1937 the medical holdings in the university's main library were moved to the reading room in the new medical building. Miss Ross Jeffress, who came to Ole Miss from the New York City Public Library, was the medical library's first director.

Among Dean Guyton's most enduring contributions to academic medicine was the establishment of the Rowland Medical Library and his appointment of Dr. Peter W. Rowland as librarian plenipotentiary. This remarkable man, born on the eve of the American Civil War, said on the eve of World War Two, "I still have some good years in me." Dr. Rowland's methodology may have been unorthodox, but his acquisition skills are legendary. Though the numbers of new journals and books he acquired are modest by present standards, the acquisitions campaign and the establishment of an organization called Friends of the Library were means of encouraging practicing physicians in Mississippi to get involved in the affairs of their medical school. In recognition of Dr. Rowland's singular devotion to building the medical library's holdings, Dean Guyton asked the board of trustees in 1939 to name the new facility the Rowland Medical Library. If Dr. Rowland could see the Rowland Library today, now under the capable direction of Ada Seltzer, he would not be surprised. When we admire this facility, it is his vision that we see, and the handiwork of Friends of the Library.

While Dean Guyton was running one medical school he was planning another one. In a letter to a Vicksburg physician dated May 24, 1941, which was one of many similar letters he wrote on this subject, Dean Guyton outlined the organizational procedures, the public support, the prospects for accreditation, and the financial requirements that would be necessary if Mississippi established a new four-year degree-granting medical college and a teaching hospital. He was cautious but optimistic that Mississippi could and would be willing to allocate the resources necessary for such an ambitious plan. "We have," he wrote, "a very complicated situation to face when a four-year school is attempted. Nevertheless, I think it could be put over all right if we can get the proper support of the legislature from year to year."

Two years after writing this letter, Dean Guyton gave up the "particularly trying post" and returned to his Oxford home and private practice. But when the opportunity came to face the complicated situation of organizing a four-year medical school, Chancellor John D. Williams asked Dean Guyton to serve with Dean David Pankratz and Dr. David Wilson, chairman of the Commission on Hospital Care, to design and plan a modern state-of-the-art medical college and teaching hospital. The vision of these three men, along with many others, has become what Lucie Bridgforth has called a "city within a city."

In recognition of his many contributions to medical education in general, and to the University of Mississippi Medical School in particular, the board of trustees named Billy Guyton Dean emeritus in 1951, an honor he retained until his death in 1971.

How then shall the legacy of Billy Sylvester Guyton be measured? Perhaps by laboratories and libraries and classrooms, and books and bricks and buildings. Better still, it could be measured in the achievements of his children and grandchildren. Or the lives of the young men and women whose lives he touched and changed, like Dr. Julius Cruse, who knew him as a young man and honors him in his maturity, and like Dr. Verner Holmes, who studied with him at Ole Miss and for whom this building we now occupy is named, and by the lives they touched and changed, and by the sick they have healed.

His legacy is an expanding community that has been uplifted by the healing art that was learned and taught at the University of Mississippi Medical Center that he saved. Mississippi, indeed the world, is a healthier place because of Billy Sylvester Guyton. That is his legacy.

22

In Remembrance of Mayor John Leslie, March 27, 2012

Like many others, including many of you here today, John Leslie, our late and beloved mayor, greatly admired Peter Marshall, the renowned Presbyterian minister and chaplain of the United States Senate. And Elizabeth, his loving wife, asked me to read a few of John's favorite passages from *A Man Called Peter*, Catherine Marshall's biography of her famous husband.

Christians have this thing called hope.

The Christian has hope—not in himself, but in God.

They are marching to Zion, the beautiful City of God.

They are bound for the promised land joyfully anticipating the meeting "in the sweet bye and bye."

This hope gave courage to our grandparents. It dried their tears. It made their sad hearts sing.

They need not fear death—

Who trust in Jesus Christ

Who have committed themselves into His care and keeping.

For we are souls in living bodies.

Jesus Christ, who conquered the last fortress on the frontier of life, made us these promises:

"He that believeth in me, though he were dead, yet shall he live."

Mayor John Leslie

"And whosoever liveth and believeth in me shall never die."

"Because I live, ye shall live also."

"In my Father's house are many mansions, if it were not so I would have told you."

"I go and prepare a place for you. I will come again, and receive you unto myself; for where I am, there ye may be also."

"Let not your heart be troubled, neither let it be afraid."

MAYOR JOHN LESLIE, OXFORD, MISSISSIPPI

These two phrases just go together, it is hard to say where one leaves off and the other starts up.

During John Leslie's twenty-four years as mayor, both the physical and cultural landscape of Oxford was literally transformed.

Under John Leslie's leadership, one of the world's most famous squares was refreshed and refurbished. Parking bays were added; the parking meters were consigned to oblivion; restaurants and eateries lined the square, and the city hall was relocated from a tiny white building a few blocks away to that towering structure that now anchors the square, and where Bill Beckwith's statuary of William Faulkner keeps a watchful eye on his "little postage stamp of native soil." John Leslie understood and promoted Oxford's special place in history and in literature. John Leslie was by profession a pharmacist but by instinct and inclination, he was a man of learning and sophistication. He knew what a special place Oxford was, and as mayor he added much to its lore and traditions.

Just as Mayor John Leslie was a man who understood what used to be and what could be, he was also a mayor who understood what should be. John Leslie was the mayor of everyman, and he was esteemed by all of his constituents, young and old, black and white, college students and town folks, by college professors and carpenters.

John Leslie was a big-city mayor of a small Mississippi town, and he was driven by a compulsion to make Oxford a better place for all its citizens. He secured federal and state funds, levied local-use taxes to rebuild old neighborhoods, to modernize its streets and infrastructure, to build a public library, a swimming pool, tennis courts, and one of the finest community baseball stadiums in the Deep South. These and many other public facilities decorate the Oxford landscape and make it a better and happier place.

As notable as these and other public facilities are, perhaps John Leslie's most enduring contribution to Oxford cannot be seen; it must be sensed, experienced, and felt. The town and gown relationship between Oxford and Ole Miss has always been idyllic, but John Leslie elevated that relationship to another level. In my history of Ole Miss I regaled the historic relationship between the state university and the county seat. Its very name, Oxford, was chosen in the hope of inducing the legislature to locate the university here.

And I wrote that the election of Mayor John Leslie was the beginning of a new era in Oxford's history.

Think about that; that is the highest accolade a historian can bestow on anyone.

In the 1970s, during the early years of John Leslie's tenure in office, the restoration of Rowan Oak, the inauguration of the annual Faulkner Conference, the Willie Morris writer in residence program, the Chancellor's Symposium on Southern History, and the founding of Square Books spawned a literary renaissance at Ole Miss and Oxford. Mayor Leslie not only embraced this literary renewal, he championed it, and Oxford became a cultural oasis in the heartland of the Old Confederacy.

The Oxford that we now know and love and call our home, the Oxford that our children and grandchildren are loathe to leave and love to come back to whenever they can, the Oxford that is named in national publications as one of America's favorite places to live happily ever after, this Oxford, that the Ole Miss alumni think of as hallowed ground, is one of the legacies of Mayor John Leslie.

One of John Leslie's constituents was complaining about something on one occasion, and after reciting her litany of grievances, she said in exasperation to the man who had been mayor for more than twenty years, "Oh, I don't know why I'm talking to you; you're not even from here."

In the finest and truest sense of the word, John Leslie was indeed from here. John was stationed at Ole Miss in a naval program during World War II. After the war John came back to Oxford, married his sweetheart, Elizabeth, and they lived happily ever after here in Oxford.

No one is from here, so much as those who come here and never leave. There is no one from here so much as those who devote their lives, their talent, time, and energy to this special place. And one of John Leslie's special gifts was that he would make you feel at home, a part of this place, and would not only allow you but expect you to give back to Oxford.

It was my good fortune to know Mayor John Leslie. I knew him well, and of all the people I have known in my lifetime, there were few whom I liked more than I liked John Leslie. John had this gift of making you feel like somebody, somebody important, at least to him. I used to love to go into his drugstore for morning coffee, where I thought for several years that the city council and a public caucus were in continuous session.

And if John Leslie were here with all of us today, he would say,

"Mourn my death, but celebrate my life, and yours, be kind to your neighbor, love one another, live your life to the fullest, and be not afraid."

BILL WALLER

STRAIGHT AHEAD

The Memoirs of a Mississippi Governor

"When Bill Waller was elected governor in 1971, Mississippi was emerging from a long period of racial turmoil and isolation. With courageous and enlightened leadership Governor Waller brought Mississippi back into the mainstream of American life and politics."—PRESIDENT JIMMY CARTER

23

GOVERNOR BILL WALLER
EULOGY

FIRST BAPTIST CHURCH,
JACKSON, MISSISSIPPI

DECEMBER 3, 2011

Bill Waller was a man of faith and family. He was a member of this congregation for more than fifty years, and his contributions are without number. He loved and honored his wife, Carroll, and their children and grandchildren. And he loved Mississippi.

Governor Waller was also a man of vision. He could see things that others could not, or would not see, and he had a deep and abiding commitment to make the world, especially Mississippi, a better place.

A fifth-generation Mississippian, he was born and grew up on a working farm in Burgess, a small rural community along Clear Creek in Lafayette County. It was there that his world view was formed. In his memoirs, *Straight Ahead*, which he published in 2007, he writes of a Sunday afternoon riding club. He wanted to let all the kids in the neighborhood who had a horse join the club, but a few of the older boys took it upon themselves to decide who could and could not belong to the club. "That riding club experience," he wrote, "was my first encounter with ringleaders, and for much of the rest of my life I would be battling the ruling elites."

When Bill Waller announced his candidacy for governor in 1971 Mississippians were mired in the social and racial turbulence of the 1960s, and they longed for someone to lead them, and not follow them. In Bill Waller they found an unpretentious and plainspoken politician who promised to lead them out of the horse and buggy age into the modern era. And he pledged to open up public affairs to the rich and the poor, to rural and urban, to blacks and whites, and to women and to men.

In perhaps the greatest upset in a Democratic Party primary in the history of Mississippi, Bill Waller won the Democratic nomination for governor and then went on to win the general election in 1971. Perhaps the most dramatic and sweeping era of change and progress in the state's history was the four years from 1972 to 1976 that Bill Waller served as governor of Mississippi.

One historian has written that Bill Waller's administration was a "transformational period in Mississippi history." A leading journalist wrote, "the most significant new era in Mississippi politics began that day in 1972 when Bill Waller took office." One of Governor Waller's successors said:

"Every governor... has benefited from his leadership. So have the citizens of the state."

We are all beneficiaries of his life and times, and as we mourn the passing of this great man, it is altogether fitting that we celebrate his life and recount his legacy.

Bill Waller's courageous prosecution of the man who murdered Medgar Evers, his appointment of African Americans to one out of every four state boards and agencies, and his veto of the appropriation for the State Sovereignty Commission was the beginning of a new era of race relations in Mississippi.

The creation of a drug rehabilitation program along with the establishment of a modern crime laboratory, the integration of the highway patrol, and the state law allowing sheriffs to succeed themselves brought an end to the "good old boy" network and professionalized Mississippi law enforcement. During his administration Mississippi led the nation in the reduction of traffic fatalities.

The establishment of trade missions to Europe, Asia, and South America, which opened up new markets for Mississippi products, the creation of the Mississippi Economic Development Corporation, the Mississippi Film Commission, and the implementation of other economic programs increased the gross state product by 55 percent and resulted in 54,000 new jobs in Mississippi. He also created the Office of Minority Business Enterprise, the first such agency in the nation.

Bill Waller fulfilled his campaign promise to link the small Mississippi towns with the major interstate corridors. He initiated a $600 million highway construction program that built or contracted for more than 235 miles of four-lane and two-lane highways, and during his administration Interstate Highway 55 and Interstate 20 were completed through the state.

Health, education, and recreation were high priorities for Governor Waller, and he devoted special attention to those services.

In addition to reorganizing the State Board of Health, he established a Department of Mental Health and a Department of Youth Services. He also created nutrition programs for the elderly, the first such program in the nation, and expanded other community-based programs for the elderly.

Perhaps Governor Waller's highest priority was education. During his administration he established the Governor's Office of Education and Training. Funding for public education increased by 64 percent; per-pupil expenditures increased by 48 percent; and teachers received the largest pay increase in the state's history up to that time. Appropriations for colleges and universities increased by 8 percent and 100 percent for community colleges. Under Governor Waller's leadership a school of dentistry, veterinary science, and a school of architecture were established, and the five public colleges were elevated to university status. He also persuaded the medical school to increase the size of the entering class to provide more doctors for the state.

Among Bill Waller's proudest achievements were the network of state parks, wildlife management areas, and other recreational facilities that were enlarged and enhanced during his four years in office. As an avid sportsman Governor Waller was protective of Mississippi's natural habitat. His commitment to protect the environment, he said in his memoirs, "was formed during those carefree summer days [of my youth] when we played on the sandy beach of Maybelle's Lake and went fishing in Clear Creek."

Perhaps his crowning achievement in environmental protection was the acquisition of 32,000 acres of pristine hardwood bottomland along the Pascagoula River. The Pascagoula purchase was the largest tract of land dedicated to wildlife management ever acquired by any state using only state funds, and it is the largest bottomland overflow swamp in the lower forty-eight states that has protected status.

In the 1971 gubernatorial campaign Bill Waller promised, "I will always work to see that clean air, pure water, and other [natural] resources will be here for our children and the generations of Mississippians yet unborn." Our generation and generations yet to come have and will continue to benefit from the vision and commitment of this good and noble man, Governor Bill Waller.

One of the most visible and tangible legacies of Carroll and Bill Waller is Mississippi's historic Governor's Mansion. During the 1971 campaign the incumbent governor and his family vacated the 1842 Mansion because it had deteriorated and was unsafe. While she was actively campaigning with her husband, Carroll Waller asked the people of Mississippi to help her save and restore the "Historic Home of Our Heritage." After the election Carroll Waller preserved the Governor's Mansion, and in cooperation with the Mississippi Department of Archives and History, she conducted a major restoration project that led to the designation of the Mansion as a National Historic Landmark. Whenever you pass the Governor's Mansion, remember that without Carroll and Bill Waller, there might be a motel or a service station on that historic site.

God bless the Waller family and his legion of friends.

24

First Lady Carroll Waller Eulogy

First Baptist Church, Jackson, Mississippi

October 31, 2014

If I were asked to define the ideal of motherhood, I would need to use only two words: Carroll Waller.

If I were asked to describe the traits of a great lady, I would need to use only two words: Carroll Waller.

She was a loving, caring, and giving person. She was gentle, and kind, but she was also strong, and determined and dedicated.

She set a high bar for herself but was forgiving of others.

When Chief Justice Bill Waller, Jr., asked me to present a eulogy of First Lady Carroll Waller, Proverbs 31 immediately came to my mind:

Who can find a virtuous woman? Her price is far above rubies. The heart of her husband doth safely trust in her. She will do him good and not evil all the days of her life. She riseth also while it is yet night, and giveth meat to her household, and a portion to her maidens.

First Lady Carroll Waller

She stretcheth out her hand to the poor; yea, she reacheth forth her hands to the needy. She is not afraid of the snow for all her household are clothed with scarlet. Her husband is known in the gates, when he sitteth among the elders of the land. Strength and honour are her clothing; She openeth her mouth with wisdom; and in her tongue is the law of kindness. She looketh well to the ways of her household, and eats not the bread of idleness. Her children rise up, and call her blessed; her husband also, and he praises her. Many daughters have done virtuously, but thou excellest them all. Favour is deceitful, and beauty is vain: but a woman that feareth the Lord, she shall be praised.

Every person who came within the embrace of Carroll Waller's sweetness and goodness is better for it.

And I was one of those fortunate.

I virtually owe my academic career to her and to her distinguished husband, Governor Bill Waller.

When I was a young, untenured, junior history professor at The University of Mississippi in 1972, Mrs. Waller was First Lady of Mississippi. There were many young untenured history professors, but there was only one First Lady of Mississippi. How fortunate was I when she asked me to work with her in writing a history of the Governor's Mansion.

Carroll Waller had been actively engaged in Bill Waller's 1971 campaign, and she often discussed the future of Mississippi's historic Governor's Mansion. That 140-year-old building had been recently vacated because of its dilapidated condition. During the 1971 campaign she asked the people of Mississippi to help her save and restore this "historic home of our heritage." She was very popular on the campaign trail, and one newspaper even speculated that maybe she should be running for governor, and Bill Waller should be politicking for her.

After Bill Waller's election, at his and the First Lady's request, the legislature appropriated one million dollars to repair and restore the Mansion. To keep the people informed about the progress of the restoration, Mrs.

Waller wrote a weekly article, "News from the Mansion," which appeared in newspapers across the state. She also wanted to involve Mississippi schoolchildren in the restoration project. With a fundraising program called "Dimes for the Mansion," she visited schools around the state and invited the children to donate dimes to the Mansion project.

At a grand ceremony on June 8, 1975, celebrating the restoration of the Governor's Mansion, Mrs. Waller announced that the United States Department of the Interior had officially designated the Governor's Mansion a National Historic Landmark. More than two thousand visitors attended the reopening ceremony and toured the Mansion.

But Mrs. Waller was not content with just restoring and rejuvenating the Mississippi Governor's Mansion, which was the second-oldest governor's mansion in the United States. She wanted to write a full-length history of this "historic home of our heritage," and she asked me to help her.

All I can say is, "Oh, happy day!"

I loved and admired Mrs. Waller from the first minute of our first meeting.

I admired and respected Governor Bill Waller, but I loved the First Lady of Mississippi.

She was kind and considerate of this young professor who had never written a book.

There are a lot of stories about Mrs. Waller that I could recall, but I have time for only one, which reveals so much about this great lady.

As we began the research on the history of the Mansion we agreed that I would conduct the scholarly research of the documentary history of the Mansion in the Department of Archives and History, and Mrs. Waller would interview former governors and their families who had lived in the Mansion.

One day as we met to discuss the progress of our research, she said to me, "Professor," she always addressed me as professor, never as David, "Professor," she said, "I learned something yesterday that is not very complimentary to," and she mentioned the name of the governor and his family. And then she asked, "Do we have to tell everything we know about the First Families?"

Governor Waller happened to be in that meeting, and he said, "Now, Carroll, you let the professor decide what we will include in the book." The professor decided not to include that tidbit of information.

The four-year administration of Governor Bill Waller and First Lady Carroll Waller was a transformative period in Mississippi history. Historians are in unanimous agreement that the Waller administration was a bridge from yesterday to tomorrow.

The role that Governor Bill Waller and First Lady Carroll Waller played in initiating that new era in Mississippi history is chronicled in my 2013 Mississippi history textbook. In that textbook is a four-page section on the Waller Administration that highlights the enduring contributions of Governor Bill Waller and First Lady Carroll Waller. They literally led Mississippi out of the horse and buggy age into the modern era.

There is no other four-year period in Mississippi history quite like it.

Governor Bill and First Lady Carroll Waller leave an enduring legacy to their children, grandchildren, and to generations of Mississippians yet unborn.

God Bless the Waller family, and their legion of friends.

Dr. Ron Borne

25

In Celebration of the Life of Dr. Ronald Francis Borne

October 23, 2016

W hen Elizabeth and I and our three children came to Oxford and Ole Miss nearly fifty years ago, Ron Borne was one of the first people we met, and in those intervening and happy years Ron became one of the best and dearest friends we have ever had.

Ron and I share so many things. And I am going to use the present tense and not the past tense because I just can't let him go quite yet.

The most enduring thing we share is the love and devotion for our children and grandchildren. I cannot count the number of times I have suggested to Ron that we do this or that, and he would say that he couldn't because he was going to Virginia, or St. Louis, or Jackson, or wherever, to see one of his children or grandchildren. Ron also loves my children as I do his.

To know Ron Borne is to love Ron Borne.

Ron and I also share an intellectual curiosity and a boundless love for teaching and for our students. As a professor of medicinal chemistry in the School of Pharmacy, Ron Borne has received virtually every local and national teaching award presented in his field of study. He has also served as chairman of various departments in the School of Pharmacy and as vice chancellor for research. In 1988 Dr. Borne received a National Service Award from the National Institutes of Health and was visiting professor of pharmacology at the University of Edinburgh in Scotland.

But Ron Borne's intellectual interests are not limited to science. He loves knowledge and books, and he and I share a love of history. He has read the manuscripts of several of my books and has made many significant suggestions. Ron has also written several books far afield from chemistry and pharmacy.

His biography of Assistant FBI Director Hugh Clegg published by the University Press of Mississippi has garnered praise from a wide variety of viewers. I mention the publisher because the University Press of Mississippi is one of the most prestigious university presses in the United States and has rigorous standards for the books it publishes. Dr. Borne also has recently completed a manuscript on the life and times of Coach James Carmody that Neil White of Nautilus Publishing will publish. (That biography of Coach Carmody titled, *Big Nasty*, was published in 2017.)

For the last fifteen years or so, Lib and I have gone to Taylor Grocery for dinner on Sunday night with Ron and Debra. I don't have to tell this audience who Debra is; we all know her, and like Ron, we all love her. But what I really want to say is that we have trouble eating our dinner at Taylor because so many friends and former students stop by the table to say hello and to tell Ron Borne how much he meant to them when they were in his classes.

Ron Borne and I also share an abiding love for The University of Mississippi and the Ole Miss Rebels. Ron was a member of the athletics committee for several years.

Our families and friends sanctified a tiny place on this earth more than forty years ago when we began tailgating in the southeastern corner of The Circle. And we have all agreed to keep it sacrosanct for those who come after us. I hope this does not sound maudlin to you, but Ron and I have seen our children and grandchildren learn to walk, and talk, and grow up and build enduring relationships beneath those towering oaks.

Ron Borne in a remarkable person and will live on in the hearts and minds of all the lives he has touched and blessed when he walked among us.

26

THE STATE-OLE MISS RIVALRY

In the January 26, 2006, issue of the Jackson *Clarion-Ledger*, Meridian High School principal R.D. Harris complained that never in his 40 years in Mississippi schools had he seen the State-Ole Miss rivalry sink so low. "When it comes to those two recruiting, there's always been a war," he said, "But now it's just at a sad level. All these rumors, accusations…all the bad information has really gotten out of hand."

By the summer of 2003 the rivalry between Mississippi State University and Ole Miss had become so bitter, so public, and so damaging to both institutions that Rick Cleveland, the Jackson *Clarion-Ledger* columnist and Dean of Mississippi Sports Writers, called for a high-level summit of the university presidents, coaches, athletic directors and other college officials "to come up with a plan to tone down the animosity and encourage fans and alumni to do the same." On the eve of the 2003 Egg Bowl, Cleveland said that a healthy and heated rivalry is good for college football. But the Mississippi State-Ole Miss rivalry, he said, "is no longer healthy for either. Over the last few years it has become, in fact, detrimental to both programs, both universities." After an NCAA investigation of the Mississippi State football program became public in the spring of 2003, Cleveland wondered if the fans hated the other school more than they loved their own.

State and Ole Miss officials did not hold a summit, but Mississippi State University President Charles Lee and Mississippi State Athletic Direc-

tor Larry Templeton both expressed their extreme frustration over the tone of the rivalry. President Lee complained that the State and Ole Miss rivalry had gotten completely out of hand and blamed the fans and supporters who "not only want their team to win on the playing field, but… seek to discredit their rivals through the media and through NCAA investigations." The "cultural environment for football [in Mississippi]," he said, "coupled with the instantaneous power of the internet, is making allegations, character assassination, and innuendo an accepted behavior."

"The mudslinging is going both ways," Larry Templeton admitted, "and it needs to cease." He added, "There's a feeling among the key individuals who support both programs that we're going to be more positive. But I don't know if we'll ever be able to control all the fans. I have real concern over what's taking place on the internet."

In November 2002, *Sports Illustrated.com* had already noted that "the normally contentious relationship between the fan factions at Ole Miss and State has grown virulent." The popular online magazine said State fans blamed Ole Miss for its "season of discontent [and] suspect the Rebels had something to do with the suspension of Mississippi State quarterback Kevin Fant for the first game of the season." *Sports Illustrated.com* also quoted Doug Colson, a talk radio personality in Jackson, as saying, "A lot of Mississippi State fans think Robert Khayat wears a black hat while sitting in his office scheming against the Bulldogs."

Many Ole Miss fans considered Coach Jackie Sherrill "The Prince of Darkness" and despised him for refusing "to utter the words Ole Miss." To University of Mississippi fans and alumni "Ole Miss" is a term of endearment for their alma mater, and they were insulted by Coach Sherrill's refusal to use the term.

Football is the focus of the State-Ole Miss rivalry, but it is about more than just football. The rivalry has even reached the city halls of Oxford and Starkville, and the mayors of both towns have found themselves answering questions about the other town. After Starkville legalized cold beer in August 2005, Oxford was the only college town in Mississippi that still banned cold beer. The mayor of Starkville said the new ordinance would "present a more favorable image of Starkville." After this statement was publicized in the Mississippi press, the mayor of Oxford was besieged by newspaper reporters and a Tupelo television station asking for his reaction. The immediate press reaction, according to the Oxford mayor, "is a fair indication of how evident and public the rivalry is." After he was quoted in the *Clarion-Ledger* as saying the people in Oxford "don't wake up on Wednesday morning wondering what Starkville did on Tuesday, though they may sometimes feel that way about us," the residents of Starkville "bristled at the comparison with Oxford" and flooded the mayor with "angry emails."

The mayor of Oxford also bristled at the Starkville mayor's perception of the two towns. The Starkville mayor implied that while Oxford is becoming a sleepy retirement community, his town is attracting a younger, more creative and productive class of citizens. "But there you have it," said the Oxford mayor, "in Mississippi, Starkville and Oxford in particular, [the rivalry] is a big deal, much bigger than anyone outside Mississippi can realize." As one writer said, most schools feud all season, but State and Ole Miss feud all the time.

The ESPN television sports network considers the State-Ole Miss game one of the top-ten rivalries in college football. *Sports Illustrated* said it was the "saddest" college rivalry, and *Lordsutch.com* considers it the "nastiest," noting that there have even been fights between the cheerleaders. There is almost never any unanimity between these rivals, but both sides agree that the internet and the lawless universe of cyberspace has vulgarized the rivalry. A Google search of the "State-Ole Miss rivalry" yielded more than 87,000 citations on the web. Among those citations is a growing number of sports blogs where State and Ole Miss fans can hurl invectives and accusations at each other. On October 18, 2003, *allsports.com* announced that Jackie Sherrill would retire at the end of the season and invited its readers to "Be the first to POST A COMMENT on this story." And the race was on.

This storied rivalry is considered among the fiercest in college football and has been the subject of two full-length hardbound books, a scholarly paper in a refereed journal, a frequent topic in America's premier sports journals, countless articles in American newspapers, the subject of endless analysis by amateurs on talk radio and commentators on television. The rivalry is also the frequent topic of heated discussions at family dining tables around the state, especially in homes of mixed marriages, which in Mississippi does not mean unions between Catholics and Protestants but marriages between a State and an Ole Miss alumni.

W.G. Barner's 1982 history of the State-Ole Miss football rivalry is entitled *Mississippi Mayhem*. The American Collegiate Dictionary defines mayhem as "a state of disorder, riotous confusion; and havoc." The term mayhem is obviously and intentionally an exaggeration, but it is an exaggeration of the truth. The annual State-Ole Miss football game is the most visible and public manifestation of a fierce rivalry, but as Ed Hinton wrote in Sports Illustrated in December 1991, when these two teams meet "there is far more at stake than mere gridiron supremacy." The rivalry between State and Ole Miss and their ardent, avid supporters is deep and bitter and has a long history.

Before 1848 the sons of Mississippi's aristocracy were sent off to school at Harvard, Yale, and Princeton. But the sectional crisis and the slavery controversy convinced the state's leadership that they should keep their sons at home, so they founded the University of Mississippi. Tuition scholarships were available at the university, but there were few takers because no self-respecting member of the gentry would admit that he needed help in paying for his son's education. The university's classical curriculum, known as the "genteel tradition," was not designed to educate the masses but to produce Southern gentlemen.

After the Civil War technical and vocational training became an American educational priority, and with the aid of federal funding, agricultural and mechanical colleges were opened all across the country. In Mississippi, Alcorn Agricultural and Mechanical College was established for African American students, and a bachelor's degree in agriculture was established at the university in Oxford. Two professors were hired; a ninety-acre demonstration farm was acquired, and the library subscribed to agricultural journals. But few students came. Only one student enrolled when the agricultural department opened in 1872, and the enrollment leaped to four during the next three years.

Farmers' organizations and the agricultural press spoke "contemptuously" of the "sideshow" up at Oxford. A letter to the editor in the Jackson *Clarion-Ledger* said, "tacking on to the tail end of Oxford an agricultural department" was a "humbug and delusion." The writer also reported that the sons of the gentry "sneered" at the sons of the farmers and called on the legislature to "abolish the farce." According to John K. Bettersworth, the historian of Mississippi State University, the history of the agricultural department at Oxford was "brief and tragic."

In 1876 the university discontinued its agricultural program, and in 1878 the legislature established Mississippi Agricultural and Mechanical College at Starkville. There would be no relics of the old aristocracy at A&M. Greek fraternities were banned, and students wore uniforms. Mississippi A&M opened higher education to the sons of Mississippi's industrial class, and it came to be known fondly as the "People's College." The fact that the Oxford representative in the state legislature tried to kill the bill establishing the college validated the industrial class's suspicion and distrust of anyone from Oxford and Ole Miss, a feeling that still lingers in the minds of some Mississippi State supporters.

The tension between the farmers and the gentry was further aggravated in 1880 by a special legislative appropriation to the state university. That special annual appropriation of $32,000 was a good faith effort by the legislature to restore to the university the proceeds from an 1819 federal land grant that had been squandered, stolen, and otherwise depleted. On the other hand, Mississippi A&M was receiving only about $4,000 from a federal land grant Mississippi had received in 1871. The special appropriation to the university smacked of favoritism, and it infuriated the friends and supporters of Mississippi A&M.

United States Senator James Z. George, a member of the Mississippi A&M Board of Trustees, lashed out at the legislature and the university, calling the appropriation "a fraud on the people of the state" and accusing the university of making "forays on the treasury whenever it suits its convenience or its tastes to do so." In a rejoinder, Ole Miss Chancellor Edward Mayes accused Senator George of being "jealous… and anxious to find fault" with the university. This public and prolonged debate between the supporters of the rival institutions was conducted in the press and in pamphlets and went on and on for several months.

The exchanges between Senator George and Chancellor Mayes reveal much about the origins of the rivalry between State and Ole Miss. That public dispute was ostensibly about money, but there was more to it than just money. Senator George not only represented Mississippi A&M, he personified the People's College. He was a son of the industrial class, and his aristocratic detractors often chided him for his country manners. Without the benefit of a college connection, Senator George was a self-made man in a time and place where lineage was prized above self-reliance, and he was often taunted for his lack of ancestry. His official biography in the *Congressional Directory* does not list any of his forebears and states only that he "moved to Mississippi with his mother when a lad."

Chancellor Mayes was a study in contrast. He had a distinguished Virginia ancestry. His father served in two branches of government and held the chair of law at Transylvania University. Mayes began his college education in Virginia and earned two degrees from the University of Mississippi. He married the daughter of L.Q.C. Lamar, and through Lamar he entered the lineage of the Longstreets. In his dialogue with Senator George, Chancellor Mayes betrayed a contempt for his adversary and a condescension that smacked of class. That contempt was directed not just at George but also at the institution whose interests he defended.

Chancellor Mayes referred to the university as the state's "most precious possession" and as such, it warranted the special appropriation. The chancellor's logic was simple and unassailable. If the university was the state's most precious possession, the agricultural college was less precious; therefore, it must occupy a lower level in Mississippi's educational hierarchy. In the minds of friends of Mississippi A&M, that special appropriation to the university was evidence that an educational hierarchy existed, and they were incensed by it. Again, it was more than just the money. It was the insinuation that the university, and the rich kids, the sons of the old aristocracy, still came first. They came first because they were better than everybody else.

The university came first because it was the school for the lawyers and the doctors and the politicians. To those people, Mississippi A&M was just a "cow college." The students over at Starkville were like their "poor relations" or their "country cousins."

The presumption that the university was the preeminent institution of higher learning in Mississippi was articulated by a legislative committee in 1886:

> *Nothing is better calculated to detract from the merits of the [uni-versity] than unfriendly remarks. ... It should not be regarded by other schools or colleges as a rival but looked up to… as pre-eminently supe-rior to all others, and to which all others should be tributary.*

This committee's scolding of those who criticized the university did not quiet the controversy over the special allocation, and the Mississippi Grange and other farm organizations demanded that A&M's appropriation be in-creased. The president of A&M also accused the friends of the university of "aiding in establishing a strong undercurrent against this institution." He also complained that although the enrollment at A&M was higher than Ole Miss's enrollment, A&M received a smaller state appropriation.

While the adults were arguing over such weighty matters as funding, the student press of both institutions was engaged in a more lighthearted if not always good-natured banter. The first expressions of the rivalry between students at Ole Miss and Mississippi State were not on the playing fields but on the pages of their student publications. In December 1895 *The Uni-versity of Mississippi Magazine* chided the *College Reflector*, its counterpart at Mississippi A&M, of bragging too much about its baseball team. The *University Magazine* was dismissive of its counterpart and said that the only good feature of the *College Reflector* was its joke section.

In the late nineteenth century, while State and Ole Miss students were chiding each other in the student press, there were two major political fac-tions competing for control of state government. The ruling elite, which came from the Delta, the wealthy counties along the Mississippi River and the black prairie region, had controlled state government since Mississippi's admission to statehood in 1817. But in the late 1880s the dirt farmers and day laborers mounted a challenge to the ruling class. These two political factions were, more or less, the basic constituencies of State and Ole Miss. The farmers and laborers were derided as "rednecks" by the aristocrats, but James K. Vardaman and Theodore G. Bilbo turned that taunt into a rallying cry.

James K. Vardaman was elected governor in 1903 largely by the "rednecks," and he promised them that he would drive the wealthy elite from their positions of power and privilege. When Bilbo was campaigning, he always wore a red tie and red suspenders. He said he wore the red necktie to keep his courage up and the red suspenders to keep his pants up.

Two years after Vardaman's election, an irate law student at Ole Miss published a pamphlet to inform the "common people" of Mississippi that their university was still catering to "the so-called upper classes." Like the common people he championed, Governor Vardaman considered the state university the last bastion of the old aristocracy, and he was determined to democratize it. A temporary democratization of the university was accomplished in 1906 when Governor Vardaman forced the Ole Miss chancellor to resign and installed one of his own political supporters. But Vardaman's appointee later resigned amid charges of corruption and mismanagement.

As the University of Mississippi was being democratized in the early 1900s, American higher education was being fundamentally changed by the rising tide of intercollegiate athletics and the expanding reach of the alumni movement. "The alumni movement," Frederick Rudolph wrote in his classic study of the American college and university, "had its own rationale, its own purposes, its own life, and was remote from the purposes of the professors." John Maynard Hutchins, president of the University of Chicago, explained how intercollegiate athletics and the alumni movement intersected and interacted with each other. "Consider the alumnus," Hutchins wrote, "his college career represents one of life's climactic experiences, and it grows rosier in memory as it recedes in time. As youth itself is overvalued, so also are the events that linger in memory. In some as-yet-undefined way renewed contact with intercollegiate athletics revives his youth as no other experience could." With the emergence of intercollegiate athletics and alumni societies, the State-Ole Miss rivalry took on an added dimension and intensity.

The Ole Miss chancellor was hesitant about establishing intercollegiate athletics at the university but finally decided that sports might serve as "a safety valve to the exuberance of youthful spirits that would frequently find vent in some harmful way." With the chancellor's blessing, Ole Miss organized its first football team in 1893, and Mississippi State fielded its first team two years later. It is not clear why they did not play earlier, but the two schools did not meet until 1901 in Starkville. The problem that has long plagued the State-Ole Miss rivalry was present at its creation. The 1901 game started late and was called early on account of darkness, because an argument over the eligibility of a State player delayed the kickoff for nearly an hour.

Recognizing that an institution's academic standing and integrity could be compromised by a rogue coach who skirted the rules, State, Ole Miss, and several other colleges and universities formed the Southern Intercollegiate Athletic Association in 1894 "to regulate, supervise, and purify college athletics throughout the South." The SIAA was invested with the authority to sanction member institutions that did not abide by the rules formulated by the association. Eventually, the larger schools of the SIAA withdrew and established the Southern Intercollegiate Conference in 1921. Two years later its name was changed to the Southern Conference, and in 1932 the Southern Conference, which included schools from the Atlantic Coast to Texas, was divided into the Southeastern and Southwestern conferences. The National Collegiate Athletic Association had been formed in 1906 in response to President Theodore Roosevelt's threat to outlaw college football unless the rules were changed to make the game less rugged and violent. Virtually all American colleges and universities are voluntary members of the NCAA, which has the power to place sanctions against member institutions.

When State and Ole Miss played their first game in 1901, college football was in its ascendency, and by the end of the first decade of the twentieth century, college football had become America's game. In 1906 the *Mississippi Magazine*, a student publication at Ole Miss, wrote that college football had "found a unique place in the hearts of the American people. Greece had the Olympics; Rome had its Coliseum, and American colleges will have the struggle of the gridiron." Ole Miss students cheered for the Red and Blue, and like students at Mississippi State who cheered for the Maroon and White, college students across America lionized "Autumn's Hero" in cheers and verse:

Hero of the gridiron! Who has sung your praise?
Who has lined in marble the beauty of your ways?

However much college officials might not want to admit it, alumni correctly argue that the success of an institution's athletic program is an important factor in student enrollment and alumni contributions. Shortly after World War II a group of Mississippi Southern College alumni met in Hattiesburg to promote the growth and expansion of their alma mater. The first resolution they passed was a recommendation for the enlargement of the college's football stadium. To many alumni, the standing of their alma mater is measured by the seating capacity of its football stadium.

Football captivated American college students, and alumni societies became a link back to the balmy days of youth. Alumni societies are useful to their alma maters so long as they maintain that delicate balance between involvement and interference. The Mississippi State alumni actually saved their alma mater on one occasion, and the Ole Miss alumni may have saved theirs three times. In 1920 a bill was introduced in the state legislature to consolidate Mississippi A&M and the university into one institution of higher learning to be located in Jackson. The bill was endorsed by the governor, the lieutenant governor, and the speaker of the house of representatives. But the combined unified opposition of the alumni associations of both institutions defeated the bill.

Twelve years later several bills were introduced in the legislature to reorganize higher education in Mississippi. One measure would have moved the university to Jackson, but the overwhelming opposition of the Ole Miss alumni defeated that bill. Another measure, which passed with virtually unanimous support of A&M alumni, expanded its curriculum and increased its course offerings in the liberal arts. Uniforms were abandoned; coeducation was reestablished after its discontinuation in 1912; Greek fraternities were now welcomed to the campus, and the institution's name was changed to Mississippi State College. The friends and supporters of the institution wholeheartedly supported these innovations and celebrated this fundamental change in the character of their alma mater.

The Ole Miss student newspaper might still claim that "the finest families of the commonwealth are represented among Ole Miss students," and its detractors might still call Mississippi State a "cow college," but its students could now take courses in Shakespeare, get a degree in elementary education, or they could even take a pre-law course and then go over to that other school and get a law degree.

Those changes took the competition between State and Ole Miss to another level, but there were still significant distinctions between the two old rivals. In the 1930s, with the tacit approval of the state's political and educational leadership, the college board established a priority pyramid and a funding mechanism with the university as the "capstone of public education in Mississippi." Mississippi State came next, then Mississippi State College for Women, then Delta State and Mississippi Southern, and finally Alcorn A&M. That "pecking order" was never acknowledged by public officials and certainly not by members of the board of trustees. But it was a reality that Mississippi State and its alumni had to live with. Mississippi State was still playing "second fiddle" to the university, at least for the time being.

Priority pyramids, pecking orders, and impending wars notwithstanding, State and Ole Miss students and alumni continued their homage to "autumn's hero." On their way to Oxford for the 1939 Egg Bowl, with Hitler threatening to overrun all of Europe, Mississippi State students proclaimed "To hell with Hitler and Ole Miss." Only days before the attack at Pearl Harbor Mississippi State and Ole Miss played at Oxford for the SEC championship for the first and only time. Mississippi State won 6 - 0. Two years after Mississippi State defeated Ole Miss for the championship, college football was cancelled in Mississippi because of the war.

World War II has been called the war that changed everything. It certainly changed higher education in Mississippi. Initiated by rising expectations among women and blacks, and sustained by the GI Bill, a postwar enrollment explosion revolutionized the American collegiate system. Students "took charge of change," and by their sheer numbers they remodeled the American college and university.

After World War II American colleges became social and cultural institutions where fun and games and growing up paralleled and sometimes overwhelmed the learning process. Mississippi State's enrollment soared from 761 in 1945 to nearly 4,000 in 1949. In the first five years after the war Mississippi State multiplied its course offerings, adding 417 new courses to meet the almost insatiable demand of a new generation of students. In the aftermath of World War II the faculty and friends and alumni of Mississippi State decided that it was no longer Ole Miss's prerogative to be "the capstone of public education in Mississippi." Although the University of Mississippi experienced similar enrollment growth and academic expansion, by 1958 Mississippi State had outstripped the university in enrollment, broadened its course offerings, upgraded its academic programs and library facilities, and was elevated to university status.

Mississippi State University was now a peer, not a rival, of the state university, a fact that Ole Miss officials seemed unable or unwilling to accept. After Mississippi State's designation as a university, Ole Miss "unofficially" added "The" to its title and its new "unofficial" name was "The University of Mississippi." Ole Miss officials also proclaimed "The University" as the "flagship" of Mississippi institutions of higher learning. The implication was clear. Mississippi State may be called a university, but to its friends and alumni, Ole Miss was still "The University of Mississippi."

In the aftermath of the war's aftermath, the 1960s, Mississippi's collegiate system was desegregated, and the social turbulence spawned by the Meredith crisis had long-term repercussions on the recruiting wars between Mississippi State and Ole Miss. In the weeks prior to Meredith's admission in 1962, Governor Ross Barnett had made a thinly veiled threat to close the university to prevent its integration. Quietly and behind the scenes, a powerful group of Ole Miss alumni informed the governor that they would not allow the university to be closed. They may very well have saved the university.

Prior to the State-Ole Miss game on December 1,1962, which came only three months after James Meredith had been admitted to the university, there were wild rumors that some Mississippi State students had captured several live "coons" and were going to sneak them into Hemingway Stadium and release them just before kickoff. Chancellor J.D. Williams was so concerned about the prank that he called President D.W. Colvard at Mississippi State to discuss it with him. Both men agreed to closely monitor the situation. The dreaded possibility did not materialize, and the game was played without incident. Ole Miss won 13-6 and went undefeated that season, won the SEC Championship and was named National Champion. In his memoirs Coach John Vaught claims that the excitement generated by that year's undefeated football team may have saved the university. Apparently, to many Ole Miss supporters a winning football program was more important than racial segregation.

In the 1970s the competition for Mississippi's limited number of high quality athletes intensified, and Mississippi State was the first to be wounded in the recruiting war. The NCAA placed State on probation for offering illegal inducements to a football recruit. To add insult to injury, the SEC also issued a mandate against the use of cowbells at SEC games. Students of both schools took notice of these developments, and at the 1975 Egg Bowl, Ole Miss students unfurled a banner that read:

State—The Worst Team Money Can Buy.

Proudly, Mississippi State responded with this banner:

We're on Probation,
We don't have a bell
But we can still say
Ole Miss—Go to Hell

By the 1990s this good-natured banter had given way to a street fight between State and Ole Miss football recruiters. In *Sports Illustrated*, Ed Hinton explained that Ole Miss's tradition of first choice among Mississippi athletes was lost during that long night of violence when federal troops had to put down a riot at Ole Miss and force the university to admit its first black student.

Mississippi State integrated its athletic program before Ole Miss did, and as the two institutions began to recruit black athletes, it became obvious that the integration crisis at the university and the Old South symbols like Dixie, Colonel Rebel, and the Confederate flag could be used against Ole Miss, if not with the students themselves, certainly with their parents.

The use of Ole Miss's racial history and its Old South symbols by Mississippi State football recruiters, according to Ole Miss fans and supporters, was prominent, frequent, and effective in the recruiting wars of the 1980s and 1990s. And they claimed that Jackie Sherrill was even more guilty of that tactic than his predecessors, and that there was proof of Sherrill's use of Ole Miss's racial troubles in recruiting black athletes. Coach Sherrill was fond to say that "When the National Guard was on the doorsteps of… Mississippi, black students were being admitted here." Although Mississippi State did not admit black students until two years after Meredith graduated from Ole Miss, and Coach Sherrill's statement was incorrect, Ole Miss coaches and supporters were deeply offended that Coach Sherrill would still use such tactics thirty years after the integration crisis and twenty years after a black football player had been elected Colonel Rebel by the student body.

In an angry outburst in May 1991 Coach Billy Brewer publicly accused Coach Sherrill of trying to persuade a former Ole Miss athlete at Texas A&M to convince a black athlete to transfer from Ole Miss to Texas A&M. After Coach Sherrill denied that he had tried to do so, Brewer called Jackie Sherrill "a habitual liar" and said he knew for a fact that Sherrill had done it. Coach Sherrill retorted that Billy Brewer probably did not know what the word "habitual" meant. The SEC Commissioner reprimanded Coach Brewer for causing such a public squabble.

As the student bodies at State and Ole Miss became more diverse with the increasing enrollment of students from varied ethnic, social and economic backgrounds, the class-based taunts were not as frequent or as ugly as they once were. But the intensity of the rivalry did not diminish; in fact, the rivalry intensified.

In a hilarious *Clarion-Ledger* article just before the 1986 Egg Bowl, a sports writer profiled the student body of both schools. State students drank Budweiser beer; Ole Miss kids drank gin and tonics. Ole Miss students included Mr. Beauregard, III, and they drove BMWs; State students were named Billy Bob and Betty Jane, and they drove to the game in their pickups.

The overtones of class have not yet completely disappeared from the Ole Miss student section, which often characterizes the State-Ole Miss grudge match as a clash between "culture and agriculture." There was a popular sweatshirt among Ole Miss students that read on the front, "We're not snobs," and on the back, "We're just better than you." The rivalry between the student bodies is focused more than ever on athletics in general and football in particular. The fanaticism of the rivalry has not changed, just the terminology and its focus. In fact, the rivalry among students, alumni, and supporters of the two institutions may never have been more intense.

One of the reasons the State-Ole Miss rivalry was refocused on football was the return of the annual Egg Bowl to the college campuses. In 1991 the annual State-Ole Miss game was brought back to the campuses from the neutral field in Jackson's Memorial Stadium. And home-field advantage was a major factor in refocusing the State-Ole Miss rivalry on football.

Another reason for the escalation of the rivalry was the resurgence of Mississippi State's football program. Coach Sherrill took them back to the big time, to an SEC championship game, back into the national rankings, to bowl games, and to seven wins against six losses to "that other school."

Coach Sherrill did for State in the 1990s what Billy Brewer had done for Ole Miss in the 1980s, before Coach Brewer lost his job following the second of two NCAA investigations of recruiting violations. Both programs enjoyed great success, but each was tarnished by NCAA probation.

In the summer of 2002 the SEC added another wrinkle to the State-Ole Miss rivalry when the SEC president's council voted to ban cowbells from all SEC games. The Mississippi State president cast the lone vote against that measure. State fans naturally blamed Ole Miss for that infamous rule that authorized game officials to penalize the team whose supporters were ringing cowbells. A similar action had been taken in 1974 but it had not been rigidly enforced. In 2010 the SEC revisited the issue, and Mississippi State supporters were allowed to ring cowbells "during pregame, timeouts, halftime, and after the Bulldogs scored."

In the spring of 2003, while Coach Sherrill was trying to rally the troops, who were growing restless after two losing seasons, Mississippi State University received a preliminary letter of inquiry from the NCAA. Over the next several months the NCAA conducted an investigation of possible rules violation by the MSU football program. This inquiry came after two straight three-win seasons by the State football team. Coach Sherrill refused to talk to the NCAA's primary investigator because, he said, "I think there is a group of people that went after Mississippi State. The investigator didn't want to know the truth when he was given information." Coach Sherrill also complained that boosters of the Ole Miss football program hired private investigators "in attempts to uncover violations to be used to place [Mississippi State] on NCAA probation."

The NCAA investigation was conducted "against a backdrop of swirling rumors and innuendo fueled by media reports and internet chat boards reverberating with the exchange of insults and threats between supporters of competing teams." While the NCAA investigation was still in progress, and long before any findings were released, Coach Sherrill announced that he was retiring from coaching at the end of the 2003 season and described the State-Ole Miss rivalry:

> *Mississippi State and Mississippi is a different rivalry than Texas-Texas A&M or Michigan-Ohio State or UCLA-USC. Those teams play each other, and then go home. It doesn't mean the game isn't important. But in the state of Mississippi, it's 365 days a year. One school*

wins that game a couple of times, and that winning coach is hated;
he's the villain. It's a big deal in the state of Mississippi for that fan to
pick up his coffee cup in the morning with his school logo on it and be
proud.

In a November 25, 2005, article entitled "Rebs, Dogs toil in field of futility," *Commercial Appeal* sports columnist Ron Higgins wrote about the destructive effects of the long rivalry and referred to State and Ole Miss as "cutthroat cousins." After noting that State and Ole Miss had not played each other for the SEC championship in more than fifty years, and that both teams had more NCAA probations than ten-win seasons in the last thirty years, Higgins wrote, "There's an underlying reason why the Bulldogs and the Rebels can never maintain championship consistency… every time one of the schools starts stringing together winning seasons, envious fans of the school on the down slope begin digging up dirt to hand over to NCAA investigators."

After the NCAA investigation of the Mississippi State football program became public in the summer of 2003, *Clarion-Ledger* sports writer Rick Cleveland recapped an old rivalry:

State fans—and officials—blame Ole Miss for the ongoing NCAA
investigation of State football. Ole Miss fans believe Sherrill is deter-
mined to take Ole Miss down with him.

And so it goes, on and on, and on.

During the 2016-2017 NCAA investigation of the Ole Miss football program, allegations and accusations entangled Ole Miss and Mississippi State that are reminiscent of yesterday, and the day before, and the day before.